Mobile Forensics – Advanced Investigative Strategies

Master powerful strategies to acquire and analyze evidence from real-life scenarios

Oleg Afonin
Vladimir Katalov

BIRMINGHAM - MUMBAI

Mobile Forensics – Advanced Investigative Strategies

Copyright © 2016 Packt Publishing

First published: September 2016

Production reference: 1260916

Published by Packt Publishing Ltd.
Livery Place
35 Livery Street
Birmingham
B3 2PB, UK.
ISBN 978-1-78646-448-4

www.packtpub.com

Credits

Authors

Oleg Afonin

Vladimir Katalov

Reviewer

Shafik G. Punja

Commissioning Editor

Kartikey Pandey

Acquisition Editor

Divya Poojari

Content Development Editor

Siddhesh Salvi

Technical Editor

Manthan Raja

Copy Editor

Vibha Shukla

Project Coordinator

Nidhi Joshi

Proofreader

Safis Editing

Indexer

Aishwarya Gangawane

Graphics

Kirk D'Penha

Disha Haria

Production Coordinator

Arvindkumar Gupta

Foreword

Hello reader. I welcome you to a book of knowledge. When Vladimir Katalov offered me an opportunity to write a foreword for their book, I was surprised and also humbled. I have never written a foreword to a book, much less participated in the authoring of a book. I accepted Vladimir's offer. So here goes.

In the field of digital forensics, there is an overwhelming amount of information to learn and comprehend. Many years ago a highly respected colleague said to me: *No man is an island*. What did he mean by this statement? From my perspective, this means that you cannot know it all. We as examiners and practitioners in the digital forensics field must learn to impart knowledge responsibly, and share so that we can all learn. In essence, a collective digital forensics knowledge hive, where the answers to our challenges lie within the knowledge hive. This book then is a part of this hive. It is important also not to focus only on the analysis tool, but also on the understanding of the devices and technologies and the methodology used to successfully get the data. This book will also help you understand the underlying technology and methodology.

In the end, I leave you to carry on your journey in this book. I hope you enjoy reading and learning from it as much as I have.

Shafik G. Punja

Police Officer, Digital Forensics Team

About the Authors

Oleg Afonin is a researcher and an expert in digital forensics. He is a frequent speaker at industry-known conferences such as CEIC, HTCIA, FT-Day, Techno Forensics, and others. Oleg has co-authored multiple publications on IT security and mobile forensics. With years of experience in the digital forensics and security domain, Oleg has led forensic training courses for law enforcement departments in multiple countries.

Vladimir Katalov is CEO, co-founder, and co-owner of ElcomSoft Co. Ltd. Vladimir manages all technical research and product development in the company. He regularly presents at various events and regularly runs security and computer forensics training both for foreign and domestic (Russian) computer investigative committees and other law enforcement organizations.

Special thanks to **Oleg Davydov** *whose help and advice was truly invaluable. Without Oleg's deep understanding of Android internals, this book would not be the same. Oleg Davydov is a co-founder and CTO of Oxygen Software. Since 2000, he has been involved in software development related to mobile forensics. For the last 10 years, Oleg has been busy developing mobile forensic tools. Oleg is an expert in cryptography, IT security, software development, mobile forensics, and reverse engineering. Oleg works in the mobile forensics industry, using his experience and understanding of smartphone internals to help law enforcement.*

Special thanks to **Shafik G. Punja** *who caught things that we missed. His expertise in acquiring BlackBerry devices was an invaluable help.*

About the Reviewer

Shafik G. Punja is a police officer with the Calgary Police Service, having served for over 20 years. He has been working in digital forensics since 2003 and is currently assigned to the Digital Forensics Team (Cyber/Forensic Unit). He has qualified in the Canadian legal system as an expert in the area of digital forensics, and has previously served as guest instructor for the Technological Crimes Learning Institute (TCLI) at the Canadian Police College, in Ottawa, Ontario. His private sector work involves R&D partnerships with various law enforcement colleagues and digital forensics training.

www.PacktPub.com

For support files and downloads related to your book, please visit www.PacktPub.com.

Did you know that Packt offers eBook versions of every book published, with PDF and ePub files available? You can upgrade to the eBook version at www.PacktPub.com and as a print book customer, you are entitled to a discount on the eBook copy. Get in touch with us at service@packtpub.com for more details.

At www.PacktPub.com, you can also read a collection of free technical articles, sign up for a range of free newsletters and receive exclusive discounts and offers on Packt books and eBooks.

https://www.packtpub.com/mapt

Get the most in-demand software skills with Mapt. Mapt gives you full access to all Packt books and video courses, as well as industry-leading tools to help you plan your personal development and advance your career.

Why subscribe?

- Fully searchable across every book published by Packt
- Copy and paste, print, and bookmark content
- On demand and accessible via a web browser

Table of Contents

Preface

Smartphone and tablet technology has changed dramatically and rapidly in the last several years and continues to do so at an astounding pace. These smaller computing devices are so common, with the ability to replace their desktop counterparts in human-to-computer interactions. Sit in any café, airport, or public place that offers Wi-Fi and you will see humans with their faces ostensibly glued to their device screens, interacting on their device with such focus, seemingly oblivious to their own physical environment.

Smartphone and tablet devices have become large digital storage vaults that store our personal and professional secrets. Strangely enough, with little faith, we have also begun to allow ourselves to accept backup up of this data to the *cloud* so that important aspects of our local device storage are now also in *cloud storage*. Why did I mention cloud storage? Cloud backup data can be accessed outside of the device itself through other processes, when access to the device data itself may be obstructed due to security mechanisms. This book addresses *cloud forensics* from the various smartphone platforms.

Whilst this could be considered a highly technical book, it is an excellent read for both novices and experienced examiners alike. For those that have read any of the blog articles that have been published by Elcomsoft, you will find a comfortable approach to the way this book has been written.

The authors of this book strive to provide essential information about a number of concepts including the following:

- NAND eMMC flash memory
- A brief summary of JTAG forensics
- NANDroid backups
- iOS security and acquisition method
- Password breaking on iOS backups
- Windows Phones security and acquisition
- BlackBerry 7 and BlackBerry data acquisition methods and password breaking

There are of course references to customized tools that are developed by the authors and their colleagues. What this highlights to anyone reading this is that in the field of mobile forensics, no one tool can do it all. I know and say this from experience because I have used all the tools mentioned in this book. All tools have their strengths and limitations. But to be effective, an examiner must have at least several tools to cover the broad range of technology in mobile forensics.

What this book covers

This book is written to represent a natural flow in the e-discovery process, covering the different stages of mobile forensics from seizing the device to acquiring the data and analyzing evidence. The book covers basic handling, acquisition, and analysis techniques for smartphones and tablets running the most popular operating systems: Android, iOS, Windows Phone, Windows 8, 8.1, and RT, and BlackBerry. The following topics are covered in detail:

Seizing techniques:

- Shielding the device: the use of the Faraday bag
- Preserving volatile memory and capturing memory dumps

Acquisition techniques:

- Physical acquisition (via USB connection)
- Logical acquisition via data backups
- Over-the-air acquisition and cloud analysis

Evidence discovery and data analysis:

- Finding, viewing, and analyzing evidence

Tools for mobile forensics:

- Acquisition and analysis tools overview
- Tools for acquiring iOS devices
- Tools for acquiring Android, BlackBerry, and Windows Phone devices
- Tools for discovering and analyzing evidence

It is important to note the bits that this book does **not** cover. These include:

- JTAG acquisition
- Chip-off imaging
- Disk imaging tools
- Tools for acquiring Windows 8 and 8.1 devices

We will **not** go into any technical detail, such as which hex code at what address means what, or how to calculate UDID, or how to use ADB to break through passcode protection on Android 2.1. We believe these things are meaningless for a law enforcement officer, and should only interest technicians working in an acquisition lab – and this book is not for them.

Chapter 1, *Introducing Mobile Forensics*, introduces the concept of mobile devices as a source of valuable evidence. The chapter describes what types of evidence are generally available in mobile devices. It also outlines acquisition options depending on whether the reader has access to the actual device, knows the user's login and password (such as an Apple ID or Google Account password), or has access to the computer that was used to sync the mobile device. This chapter also discusses the various techniques used by suspects to counter forensic efforts, and suggests methods to overcome such efforts. This chapter is essential to understand what, why, and how the expert is trying to achieve when investigating mobile devices. After reading this chapter, you will understand the big picture of mobile forensics and realize that there is no single straightforward path to acquiring mobile evidence, and understand that available acquisition options strongly depend on various factors. You'll get an idea of how to seize and store mobile devices and how to detect and counter anti-forensic efforts.

Chapter 2, *Acquisition Methods Overview*, gives an overview of the acquisition methods available for different mobile platforms. With the wide range of mobile devices around, multiple acquisition methods exist. There is no single universal acquisition method available for all models. Some acquisition methods depend on the phone's lock and encryption status, OS version, type of available storage, and so on. Investigators have to work their way through the investigation to discover what acquisition methods are available for a particular device.

Chapter 3, *Acquisition – Approaching Android Devices*, discusses the options available for acquiring information from Android devices, providing a detailed outline of physical, logical, and over-the-air acquisition methods for Android smartphones and tablets. In this chapter, the reader will learn what acquisition methods are available for the Android platform, which acquisition techniques are available in what circumstances, and how to choose the appropriate acquisition method for a given device. This chapter also covers one of the most challenging aspects of mobile forensics: the ability to recover destroyed evidence. In this chapter, we discuss exactly how modern smartphones handle deleted data, depending on the operating system (Android, iOS, Windows) and encryption status. We'll address the differences between internal (eMMC) and external (SD) storage of the device in the context of being able to recover information from unallocated areas.

Chapter 4, Practical Steps to Android Acquisition, discusses the massive amounts of information collected by Google, and explains how to extract this information from Google servers. We'll be using forensic tools to download data from Google, view it, and examine obtained evidence. The acquisition of Google Accounts can provide a much deeper insight into user activities than what's available in a single Android smartphone. This chapter offers a detailed discussion and demonstration of various physical acquisition methods available for a wide range of Android devices, including manufacturer-specific low-level service modes (LG, Qualcomm, and Mediatek), using custom recoveries (CWM, TWRP) for dumping the data partition, making NANDroid backups, and using command-line tools such as dd for live imaging the device. In addition, this chapter discusses the issue of encryption and its effect on physical acquisition.

Chapter 5, *iOS – Introduction and Physical Acquisition*, discusses the benefits and unique features of physical acquisition, and talks about stored passwords and Apple secure storage, the keychain. This chapter provides a detailed compatibility matrix for physical acquisition, discusses which locked devices can be acquired without knowing the correct passcode, and lists forensic tools that offer physical acquisition of Apple iOS devices. It discusses the differences between 32-bit and 64-bit Apple hardware, and explains how to install a jailbreak.

Chapter 6, *iOS Logical and Cloud Acquisition*, introduces the concept of the logical acquisition of iOS devices. Logical acquisition consists of extracting existing iTunes backups or making the device produce a backup and then extracting it. The differences between encrypted and unencrypted backups are explained, outlining the benefits of producing encrypted backups with a known password over unencrypted one. This chapter outlines the basics of recovering unknown backup passwords. In addition, this chapter provides step-by-step instructions on using Elcomsoft Phone Breaker to extract iOS backups. If the backup is protected with an unknown password, detailed instructions and recommendations on recovering the password are provided. This chapter explains the advantages and applicability of over-the-air acquisition, and demonstrates how to use Elcomsoft Phone Breaker for cloud acquisition. In addition, this chapter discusses the use of binary authentication tokens to bypass an Apple ID and password, as well as two-factor authentication.

Chapter 7, *Acquisition – Approaching Windows Phone and Windows 10 Mobile*, introduces Windows Phone forensics. It outlines the available methods and approaches to acquiring Windows Phone 8 and 8.1 and Windows 10 Mobile devices. Physical acquisition, bootloader exploits, invasive (advanced) acquisition via JTAG, and chip-off are explained. In this chapter, we discuss the differences in device encryption between generations of the Windows Phone platform, and provide a detailed walkthrough of over-the-air acquisition of Windows mobile devices using Elcomsoft Phone Breaker.

Chapter 8, *Acquisition - Approaching Windows 8, 8.1, 10, and RT Tablets*, covers major points that make tablet forensics different from the traditional PC and laptop acquisition approach. We'll cover the new Connected Standby mode replacing traditional Sleep and Hibernate modes of Windows laptops, discuss Secure Boot on various Windows tablet platforms, review UEFI BIOS settings, and learn how to start the tablet from a bootable USB media. We'll also cover techniques on capturing the content of the device's RAM and imaging non-removable eMMC media. General acquisition steps for Windows RT devices are also described, as standard Windows recovery media cannot be used with RT devices.

Chapter 9, *Acquisition - Approaching BlackBerry*, provides an introduction, overview, and in-depth tutorials on acquiring BlackBerry smartphones running legacy (BB OS 1 through 7.1) and modern (BlackBerry 10) versions of the OS. BlackBerry backups and backup passwords (legacy BB OS) are explained. This chapter provides tutorials on how to extract and view legacy BlackBerry backups and recover passwords protecting these backups. The reader will learn how to use Elcomsoft Phone Breaker to decrypt BlackBerry 10 backups and view their content with Elcomsoft Phone Viewer or Oxygen Forensic Suite.

Chapter 10, *Dealing with Issues, Obstacles, and Special Cases*, covers some of the most challenging aspects of mobile forensics: the ability to recover destroyed evidence and the challenge presented by two-factor authentication. In this chapter, we discuss how exactly modern smartphones handle deleted data depending on the operating system (Android, iOS, Windows) and encryption status. We'll address the differences between internal (eMMC) and external (SD) storage of the device in the context of being able to recover information from unallocated areas. This chapter also covers the issue of two-factor authentication during over-the-air acquisition. Experts face a serious roadblock when attempting to acquire information from the suspect's cloud account over the air if two-factor authentication is enabled on their account. Cloud acquisition becomes more challenging if there is no access to the secondary authentication factor. However, there are ways to bypass two-factor authentication. These methods are outlined in this chapter, to be discussed in more detail in the more technical chapters of this book.

Chapter 11, *Mobile Forensic Tools and Case Studies*, outlines several mobile forensic tools that can be used for acquiring mobile devices. Cellerbrite UFED, Micro Systemation XRY, AccessData MPE+, Oxygen Forensic Toolkit, Magnet ACQUIRE, BlackBag Mobilyze, and the range of ElcomSoft tools for mobile forensics are listed and briefly reviewed. In addition, this chapter has several case studies on using mobile forensic tools for corporate investigations and data recovery.

What you need for this book

Modern mobile forensics is impossible without using tools. Currently, there is no single, all-in-one tool to cover the complete mobile acquisition and analysis process. Different assignments and different circumstances will require the use of multiple tools. We list the tools used throughout this book here.

For many Android smartphones, we used Oxygen Forensic Suite and Oxygen Forensic Extractor, a commercial product from Oxygen Forensics (http://www.oxygen-forensic.com/en/).

For Android smartphones, you'll need ADB and Fastboot from Android SDK Tools (part of Android Studio 2.1) as a free download from Google (http://developer.android.com/sdk/index.html).

In addition, you may need TWRP custom recovery (custom built and specific to acquisition target, http://twrp.me) or CWM custom recovery (custom built for specific acquisition target, https://www.clockworkmod.com/), the Busybox package (version depends on acquisition target's Android version, https://busybox.net/), unyaffs 1.0 (only if acquisition target uses the yaffs file system, https://github.com/ehlers/unyaffs) and Netcat 1.10 (http://nc11.sourceforge.net/). These tools are available as open source downloads from their respective developers.

For Apple iOS devices, we used the following commercial tools: Elcomsoft iOS Forensic Toolkit (https://www.elcomsoft.com/eift.html), Elcomsoft Phone Breaker (demo version downloadable from https://www.elcomsoft.com/eppb.html), and Elcomsoft Phone Viewer (https://www.elcomsoft.com/epv.html). Elcomsoft Phone Breaker and Phone Viewer were also used for acquiring BlackBerry OS, BlackBerry 10, and Windows Phone/Windows 10 Mobile devices.

Who this book is for

We wrote this book for law enforcement and IT security officers who have to deal with digital evidence as part of their daily job. We wanted this book to serve as an introduction and a general guide to mobile forensics. We are aware of the sheer diversity of ecosystems, generations of operating systems, devices, and applications on the market. We have first-hand experience with Android forks, custom ROMs, and manufacturer, operator, and user customizations that can turn a familiar device into a big question mark.

And this is why we strongly believe that there is no way one could possible know of (or even hear about) more than a few variations.

For this reason, we no longer believe in manual acquisition and analysis. We believe in tools. There is no need to invent the wheel or waste endless hours on something the right tool could accomplish in minutes. There are tens of thousands of different device models, and each model can be running a different version of the OS or use a different set of OEM or operator customizations, each with its own security implications. There are millions of applications, each implementing their own way of storing, organizing, and protecting data. It is technically impossible for a single expert to know everything. However, it is still possible to learn about methods, tools, and techniques to acquire and analyze evidence in most real-life situations.

However, even the best tools won't do any good if you don't know or don't follow the basic rules of seizing, handling, and acquiring mobile devices. Make one mistake in a single step, and you risk losing access to evidence, locking down the easier acquisition paths, or even permanently destroying the very data you were about to access. And even if you succeed in extracting evidence, if you don't stick to the guidelines, the evidence you obtained may not be admissible. This is why we'll cover the entire workflow from seizing a mobile device to acquiring its content to viewing data and analyzing evidence.

Being able to analyze a mobile device suspected in leaking sensitive information is of great importance to corporate security. However, a passcode lock in a smartphone that was used by an ex-employee may become a major problem if the company does not store recovery keys for each and every mobile device allowed in the corporate network. How do you break into an ex-employee's passcode-locked iPhone? What can you do with a BlackBerry smartphone? Is there a good reason behind not allowing jailbroken devices on corporate premises? Dealing with this sort of problem requires the use of dedicated tools, and even then a positive outcome is not a given. In this book, you'll learn about the tools and methods used to deal with information stored in smartphones and tablets.

Conventions

In this book, you will find a number of text styles that distinguish between different kinds of information. Here are some examples of these styles and an explanation of their meaning.

Code words in text, database table names, folder names, filenames, file extensions, pathnames, dummy URLs, user input, and Twitter handles are shown as follows: "The platform offers a limited capability for creating offline backups via the command line (`adb backup`)."

New terms and **important words** are shown in bold. Words that you see on the screen, for example, in menus or dialog boxes, appear in the text like this: "Additionally, using the ADB backup requires having the phone unlocked and the **ADB Debugging** option enabled."

Warnings or important notes appear in a box like this.

Tips and tricks appear like this.

Reader feedback

Feedback from our readers is always welcome. Let us know what you think about this book-what you liked or disliked. Reader feedback is important for us as it helps us develop titles that you will really get the most out of. To send us general feedback, simply e-mail feedback@packtpub.com, and mention the book's title in the subject of your message. If there is a topic that you have expertise in and you are interested in either writing or contributing to a book, see our author guide at www.packtpub.com/authors.

Customer support

Now that you are the proud owner of a Packt book, we have a number of things to help you to get the most from your purchase.

Downloading the color images of this book

We also provide you with a PDF file that has color images of the screenshots/diagrams used in this book. The color images will help you better understand the changes in the output. You can download this file from https://www.packtpub.com/sites/default/files/down loads/MobileForensicsAdvancedInvestigativeStrategies_ColorImages.pdf.

Errata

Although we have taken every care to ensure the accuracy of our content, mistakes do happen. If you find a mistake in one of our books-maybe a mistake in the text or the code-we would be grateful if you could report this to us. By doing so, you can save other readers from frustration and help us improve subsequent versions of this book. If you find any errata, please report them by visiting http://www.packtpub.com/submit-errata, selecting your book, clicking on the **Errata Submission Form** link, and entering the details of your errata. Once your errata are verified, your submission will be accepted and the errata will be uploaded to our website or added to any list of existing errata under the Errata section of that title.

To view the previously submitted errata, go to https://www.packtpub.com/books/content/support and enter the name of the book in the search field. The required information will appear under the **Errata** section.

Piracy

Piracy of copyrighted material on the Internet is an ongoing problem across all media. At Packt, we take the protection of our copyright and licenses very seriously. If you come across any illegal copies of our works in any form on the Internet, please provide us with the location address or website name immediately so that we can pursue a remedy.

Please contact us at copyright@packtpub.com with a link to the suspected pirated material.

We appreciate your help in protecting our authors and our ability to bring you valuable content.

Questions

If you have a problem with any aspect of this book, you can contact us at questions@packtpub.com, and we will do our best to address the problem.

1
Introducing Mobile Forensics

Today's smartphones are used less for calling and more for socializing; this has resulted in smartphones holding a lot of sensitive data about their users. Mobile devices keep the user's contacts from a variety of sources (including the phone, social networks, instant messaging, and communication applications), information about phone calls, sent and received text messages, and e-mails and attachments. There are also browser logs and cached geolocation information; pictures and videos taken with the phone's camera; passwords to cloud services, forums, social networks, online portals, and shopping websites; stored payment data; and a lot of other information that can be vital for an investigation.

Needless to say, this information is very important for corporate and forensic investigations. In this book, we'll discuss not only *how* to gain access to all this data, but also *what* type of data may be available in each particular case.

Tablets are no longer used solely as entertainment devices. Equipped with powerful processors and plenty of storage, even the smallest tablets are capable of running full Windows, complete with the Office suite. While not as popular as smartphones, tablets are still widely used to socialize, communicate, plan events, and book trips.

Some smartphones are equipped with screens as large as 6.4 inches, while many tablets come with the ability to make voice calls over cellular network. All this makes it difficult to draw a line between a phone (or phablet) and a tablet.

Every smartphone on the market has a camera that, unlike a bigger (and possibly better) camera, is always accessible. As a result, an average smartphone contains more photos and videos than a dedicated camera, sometimes, gigabytes of images and video clips.

Smartphones are also storage devices. They can be used (and are used) to keep, carry, and exchange information. Smartphones connected to a corporate network may have access to files and documents not meant to be exposed. Uncontrolled access to corporate networks from employees' smartphones can (and does) cause leaks of highly-sensitive information. Employees come and go. With many companies allowing or even encouraging *bring your own device* policies, controlling the data that is accessible to those connecting to a corporate network is essential.

Why we need mobile forensics

The importance of mobile forensics is hard to underestimate. Back in 2012, over 70% of web page requests originated from desktop and laptop computers (Windows 7 and Windows XP being the most popular systems). In May 2015, only 43% of requests come from desktop operating systems, while 54% of the traffic comes from Android, iOS, and Windows phone devices. If you look at the following graph, the trend is clear-the proportion of time the users spend with desktop computers is falling, while the use of mobile devices is rising:

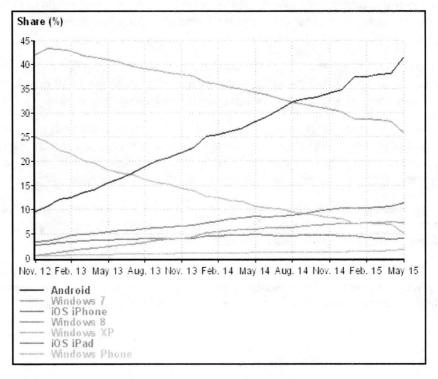

Number of visitors with different OS (source: http://www.liveinternet.ru/)

At the beginning of 2015, Apple announced that it sold over one billion iOS devices. In the first quarter of 2015 alone, the company sold 74.4 million iPhone units. Android reached a billion units sold earlier in 2014.

Smartphones and tablets are successfully competing for user's attention with personal computers. They are effectively replacing digital cameras, camcorders, book readers, newspapers, communication and navigation devices, portable game consoles, and even TV. According to Flurry (`http://flurrymobile.tumblr.com/post/115194107130/mobile-to-television-we-interrupt-this-broadcast#.VGukrIvF_Ex`), consumers spend more time with their mobile devices than they do on TV:

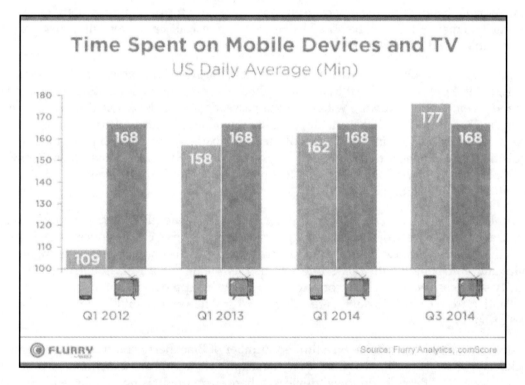

Mobile to Television (Source: Flurry)

With this amount of time spent on mobile devices, and such a vast range of activities available on them, smartphones and tablets accumulate much more information about their users than we could ever imagine. Extracting this information, analyzing the data, and turning it into solid evidence is the primary goal of a digital investigator.

Available information

Unlike personal computers that basically present a single source of information (the device itself consisting of hard drive(s) and volatile memory), mobile forensics deals with multiple data sources. Depending on the sources that are available, investigators may use one or the other tool to acquire information.

Mobile devices

If you have access to the mobile device, you can attempt to perform physical or logical acquisition. Depending on the device itself (hardware) and the operating system it is running, this may or may not be possible. However, physical acquisition still counts as the most complete and up-to-date source of evidence among all available.

Generally speaking, physical acquisition is available for most Android smartphones and tablets, older Apple hardware (iPhones up to iPhone 4, the original iPad, iPad mini, and so on), and recent Apple hardware with a known passcode. As a rule, Apple devices can only be physically acquired if jailbroken. Since a jailbreak obtains superuser privileges by exploiting a vulnerability in iOS, and Apple actively fixes such vulnerabilities, physical acquisition of iOS devices remains iffy. A physical acquisition technique has been recently developed for some Windows phone devices using Cellebrite **Universal Forensic Extraction Device (UFED)**.

Physical acquisition is also available for 64-bit Apple hardware (iPhone 5S and newer, iPad mini 2, and so on). It is worth noting that physical acquisition of 64-bit devices is even more restrictive compared to the older 32-bit hardware, as it requires not only jailbreaking the device and unlocking it with a passcode, but also removing the said passcode from the security settings. Interestingly, according to Apple, even Apple itself cannot extract information from 64-bit iOS devices running iOS 8 and newer, even if they are served a court order.

Physical acquisition is available on a limited number of BlackBerry smartphones running BlackBerry OS 7 and earlier. For BlackBerry smartphones, physical acquisition is available for unlocked BlackBerry 7 and lower devices, where supported, using Cellebrite UFED Touch/4PC through the bootloader method. For BlackBerry 10 devices where device encryption is not enabled, a chip-off can successfully acquire the device memory by parsing the physical dump using Cellebrite UFED.

You can learn more about the aforementioned method here: *BlackBerry Forensics – Physical Extraction and Decoding from BlackBerry Devices* (Cellebrite)-`http://www.cellebrite.com/Pages/blackberry-fo rensics-physical-extraction-and-decoding-from-blackberry-devic es`.

Personal computers

Notably, the user's personal computer can help in acquiring mobile evidence. The PC may contain the phone's offline data backups (such as those produced by Apple iTunes) that contain most of the information stored in the phone and available (or unavailable) during physical acquisition.

Lockdown records are created when an iOS device is physically connected to the computer and authorized through iTunes. Lockdown records may be used to gain access to an iOS device without entering the passcode. In addition, the computer may contain binary authentication tokens that can be used to access respective cloud accounts linked to a user's mobile devices.

Cloud storage

Many smartphones and tablets, especially those produced by Apple, offer the ability to back up information into an online cloud. Apple smartphones, for example, will automatically back up their content to Apple iCloud every time they are connected to a charger within the reach of a known Wi-Fi network. Windows phone devices exhibit similar behavior. Google, while not featuring full cloud backups like Apple or Microsoft, collects and retains even more information through **Google Mobile Services** (**GMS**). This information can also be pulled from the cloud.

Since cloud backups are transparent, non-intrusive, and require no user interaction, they are left enabled by default by many smartphone users, which makes it possible for an investigator to either acquire the content of the cloud storage or request it from the respective company with a court order.

In order to successfully access the phone's cloud storage, one needs to know the user's authentication credentials (login and password). It may be possible to access iCloud by using binary authentication tokens extracted from the user's computer.

With manufacturers quickly advancing in their security implementations, cloud forensics is quickly gaining importance and recognition among digital forensic specialists.

Stages of mobile forensics

This section will briefly discuss the general stages of mobile forensics and is not intended to provide a detailed explanation of each stage. There is more-than-sufficient documentation that can be easily accessed on the Internet that provides an intimate level of detail regarding the stages of mobile forensics. However, to assist the reader in the initial query, the following sources are highly recommended for further reading:

- *Developing Process for Mobile Device Forensics (Cynthia A. Murphy)*: `https://digit al-forensics.sans.org/media/mobile-device-forensic-process-v3.pdf`
- *Guidelines on Mobile Device Forensics* – **National Institute of Standards and Technology (NIST)**: `http://nvlpubs.nist.gov/nistpubs/SpecialPublicatio ns/NIST.SP.8-11r1.pdf`
- *Mobile Device Forensics: A-Z (Sam Brothers)*: `http://www.nist.gov/forensics/up load/2-Brothers-NIST-214_Slides-23-Pages-2.pdf`
- ACPO Good Practice Guide for Computer-Based Electronic Evidence, (pages 45-51): `https://www.cps.gov.uk/legal/assets/uploads/files/ACPO_guideli nes_computer_evidence[1].pdf`

The most important concept for the reader to understand is this: have the least level of impact on the mobile device during all the stages. In other words, an examiner should first work on the continuum of the least-intrusive method to the most-intrusive method, which can be dictated by the type of data needing to be obtained from the mobile device and the complexity of the hardware/software of the mobile device.

Stage 1 – device seizure

This stage pertains to the physical seizure of the device so that it comes under the control and custody of the investigator/examiner. Consideration must also be given to the legal authority or written consent to seize, extract, and search this data.

The physical condition of the device at the time of seizure should be noted, ideally through digital photographic documentation and written notes, such as:

- Is the device damaged? If, yes, then document the type of damage.
- Is the device on or off?
- What is the device date and time if the device is on?
- If the device is on, what apps are running or observable on the device desktop?
- If the device is on, is the device desktop accessible to check for passcode and security settings?

Several other aspects of device seizure are described in the following as they will affect post-seizure analysis: radio isolation, turning the device off if it is on, remote wipe, and anti-forensics.

Seizing – what and how should we seize?

When it comes to properly acquiring a mobile device, one must be aware of the many differences in how computers and mobile devices operate. Seizing, handling, storing, and extracting mobile devices must follow a different route compared to desktop and even laptop computers.

Unlike PCs that can be either online or offline (which includes energy-saving states of sleep and hibernation), smartphones and tablets use a different, always-connected modus operandi. Tremendous amounts of activities are carried out in the background, even while the device is apparently *sleeping*. Activities can be scheduled or triggered by a large number of events, including push events from online services and events that are initiated remotely by the user.

Another thing to consider when acquiring a mobile device is security. Mobile devices are carried around a lot, and they are designed to be inherently more secure than desktop PCs. Non-removable storage and soldered RAM chips, optional or enforced data encryption, remote *kill switches*, secure lock screens, and locked bootloaders are just a few security measures to be mentioned.

The use of Faraday bags

Faraday bags are commonly used to temporarily store seized devices without powering them down. A Faraday bag blocks wireless connectivity to cellular networks, Wi-Fi, Bluetooth, satellite navigation, and any other radios used in mobile devices. Faraday bags are normally designed to shield the range of radio frequencies used by local cellular carriers and satellite navigation (typically the 700-2,600 MHz), as well as the 2.4-5 GHz range used by Wi-Fi networks and Bluetooth. Many Faraday bags are made of specially-coated metallic shielding material that blocks a wide range of radio frequencies.

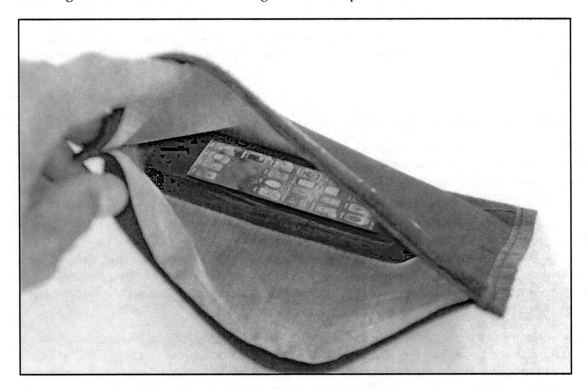

A simple Faraday bag with no charging connector

Keeping the power on

When dealing with a seized device, it is essential to prevent the device from powering off. Never switching off a working device is one thing, preventing it from powering down is another. Since mobile devices consume power even while the display is off, the standard practice is to connect the device to a charger and place it into a wireless-blocking Faraday bag. This will prevent the mobile device from shutting down after reaching the low-power state.

An advanced Faraday bag equipped with a charging connector

Why exactly do we need this procedure? The thing is, you may be able to extract more information from a device that was used (unlocked at least once) after the last boot cycle compared to a device that boots up in your lab and for which you don't know the passcode.

To illustrate the potential outcome, let's say you seized an iPhone that is locked with an unknown passcode. The iPhone happens to be jailbroken, so you can attempt to use **Elcomsoft iOS Forensic Toolkit** to extract information (refer to Chapter 4, *Practical Steps to Android Acquisition*).

If the device is locked and you don't know the passcode, you will have access to a very limited set of data:

- Recent geolocation information: Since the main location database remains encrypted, it is only possible to extract limited location data. This limited location data is only accessible if the device was unlocked at least once after the boot has completed. As a result, if you keep the device powered on, you may pull recent geolocation history from this device. If, however, the device shuts down and is only powered on in the lab, the geolocation data will remain inaccessible until the device is unlocked.
- Incoming calls (numbers only) and text messages: Incoming text messages are temporarily retained unencrypted before the first unlock after cold boot. Once the device is unlocked for the first time after cold boot, the messages will be transferred into the main encrypted database. This means that acquiring a device that was never unlocked after a cold start will only allow access to text messages received by the device during the time it remained locked after the boot.

  If the iPhone being acquired was unlocked at least once after it was booted (for example, if the device was seized in a turned-on state), you may be able to access significantly more information. The SMS database is decrypted on first unlock, allowing you to pull all text messages and not just those that were received while the device remained locked.

- App and system logs (installs and updates, net access logs, and so on).
- SQLite temp files, including **write-ahead logs** (WAL): These WAL may include messages received by applications such as Skype, Viber, Facebook Messenger, and so on. Once the device is unlocked, the data is merged with the corresponding apps' main databases. When extracting a device after a cold boot (never unlocked), you will only have access to notifications received after the boot. If, however, you are extracting a device that was unlocked at least once after booting up, you may be able to extract the complete database with all messages (depending on the data protection class selected by the developer of a particular application).

Dealing with the kill switch

Mobile operating systems such as Apple iOS, recent versions of Google Android, all versions of BlackBerry OS, and Microsoft Windows phone 8/8.1 (Windows 10 mobile) have an important security feature designed to prevent unauthorized persons from accessing information stored in the device. The so-called *kill switch* enables the owner to lock or erase the device if the device is reported lost or stolen. While used by legitimate customers to safeguard their data, this feature is also used by suspects who may attempt to remotely destroy evidence if their mobile device is seized.

 In the recent *Morristown man accused of remotely wiping nude photos of underage girlfriend on confiscated phone* report (`http://wate.com/2015/04/07/morristown-man-accused-of-remotely-w iping-nude-photos-of-underage-girlfriend-on-confiscated-phone/`), the accused used the remote kill switch to wipe data stored on his iPhone.

Using the Faraday bag is essential to prevent suspects from accessing the kill switch. However, even if the device in question has already been wiped remotely, it does not necessarily mean that all the data is completely lost.

Apple iOS, Windows phone 8/8.1, Windows 10 mobile, and the latest version of Android (Android 6.0 Marshmallow) support cloud backups (albeit Android cloud backups contain limited amounts of data). When it comes to BlackBerry 10, the backups are strictly offline, yet the decryption key is tied to the user's BlackBerry ID and stored on BlackBerry servers.

The ability to automatically upload backup copies of data into the cloud is a double-edged sword. While offering more convenience to the user, cloud backups make remote acquisition techniques possible. Depending on the platform, all or some information from the device can be retrieved from the cloud by either making use of a forensic tool (for example, **Elcomsoft Phone Breaker, Oxygen Forensic Detective**) or by serving a government request to the corresponding company (Apple, Google, Microsoft, or BlackBerry).

Mobile device anti-forensics

There are numerous anti-forensic methods that target evidence acquisition methods used by law enforcement agencies. It is common for the police to seize a device, connect it to a charger, and place into a Faraday bag. The anti-forensic method used by some technologically-advanced suspects on Android phones involves rooting the device and installing a tool that monitors wireless connectivity of the device. If the tool detects that the device has been idle, connected to a charger, and without wireless connectivity for a predefined period, it performs a factory reset. Since there is no practical way of determining whether such protection is active on the device prior to acquisition, simply following established guidelines presents a risk of evidence being destroyed. If there are reasonable grounds to suspect such a system may be in place, the device can be powered down (while realizing the risk of full-disk encryption preventing subsequent acquisition).

While rooting or jailbreaking devices generally makes the device susceptible to advanced acquisition methods, we've seen users who unlocked their bootloader to install a custom recovery, protected access to this custom recovery with a password, and relocked the bootloader. Locked bootloader and password-protected access to custom recovery is an extremely tough combination to break.

In several reports, we've become aware of the following anti-forensic technique used by a group of cyber criminals. The devices were configured to automatically wipe user data if certain predefined conditions were met. In this case, the predefined conditions triggering the wipe matched the typical acquisition scenario of placing the device inside a Faraday bag and connecting it to a charger. When the device reports being charged without wireless connectivity (but not in airplane mode) for a certain amount of time, a special tool triggers a full factory reset of the device. Notably, this is only possible on rooted/jailbroken devices.

So far, this anti-forensic technique has not received wide recognition. It's used by a small minority of smartphone users, mostly those into cybercrime. The low probability of a smartphone being configured that way is small enough to consider implementing changes to published guidelines.

Stage 2 – data acquisition

This stage refers to various methods of extracting data from the device. The methods of data extraction that can be employed are influenced by the following:

- Type of mobile device: The make, model, hardware, software, and vendor configuration.
- Availability of a diverse set of hardware and software extraction/analysis tools at the examiner's disposal: There is no tool that does it all; an examiner needs to have access to a number of tools that can assist with data extraction.
- Physical state of device: Has the device been exposed to damage, such as physical, water, or biological fluids such as blood? Often the type of damage can dictate the data extraction measures employed on the device.

There are several different types of data extraction that determine how much data is obtained from the device:

- Physical: Binary image of the device has the most potential to recover deleted data and obtains the largest amount of data from the device. This can be the most challenging type of extraction to obtain.
- File system: This is a representation of the files and folders from the user area of the device, and can contain deleted data specific to databases. This method will contain less data than a physical data extraction.
- Logical: This acquires the least amount of data from the device. Examples of this are call history, messages, contacts, pictures, movies, audio files, and so on. This is referred to as low-hanging fruit. No deleted data or source files are obtained. Often the resulting output will be a series of reports produced by the extraction tool. This is often the easiest and quickest type of extraction.
- Photographic documentation: This method is typically used when all other data extraction avenues are exhausted. In this procedure, the examiner uses a digital camera to photographically document the content being displayed by the device. This is a time-consuming method when there is an extensive amount of information to photograph.

Specific data-extraction concepts are explained here: bootloader, jailbreak, rooting, adb, debug, and sim cloning.

Root, jailbreak, and unlocked bootloader

Rooting or jailbreaking mobile devices in general makes them susceptible to a wide range of exploits. In the context of mobile forensics, rooted devices are easy to acquire since many forensic acquisition tools rely on root/jailbreak to perform physical acquisition.

Devices with unlocked bootloaders allow booting unsigned code, effectively permitting full access to the device even if it's locked with a passcode. However, if the device is encrypted and the passcode is part of the encryption key, bypassing passcode protection may not automatically enable access to encrypted data.

Rooting or jailbreaking enables unrestricted access to the filesystem, bypassing the operating system's security measures and allowing the acquisition tool to read information from protected areas. This is one of the reasons for banning rooted devices (as well as devices with unlocked bootloaders) from corporate premises.

Installing a jailbreak on iOS devices always makes the phone less secure, enabling third-party code to be injected and run on a system level. This fact is well-known to forensic experts who make use of tools such as Cellebrite UFED or Elcomsoft iOS Forensic Toolkit to perform physical acquisition of jailbroken Apple smartphones.

Some Android devices allow unlocking the bootloader, which enables easy and straightforward rooting of the device. While not all Android devices with unlocked bootloaders are rooted, installing root access during acquisition of a bootloader-unlocked device has a much higher chance of success compared to devices that are locked down. Tools such as Cellebrite UFED, **Forensic Toolkit (FTK)**, Oxygen Forensic Suite, and many others can make use of the phone's root status in order to inject acquisition applets and image the device.

Unlocked bootloaders can be exploited as well if you use UFED. A bootloader-level exploit exists and is used in UFED to perform acquisition of many Android and Windows phone devices based on the Qualcomm reference platform even if their bootloader is locked.

Android ADB debugging

Android has a hidden **Developer Options** menu. Accessing this menu requires a conscious effort of tapping on the OS build number multiple times. Some users enable **Developer Options** out of curiosity. Once enabled, the **Developer Options** menu may or may not be possible to hide.

Among other things, the **Developer Options** menu lists an option called **USB debugging** or **ADB debugging**. If enabled, this option allows controlling the device via the ADB command line, which in turn allows experts using Android debugging tools (**adb.exe**) to connect to the device from a PC even if it's locked with a passcode. Activated **USB debugging** exposes a lot of possibilities and can make acquisition possible even if the device is locked with a passcode.

SIM cloning

In certain cases, establishing a connection between the phone and the extraction tool may not be possible unless the phone has a SIM card in it. Moreover, some devices can be configured to invoke protection if a different SIM card is used. On rare occasions, devices can even be configured to wipe their content if a non-original SIM card is inserted or if a SIM card is removed. In particular, some BlackBerry devices may block extraction attempts with a message reading **SIM Not Provisioned** or **SIM Not Allowed**. In such cases, using a cloned SIM card may enable communication and allow the extraction.

SIM card memory

The SIM card holds network operator information and can identify the mobile phone number assigned to the user by the mobile device. The SIM card can contain call history, and messages. The information stored on the SIM can be obtained by most if not all mobile forensic tools.

Memory card

Most smartphone devices and tablets (except iOS devices) have the capability of increasing their storage capacity by using a microSD card. An examiner would remove the memory card from the mobile device/tablet and use either hardware or software write-protection methods to create a bit stream forensic image of the memory card, which can then be analyzed using forensic software tools, such as X-Ways, Autopsy Sleuth Kit, Forensic Explorer (GetData), EnCase, or FTK (AccessData).

Stage 3 – data analysis

This stage of mobile device forensics entails analysis of the acquired data from the device and its components (SIM card and memory card if present). Most mobile forensic acquisition tools that acquire the data from the device memory can also parse the extracted data and provide the examiner functionality within the tool to perform analysis. This entails review of any non-deleted and deleted data.

When reviewing non-deleted data, it would be prudent to also perform a manual review of the device to ensure that the extracted and parsed data matches what is displayed by the device. As mobile device storage capacities have increased, it is suggested that a limited subset of data records from the relevant areas be reviewed. So, for example, if a mobile device has over 200 call records, reviewing several call records from missed calls, incoming calls, and outgoing calls can be checked on the device in relation to the similar records in the extracted data. By doing this manual review, it is then possible to discover any discrepancies in the extracted data.

Manual device review can only be completed when the device is still in the custody of the examiner. There are situations where, after the data extraction has been completed, the device is released back to the investigator or owner. In situations such as this, the examiner should document that very limited or no manual verification can be performed due to these circumstances.

Finally, the reader should be keenly aware that more than one analysis tool can be used to analyze the acquired data. Multiple analysis tools should be considered, especially when a specific type of data cannot be parsed by one tool, but can be analyzed by another.

Summary

In this chapter, we've covered the basics of mobile forensics. We discussed the amount of evidence available in today's mobile devices and covered the general steps of mobile forensics. We also discussed how to seize, handle, and store mobile devices, and looked at how criminals can use technology to prevent forensic access. We provided a general overview of the acquisition and analysis steps. In the next chapter, we'll discuss acquisition methods in more detail. We'll overview different acquisition methods and techniques, and look at their applicability in different situations.

2
Acquisition Methods Overview

With a wide range of mobile devices around, multiple acquisition methods exist. There is no single universal acquisition method available to all models. Some acquisition methods depend on the phone's lock and encryption status, OS version, type of available storage, and so on. You'll have to work your way through the investigation to discover what acquisition methods are available for a particular device.

The following is a quick overview of the acquisition methods available for the different mobile platforms listed from the easiest to the most advanced (and labor-intensive). For more details about each acquisition method, please refer to chapters on individual platforms.

This chapter discusses existing acquisition methods and their applicability on major mobile platforms:

- Over-the-air acquisition
- Acquiring evidence from mobile backups
- Physical acquisition – availability and applicability
- Advanced acquisition methods – JTAG, ISP, and chip-off

Over-the-air acquisition

Many mobile devices come with the ability to back up their contents into the cloud. Depending on the platform, cloud backups may contain as much as the full content of the device complete with the call histories and messages (Apple iOS 7.x through 9.x, Windows RT, and Windows 8/8.1/10); as little as a list of installed applications and a few random settings (Android 4.4 and Android 5.x); or something in between (Windows Phone 8 and Android 6.0).

For some devices, cloud forensics may be the only acquisition method available due to full-disk encryption and hardware lock. For example, cloud forensics is the only viable process for locked 64-bit iPhones running iOS 8+ and some Windows Phone 8 and Windows 10 Mobile devices.

Compared to other acquisition methods in general, cloud backups tend to contain the least amount of information.

For cloud acquisition to work, the expert will have to possess the user's authentication credentials. While a login and password are the most commonly used credentials, two-factor authentication may become an obstacle if there is no access to the secondary authentication factor.

Cloud acquisition benefits are as follows:

- Device is *not required*
- Independent of device model, OS version, and jailbreak status
- Remote acquisition
- Can be performed without the suspect being aware
- Can be used to track the suspect (location tracking)
- One of the easiest acquisition methods
- No special expertise required
- Device disassembly not required
- Non-destructive process

Major drawbacks of cloud acquisition include the following:

- Limited amount of information extracted
- iOS keychain extraction may be unavailable
- Must know user ID and password (or have a binary authentication token)
- Large amount of data can be very slow to download
- Two-factor authentication presents additional challenges
- Binary authentication tokens may expire
- No unallocated space extraction

Apple iCloud

In the case of Apple iCloud, binary authentication tokens created by software on the user's computer (via Apple iCloud for Windows or its macOS counterpart) can be used in place of the login and password. The use of binary authentication tokens currently bypasses Apple's two-factor authentication. However, these authentication tokens may have limited lifespan (Apple tweaks token expirations all the time), and may have already expired when it comes to the actual acquisition. We will be giving you more information about the tokens and their expiration in Chapter 6, *iOS Logical and Cloud Acquisition.*

Windows Phone 8, Windows 10 Mobile, and Windows RT/8/8.1/10

Windows Phone 8 and Windows 10 Mobile have a comprehensive cloud backup system. Cloud backups can be downloaded with forensic tools if the user's Microsoft account login and password are known. Windows 8, 8.1, 10, and Windows RT automatically back up user data, Modern UI apps, and their data into the user's Microsoft account (OneDrive), but only if the user logs in with their Microsoft account credentials as opposed to using a local Windows account.

Google Android

A very limited amount of information from Android devices can be backed up into the user's Google Account. However, Google collects and stores a large quantity of information about its users. The data originates from all devices, Android or not, on which a particular Google service was used. As a result, large amounts of highly valuable information can be obtained from the suspect's Google Account.

Law enforcement may have an option of requesting the full content of a suspect's cloud accounts from the service provider (Apple, Microsoft, or Google) with a court order. Since cloud backups are generally not encrypted (or encryption keys are stored alongside the backup), there are no technical obstacles to obtaining the data. This may very well change in the near future, if these organizations were to implement encrypted cloud backups.

More information about over-the-air acquisition of Google Accounts is available in Chapter 3, *Acquisition – Approaching Android Devices.*

Logical acquisition (backup analysis)

Many devices (Apple iOS, BlackBerry, and a limited number of Android models, for example, Sony Xperia) are able to produce offline backups via the software installed on the user's computer. Apple iTunes, BlackBerry Link, Sony PC Companion, and many other tools can be used to produce and restore phone or tablet backups. Depending on the OS, an offline backup may or may not be password-protected. Depending on the protection status, experts may be able to extract all, some, or none of the information.

Offline backups, if available for a particular platform, tend to have as much or more information available compared to cloud backups.

Logical acquisition benefits include the following:

- One of the easiest acquisition methods
- No special expertise required
- Device disassembly not required
- Non-destructive process

Major drawbacks of logical acquisition are as follows:

- Limited amount of information extracted
- Android: Manufacturers and app developers control what is and what is not included in ADB backups
- Android: ADB backup may not work on encrypted devices
- Not available for Windows Phone 8 and Windows 10 Mobile
- No unallocated space extraction
- Backups protected with unknown passwords: No success guarantee and unknown timeframe

Apple iOS

Password-protected iTunes backups (Apple iOS) are encrypted; the expert will have to supply the correct password in order to decrypt the backup. If the password is not known, the expert can perform an attack (brute-force, dictionary, or combination) in order to recover the password. When analyzing password-protected Apple backups, experts can access items from the Apple keychain. Offline backups created without a password will be unencrypted for the most part; however, the keychain will be encrypted with a hardware key, meaning that no keychain data will be available. Making the (unlocked) iOS device produce an offline backup is a viable acquisition method. If possible, try to ensure that a backup with a known password is created (if backup password is not set, creating one before making the backup will ensure that the keychain items can be decrypted).

Backup passwords, if enabled, are more of a property of the actual iOS device rather than the backup itself. If backup password protection is enabled, the backup is encrypted on the iOS device before any data leaves the device. Once backup encryption is enabled, no unencrypted data leaves the device regardless of the tool used to make the backup. In other words, Apple iTunes is not actually creating backups; instead, the tool receives an encrypted data stream and saves it to a file.

BlackBerry 10

Backups produced by BlackBerry Link (BB 10 OS) do not have a password. Instead, they are securely encrypted on-device with a strong encryption key that is stored online. Retrieving the encryption key is possible if the user's BlackBerry ID and password are known, or by serving a government request.

Similar to Apple iOS, BlackBerry 10 devices encrypt their backups internally. No unencrypted data leaves the device. So, when the user creates a backup via BlackBerry Link or a different tool (for example, Sachesi or Darcy's BlackBerry Tools), the backup tool just passes a command to the BlackBerry device. The device handles the encryption internally and streams the encrypted data flow to BlackBerry Link (or an alternative tool). It is important to note that unencrypted data never leaves the device regardless of what tool is used.

 Windows Phone 8 and Windows 10 Mobile do not offer offline backups.

Android

Stock Android does not come with iTunes-like tools for making full-device backups. However, some**original equipment manufacturers** (**OEMs**) provide tools for making and restoring offline backups (for example, Sony PC Companion for Xperia devices).

The platform offers a limited capability for creating offline backups via the command line (`adb backup`). However, ADB backups may include a limited amount of data compared to iTunes backups. Due to Android fragmentation, manufacturers have control over what does and does not become part of the backup. As a result, some devices may back up call history, contacts, and text messages, while some other devices won't. As an example, Samsung, Sony, and HTC often omit call history, contacts, and text messages, while allowing Google Chrome data to be backed up (which, for example, will contain cached passwords and browsing history). We will discuss more on the Android logical acquisition via ADB backup in `Chapter 4`, *Practical Steps to Android Acquisition*, in the *Android physical acquisition* and *Live imaging without root (via ADB backup)* sections

Nandroid backups

Rooted Android phones with custom recoveries (CWM and TWRP) offer the ability to create so-called Nandroid backups, which contain full images of the device's filesystem. During acquisition, such devices can be booted into the Recovery Mode and instructed to produce a full Nandroid backup.

In general, the phone must have a custom recovery installed in order to produce a Nandroid backup. Installing a custom recovery (if it's not yet installed) requires an unlocked bootloader (or a bootloader hack) and/or rooting the device. Note that, in most cases, unlocking a locked bootloader will wipe all user data on the device. This Android security measure can be bypassed in certain cases via the bootloader hack.

Note that neither cloud nor offline backups include unallocated space.

Physical acquisition

Physical acquisition strikes the best balance between extraction speed, ease of use, and the amount of information being extracted. This process does not require disassembling the phone or using any special hardware. A micro USB (or Apple Lightning) cord, a PC (or Mac), and forensic software for physical acquisition (refer to the following section) are all that's required. For iOS devices newer than iPhone 4, Elcomsoft iOS Forensic Toolkit is currently the only physical acquisition solution available.

Physical acquisition extracts the maximum amount of information from the device. For unencrypted devices, unallocated space will be extracted together with the filesystem, allowing experts to carve the dump for destroyed evidence. Encrypted devices handle unallocated space differently. For example, Apple iOS always uses full-disk encryption that does not keep encryption keys to released data blocks. As a result, unallocated areas can be accessed, but cannot be decrypted in Apple devices even if the device is jailbroken and the passcode is known.

Physical acquisition benefits as are follows:

- Strikes the best balance between the amount of extracted data, speed, and ease of use
- Guaranteed timeframe
- In many cases, it can extract unallocated space (except on Apple devices)
- Operates on a high level and can overcome encryption (extracted images are decrypted on-the-fly)
- Available for select Windows Phone models
- Available for older iOS devices
- Available for many Android devices (various methods exist)
- Only requires a USB or Lightning cord and acquisition software
- Device disassembly not required
- Can be used by most forensic experts, no special skills required
- Non-destructive and non-invasive process

Major drawbacks of physical acquisition include the following:

- Limited general availability, extremely limited availability for Apple iOS devices
- May or may not support locked Android devices with USB Debugging turned off
- No unified approach, a wide range of acquisition tools and methods
- May not acquire locked devices with an unknown PIN/passcode

Apple iOS

When it comes to Apple devices, physical acquisition is fully available for 32-bit hardware, with limited support for 64-bit devices (keychain items remain encrypted when acquiring a 64-bit device, even if the passcode is known). The 32-bit acquisition process supports iPhone 4, 4S, 5, and 5C, but not the later 5S, 6, or 6 Plus. The original iPad mini can be acquired with the 32-bit process, but iPad mini 2 (Retina) already uses a 64-bit **System on a Chip (SoC)**, so physical acquisition is available via a separate (64-bit) process.

 SoC is an integrated circuit that combines electronics such as the main CPU, GPU, wireless modems, and dedicated motion and other co-processors on a single chip. A SoC packs much more than just a CPU on a single silicon chip.

Note that iPhone 4S, 5, and 5C can only be acquired via a jailbreak, so prerequisites for the physical acquisition of these devices includes either a jailbroken iPhone or a known passcode and a version of iOS that can be jailbroken. A non-jailbroken iPhone 4S, 5, or 5C locked with an unknown passcode cannot be extracted via physical acquisition; however, a limited amount of data can still be extracted even if the device is locked with an unknown passcode.

The 64-bit acquisition process supports all existing Apple devices, such as iPhone 5S/6/6S/Plus, iPad mini 2-4, iPad Air/Air 2, and iPad Pro. The 64-bit process is backward-compatible with 32-bit devices and can be used instead of the full 32-bit acquisition process if there is an error acquiring the device. However, the 64-bit process is highly invasive; it modifies the content of user and system partitions. Instead of a DMG image, the 64-bit process returns a TAR file of the filesystem (files and folders only). Finally, keychain items are acquired, but cannot be decrypted via the 64-bit process even if the passcode is known.

More about iOS physical acquisition in `Chapter 5`, *iOS – Introduction and Physical Acquisition.*

Android

Physical acquisition is probably the best extraction method available for Android devices. Physical acquisition operates on a higher level than JTAG or chip-off.

 JTAG: This is a common name for **test access ports (TAP)** standardized by the **Joint Test Action Group (JTAG)** association. These ports, among other things, can be utilized to access raw data stored in the connected device. Chip-off: This is an advanced, destructive acquisition technique where individual storage chips (for example, **embedded MultiMediaCard (eMMC)**) are removed from the device and imaged directly (by attaching wire leads to the chip contacts) or via a commercially-available adapter.

Since physical acquisition runs through the phone's controller, in many cases, dumping an encrypted device will produce a decrypted dump (which is not the case for JTAG or chip-off). In Android, the dumping process requires superuser permission to run. A rooted device is required. Commercial acquisition tools such as Oxygen Forensic Suite will automatically attempt to root the device (tethered rooting) on the expert's behalf. A different, more advanced acquisition strategy is available for certain devices via a bootloader hack (Cellebrite UFED), which does not require rooting the device or altering its content in any way. Only supported devices can be extracted with this method, which include some Motorola Android devices and selected Samsung, Qualcomm, and LG devices. While this method is mostly applicable to devices with unlocked bootloaders, Cellebrite has bootloader hacks for certain devices with locked bootloaders (for example, selected Nokia Lumia devices).

Finally, some manufacturers implement service access to the phone's storage via a special firmware update mode. These manufacturers include Qualcomm (Qualcomm HS-USB 9006 / Qualcomm MMC Storage; this works regardless of the bootloader lock status, but may not be available on all devices); LG, regardless of the chipset (LAF mode works regardless of the bootloader lock status); and MediaTek and Spreadtrum (only works on unlocked bootloaders). These modes can be utilized for forensically sound acquisition of some devices via mobile forensic tools, such as Oxygen Forensic Suite.

We will discuss more about Android physical acquisition in `Chapter 5`, *iOS – Introduction and Physical Acquisition*.

Windows Phone 8 and Windows 10 Mobile

For a long time, the Windows Phone OS remained secure against physical acquisition attacks. A bootloader-level exploit was developed for select Windows Phone devices by Cellebrite. Supported Windows Phone 8 devices can be dumped with Cellebrite UFED via a USB cord
(`http://www.cellebrite.com/Pages/windows-phone-forensics-physical-extraction-and-decoding-from-windows-phone-devices`).

The bootloader exploit works even if the device was updated to run Windows 10 Mobile.

Limitations and availability

Physical extraction is not available on BlackBerry 10, Apple iOS devices with 64-bit hardware, and a great deal of Android smartphones for which no known exploit is available.

Tools for physical acquisition

Just to mention, the following forensic tools are available and recommended for performing physical acquisition of mobile devices:

- **Cellebrite UFED** offers an extensive range of tools for mobile forensics under their *UFED* umbrella. More tools are provided by Cellebrite.
- **Micro Systemation (XRY)** offers a range of mobile forensic tools to perform physical and logical extraction from a wide range of mobile devices, extracting all available raw data (physical only).
- **AccessData (MPE+)** offers **Mobile Phone Examiner Plus (MPE+)**, an all-in-one acquisition and analysis toolkit supporting a wide range of mobile devices. The company claims support for over 7,000 device models.
- **Elcomsoft iOS Forensic Toolkit** is the only tool on the market to support physical acquisition of all 32-bit and 64-bit iOS devices.

- **Oxygen Forensic Suite** supports more than 12,000 unique device models via physical, logical, and cloud acquisition techniques. This comes with the ability to exploit unique properties of certain chip sets and OEMs that allow investigators to dump the entire content of the device while bypassing the bootloader lock and screen lock together.

- **Magnet ACQUIRE** can perform logical acquisition as well as physical acquisition of multiple Android and iOS devices. The extraction is done in a manner that is agnostic so that any analysis tool can import the extracted data for analysis.
- **BlackBag Mobilyize** can acquire Android and iOS. iOS is restricted to logical/filesystem. For Android, it can do all three levels of extraction provided on the device type and other variables such as OS, operator customizations, and so on.

JTAG

JTAG forensics is an advanced acquisition procedure that uses test access ports standardized by the JTAG association. These ports, among other things, can be utilized to access raw data stored in the connected device. The acquisition process involves using existing solder points on the device's circuit board. By using specialized equipment and a matching device-specific JTAG cable, one can retrieve the flash memory contents (less the eMMC overprovisioned area, but including addressable unallocated space) from compatible devices. Notably, JTAG acquisition is often available even for locked, damaged, or otherwise inaccessible devices. JTAG acquisition is available for many Android devices, as well as some feature phones and Windows Phone 7 and 8 devices. JTAG is not available for recent BlackBerry 10 devices. It is not available for any Apple device either.

JTAG operates on a lower level compared to physical acquisition. This has its advantages and disadvantanges.

The following are the JTAG benefits:

- It can acquire locked devices with an unknown PIN/passcode
- Supports locked Android devices with USB Debugging turned off
- Available for many Windows Phone models
- Available for devices running proprietary operating systems (for example, Ubuntu Touch, Firefox OS, and so on)
- Good chance of extracting the content of locked up, damaged, and broken devices
- Extracts data from devices not supported by any forensic tools
- Non-destructive, but invasive process

Major drawbacks of JTAG acquisition include the following:

- Cannot overcome encryption (experts may or may not be able to decrypt extracted images)
- Requires a high skill level and a good amount of expertise
- Invasive process, requires disassembling the device
- Labor-intensive
- Relatively slow acquisition speed (compared to chip-off or ISP)
- Only available for a limited number of devices with TAP ports
- Different kinds of JTAG boxes may be required to fully support all manufacturers or models, which adds significant cost

JTAG forensics is a labor-intensive and time-consuming process requiring an expert to use a well-equipped lab. As such, forensic experts tend to try JTAG acquisition after other methods prove unsuccessful.

Chip-off

Chip-off acquisition is a highly advanced, destructive extraction technique that requires attaching wire leads to the PCB contacts or physically removing (desoldering) the phone's flash memory chip. Chip-off is considered more difficult compared to JTAG; however, the amount of information acquired via chip-off acquisition is similar to the amount of data acquired by JTAGging the device. Since most smartphones use standard eMMC flash modules, the process is standardized and typically presents no surprises to the examiner.

When imaging computer hard drives, one normally attempts to go as low level as possible. In the world of mobile forensic, the lowest-level access is not always the best. While reading the chips directly produces a complete raw dump of the memory chips, the investigator may be faced with an encrypted partition with no decryption keys stored anywhere around. In the case of Apple devices, many Samsung phones, and other devices (for example, the Android 5 Nexus line), encryption is enforced out-of-the-box. This forced encryption cannot be bypassed during low-level acquisition or by attacking the offline image even if you know the correct passcode. Chip-off acquisition delivers the best result when used on unencrypted devices.

Chapter 2

Chip-off benefits include the following:

- It acquire locked devices with unknown PIN/passcode
- Supports locked Android devices with USB Debugging turned off
- Available for all Windows Phone models
- Available for devices running proprietary operating systems (for example, Ubuntu Touch, Firefox OS, and so on)
- Excellent chance of extracting the content of locked up, damaged, and broken devices
- Extracts data from devices not supported by any forensic tools
- Supports devices without JTAG ports
- High acquisition speed

Major drawbacks of chip-off acquisition include the following:

- Cannot overcome encryption (experts may or may not be able to decrypt extracted images)
- Requires disassembling the device
- Requires extremely high level of expertise
- Extremely labor-intensive
- Destructive process

Chip-off acquisition is useless on Apple iOS devices as these devices enforce encryption out-of-the-box. It's also useless on encrypted BlackBerry 10 devices; however, BlackBerry 10 does not enforce encryption and does not enable it out-of-the-box, so the encryption status of BB10 smartphones should be confirmed on a case-by-case basis.

In-system programming

In-system programming (ISP) forensics is a non-destructive variation of chip-off acquisition. ISP is an advanced acquisition process that is in between JTAG and chip-off. During the acquisition process, examiners can attempt to dump the content of the eMMC memory without removing the chip. ISP acquisition is only available for devices utilizing eMMC or eMCP-style **ball grid array (BGA)** chips. Access to the memory is obtained through access points around the BGA chip. This acquisition process is considered non-destructive in that, if all stars align, the device can be reassembled and booted after the extraction.

[39]

eMMC ISP is used to create a binary image of the device, which can be acquired and analyzed with one of the many commercially-available forensic tools, such as UFED or Oxygen Forensic Suite.

ISP benefits include the following:

- Standardized procedure for eMMC BGA chips
- Considered non-destructive (device can be reassembled and booted afterwards)
- Can acquire locked devices with unknown PIN/passcode
- Supports locked Android devices with USB Debugging turned off
- Available for all Windows Phone models

- Available for devices running proprietary operating systems (for example, Ubuntu Touch, Firefox OS, and so on)
- Excellent chance of extracting the content of locked up, damaged, and broken devices
- Extracts data from devices not supported by any forensic tools
- Supports devices without JTAG ports
- High acquisition speed

Major drawbacks of ISP acquisition include the following:

- Cannot overcome encryption (experts may or may not be able to decrypt extracted images)
- Highly invasive process, requires disassembling the device
- Still requires a high level of expertise
- Labor-intensive

Limitations of the ISP acquisition process are similar to those of chip-off. Encrypted devices are better left to other acquisition techniques, meaning that no Apple smartphone or tablet can be acquired via ISP. Technically, the technique can be used on an Apple iOS device; however, decrypting the data partition will not be possible.

Summary

In this chapter, we had an overview of existing acquisition methods ranging from fairly easy logical and cloud extraction to expert-level and labor-intensive chip-off. We also reviewed the acquisition methods that are available on the various mobile platforms, and learned about the strengths and limitations of each method. Starting with the next chapter, we'll closely look at each mobile platform. The next chapter will provide detailed technical information on acquiring mobile devices running the Android OS.

3
Acquisition – Approaching Android Devices

Approximately, 82% of mobile devices (Q1, 2016) run the Android OS. The total number of active Android devices is about 1.4 billion (although not all of these are Google devices).

Similar to iOS, the data is not stored exclusively on mobile devices. In Android 6, Google officially introduced a cloud backup option, allowing users to maintain limited automatic backups for Android devices on Google Drive. Learning what Google knows about the user can be essential for an investigation.

An excellent resource with lots of detailed (but not too technical) information exists to help forensic experts get a better understanding of Android forensics. The **Free Android Forensics** blog at `http://freeandroidforensics.blogspot.com` offers excellent insight into the Android platform, imaging tools, and techniques. The blog mostly talks about using free forensic tools and acquisition techniques, which in our opinion can limit the available acquisition options and require more time and effort than an examiner may have at their disposal. However, the information presented in the blog is an excellent read for understanding what exactly the acquisition tools do on your behalf when acquiring information from mobile devices.

In the following sections, we will discuss the options available for acquiring information from Android devices, as well as for pulling associated data from Google servers. In this chapter, we will cover the following topics:

- Android platform fragmentation and why it matters
- AOSP and GMS demystified

- Logical acquisition via ADB backup
- Dealing with unallocated space
- Overview of advanced acquisition methods

Android platform fragmentation

Android is a heavily fragmented platform. Nearly 1,300 manufacturers and over 24,000 device models introduce a huge degree of variance:

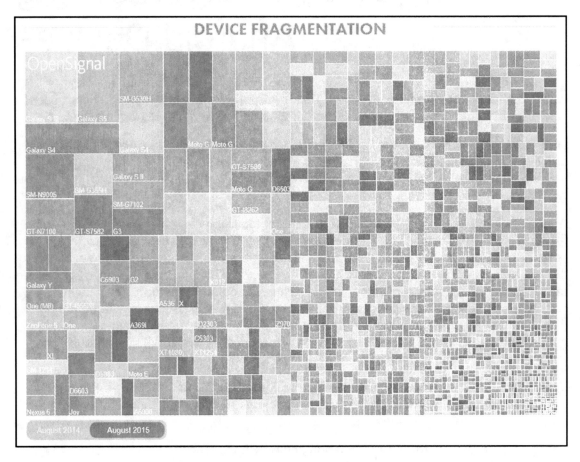

Source: http://opensignal.com/reports/2015/08/android-fragmentation/

Hardware specifications demonstrate wild variations in screen size, resolution, and display ratio, CPU, SoC, and even architectures (ARMv7, ARMv8, and Intel's x86/x64 are among the most popular Android platforms). Android devices also vary in the version of the core OS and available API's. Compare this to Apple's iOS:

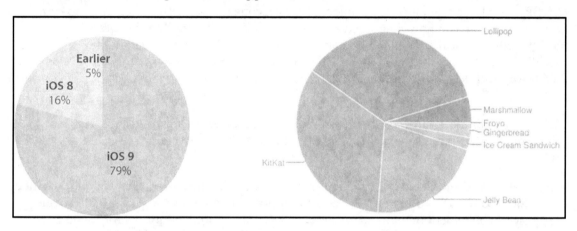

iOS and Android distribution charts (April 2016)

Android devices come with many different versions of Android and many different API levels that are available at any given time. For the purpose of mobile forensics, this means that one must either become familiar with the acquisition and protection specifics of all versions of Android or revert to using a dedicated Android acquisition product.

More information on Android fragmentation is available at the following:

- **The genius of Google Play Services: Tackling Android fragmentation, malware and forking in one fell swoop** at
  `http://www.androidcentral.com/genius-google-play-services`
- OpenSignal Android Fragmentation Report at
  `http://opensignal.com/reports/2015/08/android-fragmentation/`
- **Another Android 'fragmentation' report misses the point** at
  `http://www.androidcentral.com/another-android-fragmentation-report-mis ses-point`

AOSP, GMS, and their forensic implications

Android and Google are not synonymous. The core Android OS is developed and maintained by Google and published open source via **Android Open Source Project (AOSP)**. AOSP Android is freely available for everyone to take with no contracts to sign and no restrictions on how manufacturers can use and modify it. Manufacturers have the ability (both technical and legal) to create so-called Android forks, which are heavily modified versions of Android that may or may not be compatible with all Android apps. AOSP Android does not include any proprietary Google services (we will discuss more on that later).

Majority of Chinese smartphones sold in mainland China are based on AOSP Android, while some are running customized versions of the OS (for example, Xiaomi MIUI or Meizu FlyMe).

What makes Android devices so popular in the Western hemisphere is the Google-provided ecosystem. Google Play Store offers access to millions of games and applications. Google Maps offers convenient mapping services with free navigation and live traffic. Gmail (Google mail), Google Drive, Google Photos, Google Keep (notes), Google Chrome (browser), and a lot of other things Google comprise a closed-source ecosystem working under the **Google Mobile Services (GMS)** umbrella.

In order to preinstall GMS on their devices, manufacturers must join the **Open Handset Alliance (OHA)** and sign a very restrictive agreement. The agreement does not allow OHA members to manufacture devices based on Android forks, which makes manufacturers choose between making AOSP-based devices without Google services or shipping GMS-enabled devices. It's an either/or condition.

Google Mobile Services are included with virtually all Android smartphones sold in the Western hemisphere. Google uses its services to collect large amounts of information from GMS-enabled devices. Location reporting, Google Account details, notes, search and browsing history, stored forms and passwords, synced application data, and a lot of other information is automatically transmitted to Google services by GMS-enabled devices.

Most of this data can be acquired or requested from Google. AOSP-based devices without Google Mobile Services do not report their usage to Google servers, and therefore, are much less susceptible to over-the-air acquisition techniques.

In the U.S., Amazon is the biggest company making devices based on an Android fork. Amazon's custom Android-based OS-dubbed Fire OS empowers the company's Fire tablets, including the original Amazon Kindle Fire, Kindle Fire HD, Kindle Fire HDX 7, Kindle Fire HDX 8.9 (2013), Fire HDX 8.9 (2014), as well as the entire 2015 range. The only Amazon smartphone, Amazon Fire Phone, is also based on the Fire OS. Amazon Fire OS replaces Google Mobile Services with Amazon's in-house alternatives, offering alternative Maps, push and sync services, as well as its own app store. Older versions of Fire OS differed greatly from stock Android to the extent that Google Play Store would not run on the platform. The latest versions (Fire OS 5) are much closer to stock Android in look and feel, and offer much greater compatibility with Google services.

Google Play Services help overcome platform fragmentation by providing timely background updates to users of all versions of Android since 2.3 Gingerbread.

 The genius of Google Play Services: Tackling Android fragmentation, malware and forking in one fell swoop at `http://www.androidcentral.com/genius-google-play-services`.

Android logical acquisition

The pure Android OS offers limited support for offline backups via ADB. Google implemented the ADB backup functionality in Android 4.0 Ice Cream Sandwich. The ADB backup functionality allows examiners to extract application data to a local PC over ADB. This process does not require root and works without custom recoveries or unlocking the bootloader; however, it extracts a very limited amount of information, and should only be used as the last resort. Additionally, using the ADB backup requires having the phone unlocked and the **ADB Debugging** option enabled.

XDA developers published a complete guide for backing up the phone via ADB:

`http://forum.xda-developers.com/galaxy-nexus/general/guide-phone-backup-unlock-root-t1420351`
Additional information is available at:

`http://android.stackexchange.com/questions/28481/how-do-you-extract-an-apps-data-from-a-full-backup-made-through-adb-backup`
The following command should produce a full backup of the device, complete with all APK files, including system apps and the content of the shared (`/sdcard`) storage:

```
adb backup -apk -shared -system -all -f C:\fullpath\backup.ab
```

The complete syntax is as follows:

```
adb backup [-f <file>] [-apk|-noapk] [-shared|-noshared] [-all][-system|-
nosystem] [<packages...>]
```

The options are explained as follows:

- Write an archive of the device's data to `<file>`. If no `-f` option is supplied, then the data is written to `backup.ab` in the current directory.
- `-apk|-noapk` will enable/disable backup of the `.apks` itself in the archive; the default is `noapk`.
- `-shared|-noshared` will enable/disable backup of the device's shared storage / SD card contents; the default is `noshared`.
- `-all` means to back up all installed applications.
- `-system|-nosystem` toggles whether `-all` automatically includes system applications; the default is to include system apps.
- `<packages...>` is the list of applications to be backed up. If the `-all` or `-shared` flags are passed, then the package list is optional. Applications explicitly given on the command line will be included even if `-nosystem` would ordinarily cause them to be omitted.

For this to work, the phone must have **ADB Debugging** enabled and unlocked. The phone may display a prompt asking you to confirm the action.

 In real life, specifying certain keys may cause the backup to fail. For example, when we attempted to back up a Motorola Nexus 6 with the `-noapk` option, the backup failed. However, using the `adb backup -all -f c:\temp\nexus6.ab` command completed correctly.

Without root access, extraction via ADB backup is limited. ADB backup cannot acquire every application installed on the device. Developers can choose whether their apps allow backups or not. While the default setting is set to `on`, some developers choose to disable backups. It's worth noting that ADB backup does not capture the content of application cache. The ADB backup functionality is separate from the new cloud backups introduced with Android 6.0 Marshmallow.

While performing logical acquisition of an Android device is possible without the use of any specific mobile forensic tools by using the manufacturer-specific drivers and **Android Debug Bridge** (**ADB**), you may want to use a commercial mobile forensic tool if you already own one. For example, the following is how you perform logical acquisition of an Android device with Oxygen Forensic Suite:

1. Turn on and unlock the device.
2. Ensure that **USB debugging** is enabled in the **Developer** options, as shown in the following screenshot:

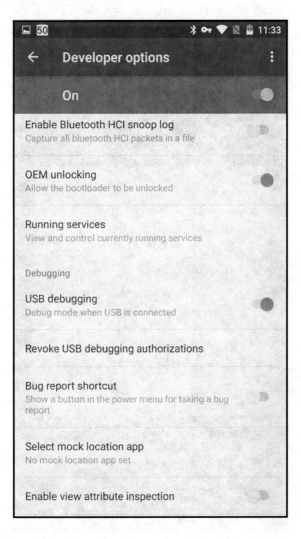

3. Connect the device to your computer via a USB cable. On some devices, you may need to switch the USB connection mode from **Charging only** to **PTP** or **MTP**.

Android offers a choice of connectivity options. You may see **Charging, File transfers (MTP)**, **Photo transfer (PTP)**, and other options. An ADB connection can only be established once you choose either **MTP** (Media Transfer Protocol for transferring files between your Android device and a Windows or Mac) or **PTP** (Photo Transfer Protocol, generally employed by devices such as printers and cameras for transferring photos). In our tests, we had a better success rate on selecting the **PTP** option.

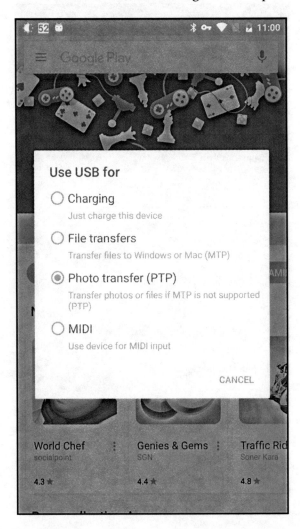

4. Select **Connect device** | **Fast backup/image extraction...**, as shown in the following screenshot:

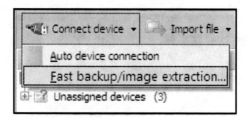

5. Select **Android backup** and click on **Next**:

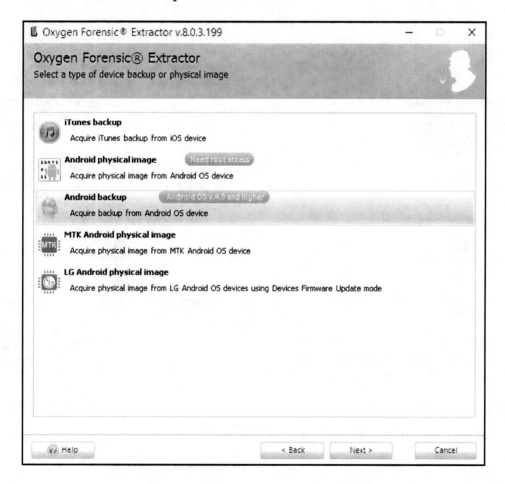

6. Connect the device and follow the instructions:

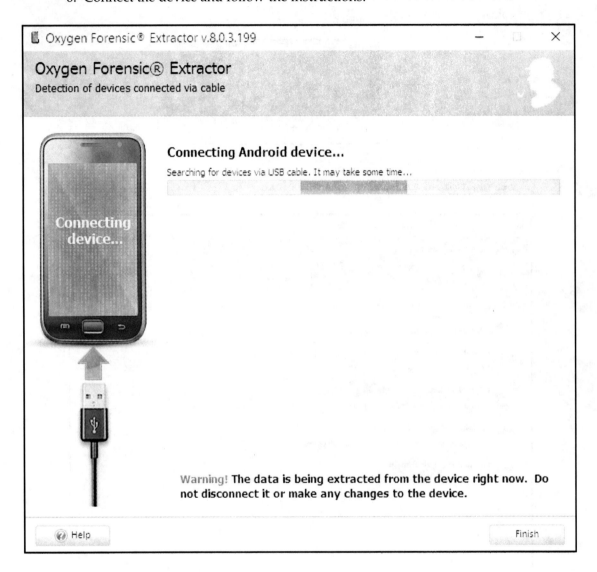

7. On the Android device, you may need to authorize your PC as a debug bridge:

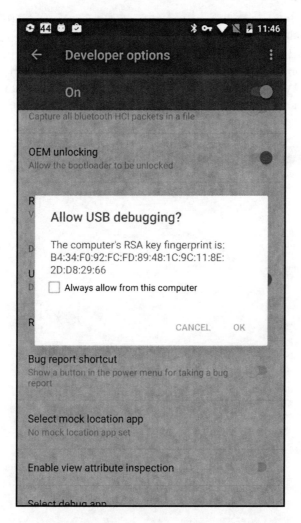

8. Oxygen Forensic Extractor will automatically establish a connection with the device and begin extracting the backup.

Additional information on ADB backups is available in `Chapter 4`, *Practical Steps to Android Acquisition*.

OEM software

Some manufacturers offer companion software to enable communication between the phone and the PC. The most common example is Apple iTunes, which is commonly used by forensic experts during logical acquisition. As an example, SONY PC Companion provides full backup and restore functionality for Xperia devices without the need to root or unlock bootloader. While using SONY PC Companion requires the user to unlock the device with the correct method (PIN, pattern, and so on), we've seen evidence of such lock measures being bypassed:

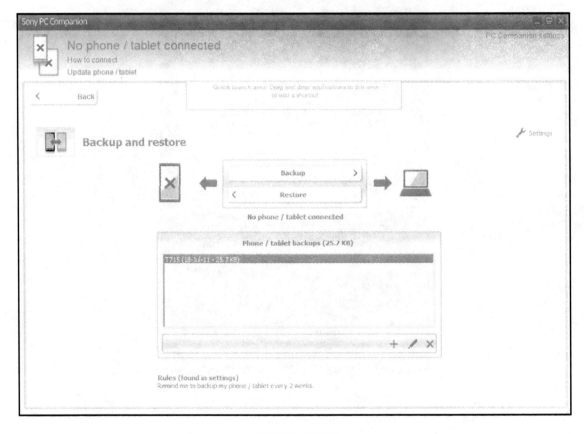

Sony PC Companion backup

In addition, some OEMs (LG, ASUS, and many others) include their own proprietary software to allow backing up and restoring the entire contents of the device. Using these tools, however, requires that the device is unlocked, in which case other acquisition methods may be available.

A backup extracted from an ASUS ZenPad S 8.0 tablet contains all of the following files:

Name	Date modified	Type	Size
com.ironhidegames.android.kingdomrus...	02-Dec-15 23:44	ABU1 File	27,878 KB
com.jackthakar.sflauncher.abu1	03-Dec-15 3:20	ABU1 File	8,358 KB
com.jm.android.frequencygenerator.abu1	03-Dec-15 5:23	ABU1 File	985 KB
com.levelup.beautifulwidgets.abu1	03-Dec-15 5:19	ABU1 File	13,895 KB
com.m4rk3t.libcopy2.abu1	03-Dec-15 4:46	ABU1 File	14,773 KB
com.microsoft.amp.apps.bingnews.abu1	03-Dec-15 3:26	ABU1 File	10,384 KB
com.microsoft.msa.authenticator.abu1	02-Dec-15 23:53	ABU1 File	5,002 KB
com.microsoft.office.officelens.abu1	03-Dec-15 3:34	ABU1 File	38,308 KB
com.microsoft.office.onenote.abu1	03-Dec-15 2:26	ABU1 File	34,449 KB
com.microsoft.office.outlook.abu1	03-Dec-15 3:18	ABU1 File	14,378 KB
com.microsoft.skydrive.abu1	03-Dec-15 4:28	ABU1 File	28,122 KB
com.momocode.shortcuts.abu1	02-Dec-15 23:44	ABU1 File	598 KB
com.mxtech.videoplayer.pro.abu1	03-Dec-15 1:47	ABU1 File	13,890 KB
com.noinnion.android.greader.readerpro....	03-Dec-15 4:09	ABU1 File	112,978 KB
com.nomotorola.MotGallery2.abu1	02-Dec-15 23:08	ABU1 File	22,463 KB
com.nuance.swype.dtc.abu1	03-Dec-15 5:28	ABU1 File	26,405 KB
com.opera.browser.abu1	03-Dec-15 3:12	ABU1 File	54,008 KB
com.painless.pc.abu1	02-Dec-15 23:44	ABU1 File	535 KB
com.paragon.tcplugins_ntfs_ro.abu1	02-Dec-15 22:29	ABU1 File	3,542 KB
com.pzolee.android.localwifispeedtester....	02-Dec-15 23:06	ABU1 File	4,281 KB
com.quoord.tapatalkpro.activity.abu1	03-Dec-15 2:44	ABU1 File	18,281 KB
com.rarlab.rar.abu1	03-Dec-15 2:39	ABU1 File	3,900 KB
com.rovio.angrybirdsspaceHD.ads.ultima...	03-Dec-15 0:32	ABU1 File	48,816 KB
com.sgg.archipelago.abu1	03-Dec-15 3:20	ABU1 File	2,292 KB
com.sika524.android.quickshortcut.abu1	03-Dec-15 5:28	ABU1 File	1,330 KB
com.sikebo.materialistik.material.icons.ab...	02-Dec-15 23:28	ABU1 File	18,522 KB
com.simusphere.robotic.abu1	03-Dec-15 5:28	ABU1 File	9,657 KB
com.skype.raider.abu1	03-Dec-15 5:30	ABU1 File	33,991 KB
com.smophix.phix.abu1	02-Dec-15 23:34	ABU1 File	16,393 KB
com.tippingcanoe.mydealz.abu1	03-Dec-15 4:17	ABU1 File	6,506 KB
com.touchtype.swiftkey.beta.abu1	02-Dec-15 22:35	ABU1 File	40,879 KB
com.tung91.meeuihd.abu1	03-Dec-15 3:16	ABU1 File	38,095 KB
com.ubisoft.adventure.valiant_hearts_ggt...	02-Dec-15 22:30	ABU1 File	46,545 KB
com.vectorunit.red.lunar.abu1	03-Dec-15 2:30	ABU1 File	55,104 KB
com.vertumus.rewun.abu1	03-Dec-15 5:35	ABU1 File	24,655 KB

Path: id Firmware and Drivers › ASUS ZenPad S › backup_sd › ASUSBackup › backup_20151202_222914

The content of ASUS ZenPad S 8.0 backup

Backups made with proprietary tools generally contain device settings, passwords (or, in certain cases, authentication tokens that may or may not have expired by the time they are restored), the list of installed applications, as well as application data (and often application binaries). These backups do not have provision for accessing unallocated space.

Android acquisition – special considerations

What happens to information that the user attempts to destroy? Deleted evidence may still be recovered—at least in Android smartphones. Rarely encrypted, Android devices are susceptible to various acquisition techniques, many of which enable access to deleted data. Let's look at how Android deletes information and what can be done to recover deleted data.

Unallocated space

In Android, unallocated space can usually be extracted along with the filesystem (which is not the case with Apple devices due to iOS full-disk encryption). However, it is important to realize that Android devices employ trim support, erasing the content of unallocated disk space every time the device is shut down. This is one of the reasons why standard acquisition techniques don't recommend turning the phone off at any time; instead, they advice putting the device on a charger and placing it into a Faraday bag.

So what happens to unallocated (or released) space inside an Android phone?

eMMC storage

Let's take a look at how recent smartphones and tablets store information. Since 2011, most Android smartphones use eMMC flash chips for non-volatile storage. Unlike the *plain* flash chips, eMMC storage integrates flash memory and controller onto a single chip planted into the phone's main board. The built-in controller is responsible for flash-specific operations to maintain data integrity while ensuring the optimum performance and lifespan of the NAND cells. The controller performs, among other things, operations such as trimming unused data blocks, remapping logical addresses to physical chips. The controller is also responsible for performing secure data erasure when requested.

Remapping and overprovisioning

Internally, the built-in controller is responsible for establishing a link between addressable (logical) storage space and physical blocks in the flash chip. In other words, each logical block is mapped to a corresponding physical block by the eMMC controller. The reverse, however, is not true—we cannot say that each physical block has a corresponding addressable logical block assigned.

eMMC chips have more actual storage capacity than they advertise to the outside world. The extra physical data blocks are therefore non-addressable until called into service by the integral eMMC controller. This feature is called overprovisioning. Overprovisioned data blocks have no logical addresses. Any *bad sectors* (unstable or unreadable data blocks) will be permanently placed into the overprovisioned area. They'll never be assigned a logical address or be visible to the operating system, or anything at all, except the built-in eMMC controller.

Important: There is no feasible way of extracting information contained in the overprovisioned area. The entire area is invisible to logical or physical acquisition tools as these data blocks are not mapped onto available address space. These data blocks are only accessible to the internal controller, there is no interface available to intentionally access their contents from the outside the eMMC chip. As a result, even performing chip-off extraction will not give you access to physical blocks from the overprovisioned area, as chip-off extraction of eMMC chips is still based on sending commands to the eMMC controller.

Wear leveling

Flash memory has several qualities unique to this type of storage. NAND flash chips have a limited lifespan by only supporting a finite number of write-erase cycles. After reaching the end of its effective lifespan, the flash chip may continue functioning, yet the data retention period may be severely affected (the data will get corrupted or disappear completely after the flash storage is powered off for a certain amount of time). As a result, the embedded eMMC controller will attempt to evenly distribute write cycles among available data blocks. This is called wear leveling.

Trimming

Another quality unique to flash storage is how they write information. Blocks must be erased before they can be written to. Erasing a *dirty* flash cell takes significantly more time than writing into an already empty block. In order to work around this issue, the eMMC controller will perform background garbage collection by trimming (erasing) released blocks when the controller is idle. In order to make a certain logical address immediately writeable after its content was deleted (and the block was advertised as available, but not yet erased), the controller may perform address remapping by pointing this logical block to an already empty physical cell. Unlike erasing, remapping happens instantly, making the block that used to contain deleted data writeable without the wait associated with erasing its content.

Due to Android platform fragmentation, trim support in Android varies between versions and among the different OEMs. Full-trim support only came to Android in version 4.3 Jelly Bean. Moreover, full-trim support is only guaranteed in devices that originally shipped with Android 4.3 or newer, which excludes devices upgrading from earlier versions of Android. While some manufacturers implemented trim support during the course of updating devices to newer versions of Android, some other OEMs never bothered. As a result, a large number of devices that originally shipped with Android 4.2 and were updated to Android Kit Kat or even Lollipop never received proper trim support.

Earlier versions of Android without full-trim support used to include a basic form of trimming. With no *live* trimming available in older Android builds, the cleanup (trimming) was performed every time the device was shut down. This is one of the reasons for the ACPO requirements to keep devices powered on instead of shutting them down. On a side note, simply removing the battery would not trigger the cleanup stage.

If you are handling an Android device, and it's one of the older ones, you may be able to dump a physical image of its eMMC chip and access information about its unallocated space.

What happens to the deleted data?

So what happens to information stored in the blocks released by the operating system? The Android OS (depending on the version) will pass a `trim` command to the eMMC controller, telling it that a certain logical block is no longer used. The controller assigns a special status of *do not care* to the physical block corresponding to this logical address, adding the physical block to the *to be erased* list and remapping the logical address to a clean physical block (either from an existing address space or from the overprovisioned area).

Notably, the controller may or may not decide to push a newly released physical block out of the addressable space and into the overprovisioned area. As a result, the content of a deleted logical block may remain available in the addressable space for a while. This phenomenon enables forensic specialists to carve information from unallocated areas.

If you need more information about what happens to information deleted from Android devices, refer to the *Security Analysis of Android Factory Resets* publication by *Laurent Simon* and *Ross Anderson (University of Cambridge)* at `http://www.cl.cam.ac.uk/~rja14/Papers/fr_most15.pdf`. In this paper, the scientists studied the implementation of factory reset on multiple Android smartphones running Android versions 2.3.x to 4.3, reviewed how Android smartphones handle deleted files, and discovered that, in many cases, user data is still available after a factory reset due to improper implementations of the function by many device manufacturers.

JTAG forensics

JTAG forensics is an advanced acquisition procedure that uses **test access ports (TAP)** standardized by the **Joint Test Action Group (JTAG)** association. These ports, among other things, can be utilized to access raw data stored in the connected device. The acquisition process involves using existing solder points on the device's circuit board. By using specialized equipment and a matching device-specific JTAG cable, one can retrieve the entire flash memory contents (less the eMMC overprovisioned area, but including addressable unallocated space) from compatible devices. Notably, JTAG acquisition is often available even for locked, damaged, or otherwise inaccessible devices. JTAG acquisition is available for many Android devices, as well as some feature phones and Windows Phone 7 and 8 devices.

JTAG forensics is a labor-intensive and time-consuming process requiring an expert to use a well-equipped lab. As such, forensic experts tend to try JTAG acquisition after other methods prove unsuccessful.

When to JTAG a device

JTAG is an invasive acquisition method since it requires disassembling the device to a certain level and soldering wires to the contacts of the test port. While being invasive, JTAG is not considered a destructive method by many experts. If JTAG is performed carefully, the device, if it was in working order prior to the JTAG procedure, will continue to work post JTAG—which is exactly what the test port is designed for. From time to time, JTAG can still result in the device being rendered inoperable. For this reason, JTAG forensics is normally used when commercial forensic tools fail to image the device, or when the device is soft-bricked or unbootable. This includes devices locked with an unknown passcode and the **USB debugging** option not enabled if no exploit is available to bypass protection.

JTAG acquisition produces a full image of the device's memory complete with unallocated space. This is how JTAG acquisition may look in a lab:

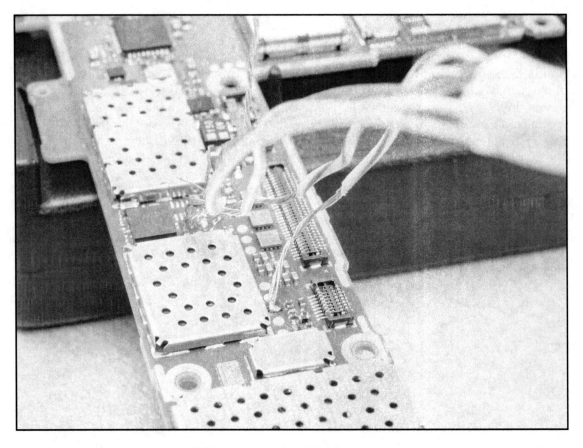

JTAG acquisition of Nokia Lumia 920. Image source: SYTECH Digital Forensics, http://sytech-consultants.com/.

Limitations of JTAG forensics

JTAG extraction is a low-level acquisition method that returns raw content of the device storage. If full-disk encryption is enabled, JTAG will extract a raw encrypted image. Breaking the encryption may or may not be an option, depending on the manufacturer (Samsung is renowned for *making things different*), phone model, and Android version.

In order to extract a decrypted image, a higher level API must be used. This, however, may require unlocking the device with the correct passcode (or an alternative method, such as pattern or knock code). Full-disk encryption is active out-of-the-box on some Samsung devices, Google-manufactured devices running Android 5 (such as Nexus 6 and Nexus 9), as well as some other flagship phones sold by leading manufacturers.

JTAG processes are minimally documented and require an expert examiner. Some manufacturers disable TAP on their devices after they leave the factory, so JTAG acquisition may not be available even if a TAP port is visibly present.

The full image extracted via JTAG does not include the overprovisioned area. JTAG will not bypass the controller and can only obtain access to the device memory area allowed by the controller of the device being acquired, unless the examiner is using an advanced form of JTAG called **Boundary Scan**. In other words, without using the Boundary Scan technique, the overprovisioned area is inaccessible with standard JTAG method. Yet, even using the Boundary Scan technique, examiners can only access as much information as can be obtained from the embedded storage. If the device uses eMMC memory, all extraction requests are still routed through the embedded controller integrated into the eMMC chip, which in turn will not allow accessing the content of flash chip(s) directly. As a result, the Boundary Scan technique is only effective if the device is equipped with plain flash chips, which is not the case for up-to-date devices (for example, majority of Android smartphones has been using eMMC chips since Android 2.3). Notably, some entry-level no-name Chinese smartphones are still equipped with plain flash chips instead of eMMC.

Despite the limitations, JTAG remains a viable acquisition method for compatible devices. Google decided to back away from encrypting new Android 5.0 devices (`http://arstechn ica.com/gadgets/215/3/google-quietly-backs-away-from-encrypting-new-lollipop -devices-by-default/`), removing the requirement to enforce full-disk encryption in existing devices receiving an upgrade to Android 5.0/5.1, as well as newly released phones running Lollipop out-of-the-box. You can use JTAG forensics on compatible phones only if they are not using whole-disk encryption.

Step-by-step JTAG acquisition

This book targets mobile forensic experts in general, so we don't discuss JTAG extraction in detail. Sending the phone to a lab specializing in low-level extractions is probably your best option. In the lab, they'll perform the following steps:

1. The expert will attempt to identify TAP by researching available service documentation for the particular device model. If no service documentation is available, the examiner will open the device and inspect its PCB for potential TAPs, and then manually probe to identify TAP connector pins.
2. The expert will then attach wire leads to the correct connector pins by either soldering the connectors or utilizing a solderless jig.
3. The wire leads will be connected to an appropriate JTAG emulator supporting the device being analyzed.
4. By sending appropriate commands to the exhibit device via the TAP, the expert will make the device dump its flash memory contents. The raw dump will be captured by the JTAG emulator and will be saved into a binary file.
5. The binary file with raw contents of the memory chips will be presented to you for analysis. The dump may or may not be encrypted, and it may or may not be possible to decrypt its content at that time even if the lock screen passcode is known.
6. At this time, you can use a mobile forensic tool of your choice to load the content of the JTAG dump and parse and analyze its content.

Chip-off acquisition

Chip-off acquisition is a highly advanced, destructive extraction technique that requires attaching wire leads to the PCB contacts or physically removing (desoldering) the phone's flash memory chip. Chip-off is considered more difficult compared to JTAG; however, the amount of information acquired via chip-off acquisition is similar to the amount of data acquired by JTAGging the device. Since most smartphones use standard eMMC flash modules, the process is standardized and typically presents no surprises to the examiner.

In the world of mobile forensics, the lowest-level access is not always the best. While reading the chips directly produces a complete raw dump of the memory chips, the investigator may be faced with an encrypted partition with no decryption keys stored anywhere around. In the case of Apple devices, many Samsung phones, and some other devices (for example, the Android 5 Nexus line), encryption is enforced out-of-the-box and may not be bypassed during or after the chip-off acquisition even if the correct passcode is known. Chip-off acquisition delivers the best result when used on unencrypted devices.

Chip-off and encryption

Chip-off often involves removing the memory chip from the circuit board and using special eMMC adapters to make a raw dump of the memory chip. If full-disk encryption was enabled on the device, on many Android versions prior to Android 5.0 Lollipop (with the default encryption scheme), it is then possible to attempt carving the raw data dump in order to locate and extract the encryption metadata. If the encryption metadata is successfully extracted, the analyst can then attempt to brute-force the passcode and decrypt the image.

Chip-off extraction is the lowest-level acquisition method available. Chip-off is often used as a last resort if both physical acquisition and JTAG extraction fail. If full-disk encryption has been used, chip-off acquisition will result in an encrypted image that may or may not be possible to decrypt.

Note that this technique does not work on many Samsung phones with fairly recent firmware, as well as on most devices running Android 5.0 and later versions of Android. Recent Samsung devices (as well as all Android 5.x smartphones) encrypt metadata with a master key, while the master key itself is stored in a protected area that cannot be accessed via chip-off.

In-system programming forensics

In-system programming forensics is a non-destructive variation of the chip-off acquisition. ISP is an advanced acquisition process that is in between JTAG and chip-off. During the acquisition process, examiners can attempt to dump the content of the eMMC memory without removing the chip. ISP acquisition is only available for devices utilizing eMMC or eMCP-style BGA chips. Access to the memory is obtained through access points around the BGA chip. This acquisition process is considered non-destructive in that, if all stars align, the device can be reassembled and booted after the extraction. This is how ISP acquisition may look in a lab:

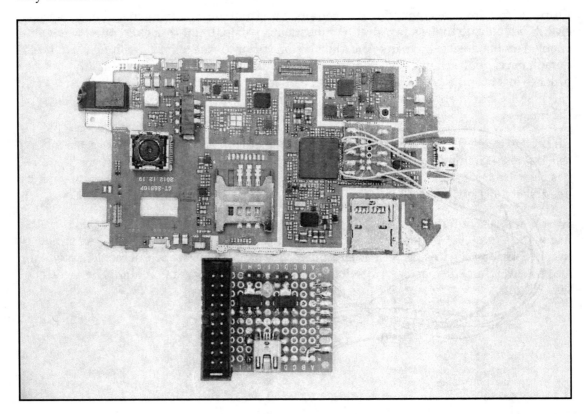

eMMC adapter attached to a smartphone PCB. Source: http://easy-jtag.com/.

The following is a schematic image of JTAG eMMC pinout (courtesy of Easy Jtag):

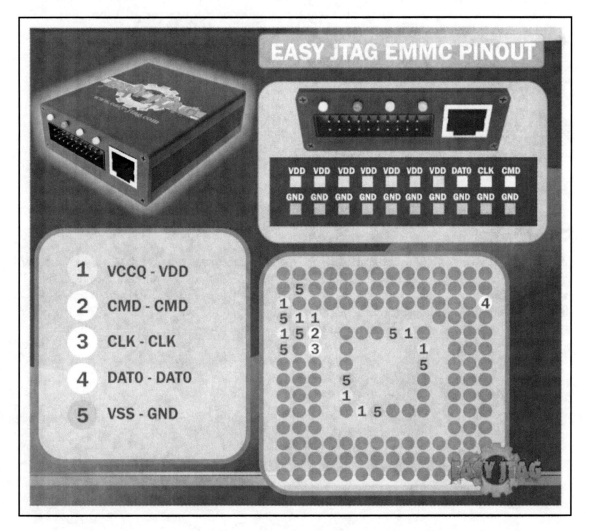

Easy JTAG eMMC box. Source: http://easy-jtag.com/.

Teel Technologies
(`http://www.teeltech.com/mobile-device-forensics-training/in-system-programming -for-mobile-device-forensics/`) lists the following benefits for ISP acquisition:

- Enables examiners to bypass lock codes and recover the complete dataset from phones that are not supported by JTAG or commercial tools
- Non-destructive practice that achieves the same results as a chip-off, while leaving the original evidence intact
- Acquires data much faster than JTAG, enabling examiners to process more phones faster
- Fewer resources and tools are required to perform an ISP download compared to chip-off

Summary

In this chapter, we looked at the Android OS from the forensic standpoint. We reviewed the various acquisition options and discussed how to perform logical acquisition of an Android device. We also took a look at the issue of deleted evidence, and discussed when and how deleted data can be recovered. In the next chapter, we'll continue working with Android devices, learning about some of the most commonly used forensic techniques—physical acquisition.

4
Practical Steps to Android Acquisition

When approaching an Android smartphone, there is no straightforward route to acquisition. Due to extremely high fragmentation of the Android platform, your approach to acquiring an Android smartphone will vary greatly between devices. Your approach will depend on who made the device and what chipset was used; what version of Android it is running and what version of Android it was originally released with; whether or not the device has an unlocked (or unlockable) bootloader, and whether it was or can be rooted. If that's not enough, you'll have different options depending on the encryption status of the device (which also depends on the device's make, model, and version of Android).

This chapter offers detailed discussion and demonstration of the various physical acquisition methods available for a wide range of Android devices. We'll discuss how to use manufacturer-specific low-level service modes (LG, Qualcomm, and Mediatek), how to use custom recoveries (**ClockworkMod (CWM)** and **Team Win Recovery Project (TWRP)**) for dumping the data partition, and how to make NANDroid backups and use command-line tools such as **dd** for live-imaging the device. We'll talk about encryption and its effect on physical acquisition.

Android physical acquisition

When approaching an Android smartphone, there is no straightforward route to physical acquisition. Is the device encrypted? Do you happen to know the passcode? Do you have a bootloader that is unlocked (or at least semi-unlocked)? Does the device have root access installed, or do you have the means to root it? Is a service backdoor available on a particular model? Depending on these factors, you may be able to pursue one or another acquisition method.

Encryption

Before we go on discussing the various physical acquisition methods, let's make one thing clear: device encryption may affect your ability to access user data. There may be a possibility to extract decryption keys, which in turn, depends on the version of Android and whether or not the phone was made by Samsung.

Prior to Android 5.0 *Lollipop*, Google used to utilize (and push to **Android Open Source Project (AOSP)**) a seriously flawed encryption method. This method was compromised as experts were able to extract decryption keys from the device and use it to decrypt user data. Decryption metadata was kept unencrypted, thus extracting the metadata made it possible to decrypt the data partition.

Samsung knew of this vulnerability and designed its own proprietary encryption scheme that encrypted the decryption metadata. As a result, encrypted Samsung smartphones are a tough call even if they are running an early version of Android (pre-Lollipop).

 Samsung devices running Android 4.0 and earlier used open decryption metadata, and can be acquired even if encrypted. Samsung Galaxy Nexus running stock Android used Google's standard encryption implementation (with open decryption metadata) and can also be decrypted.

In Android 5.0, Google adopted a much more secure encryption scheme, similar to the one developed by Samsung. In Android 5.x and 6.x, decryption metadata is no longer stored in an open form. Instead, the decryption metadata is securely encrypted. While decryption metadata can be extracted via physical imaging, JTAG, or chip-off, it is impossible to use it to decrypt the data partition since the required metadata itself is encrypted. At this time, no method exists to decrypt the required metadata off-device. Samsung is now using this encryption standard in devices running Android 5.x and newer. When acquiring an encrypted Android device, the following compatibility matrix applies:

- For **encrypted non-Samsung devices running Android 4.4 KitKat** or earlier, you may be able to recover the decryption key and use it to decrypt the user data.
- For **encrypted Samsung smartphones running Android 4.0 through 4.4**, you may be unable to extract or recover the decryption key. As a result, you may be unable to decrypt the user data. If this is the case, you can still try live imaging, logical acquisition, or cloud extraction.
- For **encrypted devices running Android 5.x or newer**, you are unlikely to discover the decryption key. Lower-level acquisition techniques (JTAG, ISP, or chip-off) will be equally useless. Attempt live imaging, logical acquisition, or cloud extraction.

Now that we have this clear, let's move on to actual acquisition techniques.

Approaching physical acquisition

When approaching a device, you may want to consider the following:

- Some manufacturers ship their devices with fully or partially unlocked bootloaders. Imaging such devices usually presents no problem (unless data is encrypted).
- Some manufacturers ship their devices with locked bootloaders, officially allowing users to unlock them (for example, Samsung, Motorola, SONY, Nexus devices, and many others). If the user unlocked the bootloader, there is a high probability of successful imaging (unless an anti-forensic technique was employed).
- In many cases, manufacturers and/or carriers restrict bootloader unlocks. In some cases, it is possible to bypass these restrictions in some models (the chipset and manufacturer of the device are important). Some chipset makers and device OEMs have backdoors (used for service-level access), while some can be exploited to bypass bootloader lock and boot into a custom recovery (which does not necessarily mean that you can permanently flash one). These devices are also relatively easy to acquire.
- Finally, some devices are really tough. Locked bootloaders, no service mode, and no known exploits make them difficult to acquire. You can still try live imaging or alternative acquisition methods.

If you are using Cellebrite UFED, you may find it useful to install their free mobile app (onto your own smartphone or tablet) to help you identify the extraction capabilities of a given mobile device. **UFED Phone Detective** is available for iOS and Android devices, and offers an easy way to view forensic extraction and decoding capabilities, as well as connectivity methods, for mobile devices supported by Cellebrite UFED 4PC/Touch/Classic. While the app can be downloaded free of charge, you will need to provide your **My Cellebrite** credentials to log in. If you don't have a My Cellebrite account, you will be able to register free of charge from within the app:

UFED Phone Detective mobile app complements Cellebrite's mobile extraction suite by enabling experts to look up mobile devices by vendor name, mobile device name, or model number. Once the device is identified, the app displays specific support information, including whether the extraction can bypass the device's lock.

 More information about UFED Phone Detective and the download links is available at `http://www.cellebrite.com/`.

We compiled a short acquisition walkthrough for your convenience.

Encryption status – Is the data partition encrypted?

Yes: If you're imaging a Samsung device, and if that device runs Android 4.0 to 4.4, or if you're imaging a Samsung or non-Samsung device that runs Android 5 or newer, try live imaging. In order to perform live imaging, you will need to unlock the device with the correct passcode (plenty of solutions are available on the market). If you are imaging an older *non-Samsung* device that runs a version of Android 4.4 or earlier, proceed to physical acquisition as you have a good chance of recovering the decryption key.

No: Proceed to physical acquisition.

Service mode available

Prior to trying other acquisition methods, let's discover whether a service backdoor is available for the device being imaged.

LG smartphones

LG smartphones ship with a proprietary service access mode called **LAF**. In LG smartphones, this proprietary mode completely replaces similar low-level access modes provided by chipset makers, such as Qualcomm or MediaTek. This bears an important consequence. If you are imaging an LG smartphone, make sure that you use the LG service mode instead of attempting to boot the device into Qualcomm 9006 or MTK service mode.

LG service mode works both ways (for reading and writing data onto the raw physical storage). As a result, you can image the complete physical storage regardless of the bootloader lock status. LG uses a proprietary protocol, so your acquisition tool must support that in order to be able to read the data. You will need to install the latest LG drivers as well. Tools that support LAF include Cellebrite UFED and Oxygen Forensic Suite. More on this method will be discussed in the *LG smartphones' LAF mode* section.

Devices based on the Qualcomm reference platform

A number of vendors build devices based on reference platforms supplied by chipset manufacturers. Using a reference platform greatly streamlines development. Manufacturers receive a ready-to-use PCB design complete with pre-selected components and drivers. In addition to this, some reference platforms expose service-access backdoors. The reference platform provided by Qualcomm, one of the largest chipset manufacturers, includes several service modes. One of these modes, **HS-USB 9006** or **mode 9006**, provides system-level access to device partitions regardless of whether the device ships with a locked or unlocked bootloader.

Generally speaking, switching into this mode is activated by turning the device off, connecting it to the computer via a USB cord while holding the volume up key, and powering on the device while still holding the volume up key (details on entering mode 9006 may vary slightly between devices). Once the device boots into the service mode, the Windows **Disk Management** console will display a list of available partitions. Note that a dedicated Qualcomm Download Mode HS-USB 9006 driver must be installed on the expert's computer for the partitions to appear. Once you see the list of partitions, you'll be able to image these partitions with a mobile forensic tool of your choice. Some flash imaging tools are also available. More on this method will be discussed in *The Qualcomm 9006 mode* section.

Mediatek-based Chinese phones

Another chipset manufacturer providing a special service backdoor is **MediaTek (MTK)**. MTK chipsets are used by most Chinese smartphone makers and include models built by Xiaomi, Meizu, Oppo, Vivo, OnePlus, Cubot, Zoppo, ZTE, No. 1, and hundreds of B-brands and C-brands. Unlike Qualcomm, MediaTek only allows accessing data via this service mode if the bootloader is unlocked. Many Chinese manufacturers ship their smartphones with unlocked bootloaders, presumably for easier servicing, which allows users of mobile forensic tools to easily image these devices by exploiting the MTK service mode. Later in this book, we'll discuss more about one of the tools, Oxygen Forensic Toolkit. More on this method is discussed in the *MediaTek smartphones* section.

Bootloaded status

Is the bootloader locked? When it comes to acquiring Android devices, this is a major question. Major brands ship their Android devices with locked bootloaders. Some vendors allow users to unlock bootloaders on some models and carrier combinations, while other vendors (models and carriers) opt for permanently locked bootloaders.

The majority of Android devices sold in the US and Europe ship with locked bootloaders; in China, the opposite is true. Some devices come with semi-locked bootloaders, allowing to boot into (but not permanently flash) a custom boot image. If you are able to boot into a custom recovery, you may be able to create a Nandroid backup or image the data partition. However, note that booting into a custom bootloader on a semi-unlocked bootloader may (InFocus m810t) or may not (ASUS ZenPad S 8.0) trigger a security reset.

Root status

Is the device rooted? Unlike iOS jailbreak, rooting the device is not a necessary prerequisite for imaging many Android devices. Whether or not the device has been rooted only affects your ability to perform live imaging of the device. However, if the device has been already rooted, you will be able to perform live imaging without attempting to root the device first, which can be iffy.

LG smartphones' LAF mode

For service purposes, LG developed a low-level protocol enabling LG smartphones to accept firmware updates over a USB connection even if the device is not otherwise accessible (*bricked*). Initially only available to authorized service centers, details of this protocol and the actual drivers and flashing tools soon became available to the general public, and made it into some mobile forensic tools such as Cellebrite UFED and Oxygen Forensic Suite (refer to the *Live imaging using Oxygen Forensic Suite* section for more information).

This service mode (LAF mode) is generally activated by powering down the device, holding the volume up key and attaching it to the PC via a USB cable. The phone will automatically boot into the download mode, ready to accept firmware updates:

In this mode, an imaging tool can extract the complete physical image of the device's physical storage. This is one of the cleanest, easiest, and most forensically sound acquisition methods available.

When using this method, select **Physical data acquisition | LG Android dump**:

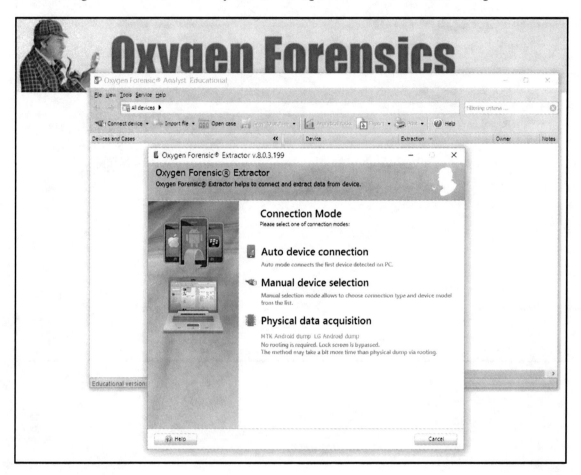

You will be prompted to download and install LG drivers, as shown in the following image:

Once the drivers are installed, carry out the instructions appearing in the following screenshot:

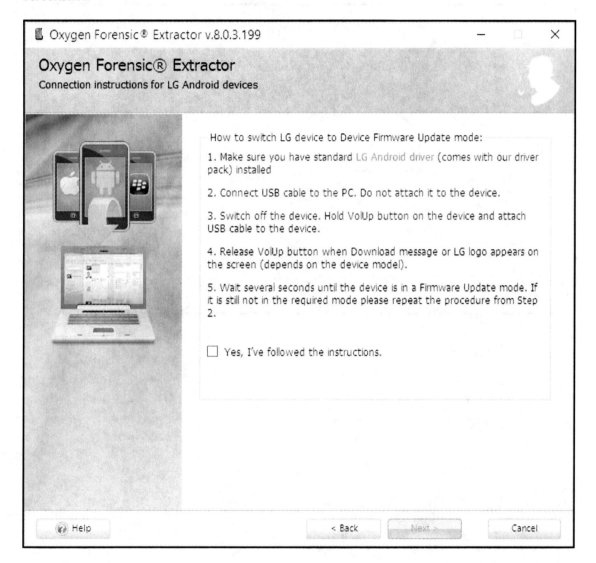

Once the LG device is connected, wait while Windows installs the corresponding driver:

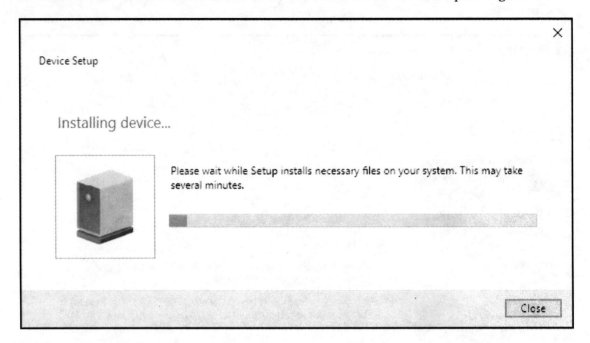

Click on **Next**:

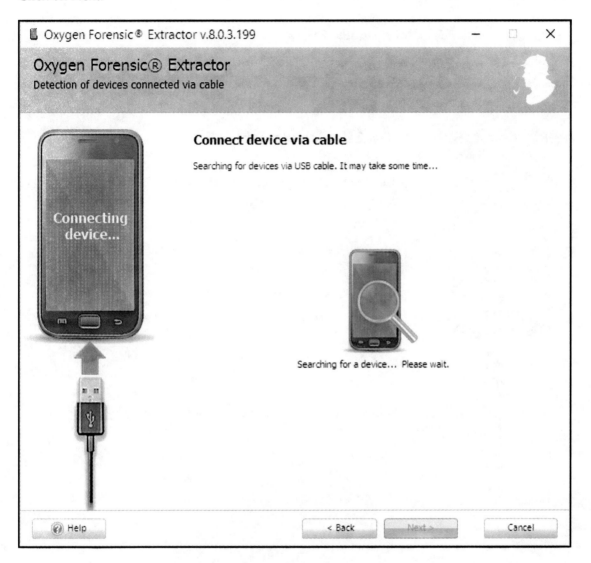

Shortly after this, you'll be able to see that your device is connected:

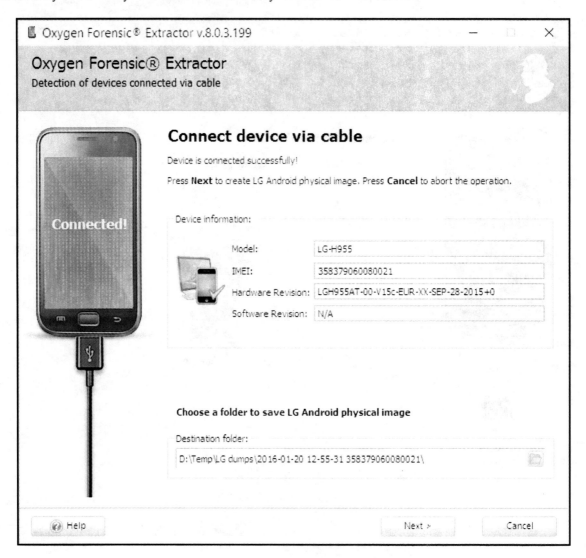

Click on **Next** to begin imaging:

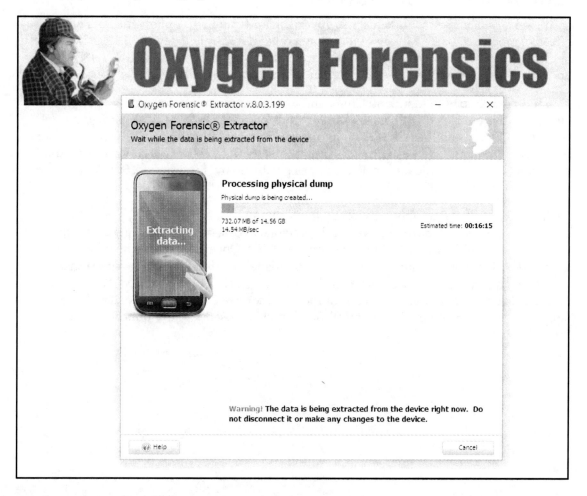

Once the process is finished, you will get a single binary file (stored at the path you specified earlier) representing a dump of the device's entire physical storage. You'll be able to open and analyze the dump in Oxygen Forensic Suite or a mobile forensic tool of your choice.

MediaTek smartphones

MediaTek is a Chinese manufacturer supplying a large number of phone makers with cost-effective mobile chipsets. Mostly used in low-end and mid-range devices, MTK chipsets can be found in smartphones and tablets produced by major manufacturers (LG, SONY, HTC, and so on), as well as a countless number of B-brand and C-brand manufacturers.

C-brand devices sold in Mainland China and available from numerous online outlets are almost always equipped with one or another chipset offered by MTK. Such devices rarely come with locked bootloaders, allowing for clean acquisition via the MTK firmware update mode. Note that only devices with unlocked bootloaders can be acquired via this method, so it won't work on bootloader-locked devices produced by, for example, SONY, HTC, or LG.

Technically, MTK service mode works by installing a virtual serial (COM) port into the system. While dedicated MTK drivers are available, in practice, these are generic Windows drivers for virtual COM ports with a custom `.inf` file. Once the driver is installed, an MTK-supplied DLL allows booting into a service bootloader, reading the device info, and extracting the storage content. This method can access both NAND and eMMC memory. New models require updated versions of the MTK service DLL and bootloader. Note that support is added for entire SoC (chipset) families as opposed to individual smartphone models.

In order to extract a device via MTK physical imaging, select the corresponding option in Oxygen Forensic Suite:

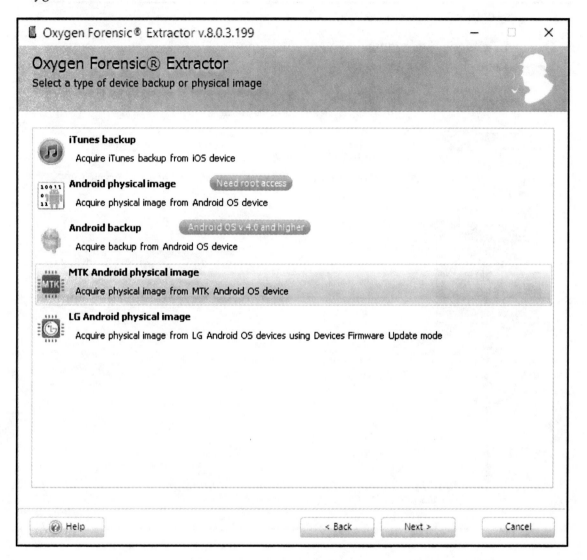

You will be prompted to download the driver and turn off the device:

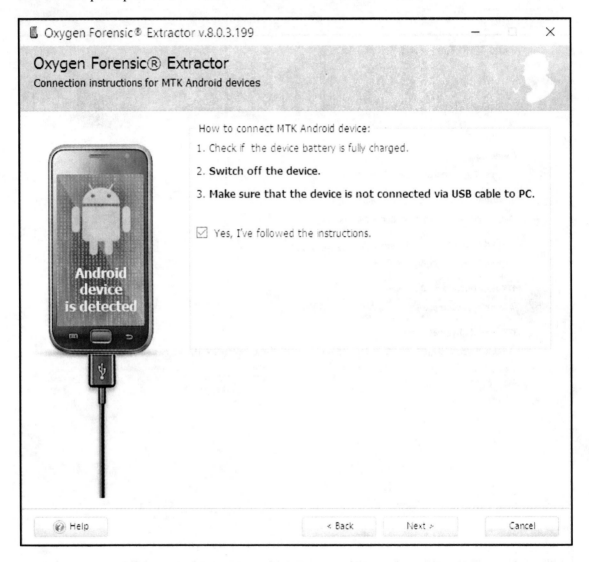

After the drivers are installed, turn on the device and follow the instructions:

Once the device is connected, you'll be able to proceed to extracting its storage.

Qualcomm bootloader exploit

Physical acquisition options are limited for locked devices featuring the locked bootloader, no root, and disabled ADB Debugging option. A bootloader-level exploit exists for some Qualcomm devices, and can be used by tools such as Cellebrite UFED to boot the device with a patched boot image to allow the tool to extract device image.

The exploit is based on a critical security vulnerability discovered in certain versions of the kernel bootloader used in Qualcomm reference devices and implemented by multiple OEMs. When processing the boot command in the fastboot mode, the affected kernel bootloader will not verify the unlock status of the device or whether the kernel is properly signed. If the device is using an affected kernel, it can be booted with a patched kernel image without verification.

Experts can use this vulnerability to boot Android devices with arbitrary kernel images via fastboot even when the target uses a signed kernel and the bootloader is locked. (Source: *Fastboot boot command bypasses signature verification (CVE-2014-4325)* at `https://www.codeau rora.org/projects/security-advisories/fastboot-boot-command-bypasses-signatu re-verification-cve-214-4325`).

Bootloader exploits are device-specific and involve using a custom boot image, built specifically for target devices. Manually building a patched boot image for a particular device being investigated is not feasible as it would require a high level of skill and a lot of time. The Cellebrite acquisition kit implements bootloader runtime exploits for multiple devices.

Bootloader attacks are tethered. They don't write anything into the device while using a patched boot image that only modifies the content of the device volatile memory (RAM) but does not alter the content of the device storage. For this reason, bootloader-level acquisition is forensically sound.

Since bootloader exploits are device-specific, they are only available for some devices (Cellebrite claims support for most Motorola Android devices, selected Samsung, Qualcomm, and LG GSM and CDMA devices). No universal bootloader exploit exists. Bootloader exploits should be used with caution as some devices are known to wipe data partition when booting into a custom recovery. At the time of writing, bootloader acquisition is exclusive to Cellebrite UFED:

In addition to bootloader exploits, a few Qualcomm-based devices are susceptible to some of the cleanest acquisition techniques via Qualcomm 9006 mode.

Qualcomm-based smartphones – HS-USB 9006

This method is applicable to certain smartphones and tablets based on one of the recent Qualcomm SoC. Bootloader status is irrelevant; devices with locked bootloaders can be successfully imaged with this method. The limiting factors are as follows: the ability to switch the device into Qualcomm Download Mode 9006, and having the correct Qualcomm HS-USB 9006 drivers for a given device.

This method is considered to be physical acquisition. It returns the full dump of either the entire eMMC storage or just the data partition. The complete raw dump is captured, including unallocated space, which makes it possible to recover the deleted files. This method is clean, safe, forensically sound (it leaves no traces anywhere in the device), and requires no specific technical expertise.

Encryption

In this mode, you are capturing the raw image of either the entire eMMC card or selected partitions. If the data partition is encrypted, you will not be prompted for a passcode. The data will be captured encrypted. You may or may not be able to decrypt it afterwards, even if you know the correct passcode. The ability to decrypt encrypted data depends on many factors, such as the version of Android the device is running, the version of Android it was initially released with, and the manufacturer of the device. For example, Samsung used particularly strong versions of custom encryption in some versions of Android. Devices that were initially released with Android 5.x Lollipop use a similarly strong encryption scheme. Devices released with Android 4.2 Jellybean can often be decrypted.

The Qualcomm 9006 mode

Qualcomm is known to provide OEMs with a number of reference platforms. Manufacturers can use these platforms, complete with low-level firmware and drivers, to quickly build smartphones and tables without spending much time on research and development.

Since Qualcomm reference platforms are implemented across a variety of devices made by dozens of different manufacturers, security exploits that are applicable to a certain reference platform can often be applied to other devices built on the same platform. Cellebrite, for one, developed bootloader-level exploits, allowing the company's acquisition tool, UFED, to successfully acquire information from smartphones with locked bootloaders. Importantly, this is applicable to devices across different platforms (Android, Windows Phone 8.x, and Windows 10 Mobile) and regardless of whether or not the device being acquired has its bootloader locked or unlocked.

Yet another low-level exploit exists, which allows downloading the entire content of the device internal storage (eMMC) by using Qualcomm Download Mode (firmware recovery mode 9006, Qualcomm MMC Storage (Diag 9006), Qualcomm HS-USB Diagnostics 9006, HS-USB QDLoader 9006, Qualcomm HS-USB 9006, or simply qhsusb 9006, depending on the device). This mode is engaged automatically if the device has a corrupt bootloader. On many devices, it can be possible to manually engage this mode by turning the device off and holding the volume down key while connecting it to a PC via a USB port. On some devices, a different sequence is required. For example, LG G Flex 2 requires holding the volume up button while connecting to the PC.

There is a notable difference between this 9006 diagnostic mode and Qualcomm HS-USB QDLoader 9008 mode. While it is easy to switch the device into the 9008 mode using Qualcomm QPST, additional files are required to boot into the 9006 mode. Imaging the device is not possible from the 9008 mode. More information is available at `http://forum.xda-developers.com/general/help/how-to-enter-qualcomm-mmc-storage-diag-t3253478`.
Also note that sometimes using QPST's eMMC Software Download Tool can help get the device from 9008 to 9006 by using additional files.

By connecting compatible devices in Qualcomm Download Mode 9006 and using specific software, it may be possible to acquire the entire content of the phone's eMMC chip without rooting the device or unlocking its bootloader. Please note that this technique may not work for all manufacturers as some of them (HTC, LG, Motorola, Sony, and so on) may tweak the reference platform to remove user access to the 9006 mode.

In Qualcomm Download Mode 9006 (provided that the correct drivers are installed and assuming you're using a Windows PC), available partitions may appear in the **Windows Disk Management** console. If this is the case, acquiring the content of the device is as simple as using an imaging tool, such as **HDD Raw Copy Tool** (`http://hddguru.com/software/HDD-Raw-Copy-Tool/`).

However, Qualcomm-specific software exists, allowing you to identify and acquire individual partitions.

Tools for imaging via Qualcomm Download Mode 9006

A variety of tools are available for programming/reading devices via the diagnostic port. One such tool is **eMMC RAW Tool**. The tool is developed by Albie Cervice, and is available as a free download at `http://www.na2nkhape.com/215/2/download-emmc-raw-tool.htm l`.

 Video: A quick video tutorial on using eMMC RAW Tool is available at `ht tps://www.youtube.com/watch?v=ESQqVqCODY` (video by `http://www.un brickandroid.com/`).

The tool can read the content of the device's eMMC storage via low-level firmware recovery mode Qualcomm HS-USB 9006. Alternatively, it can mount an Android smartphone as a generic mass storage device.

eMMC RAW Tool features include the following:

- Read full image
- Read partition structure from the device
- Read partition structure from a file
- Read selected partition from the device
- Read by address

Note that eMMC RAW Tool is a powerful tool that can also write to Android devices. This same tool is used to revive (unbrick) devices with corrupted bootloaders. It goes without saying that writing anything onto a phone being imaged is not our intention.

To use eMMC RAW Tool, perform the following steps:

1. Download and unzip the tool from the developer's website (`http://www.na2nkh ape.com/215/2/download-emmc-raw-tool.html`) or from `http://4pda.ru/foru m/index.php?showtopic=655617`.
2. Download and unzip Qualcomm drivers (the correct drivers for Qualcomm 9006 mode must be installed).
3. Install the correct driver for your version of Windows.

4. Switch your device into Qualcomm Download Mode 9006. This is the iffy part. To do this, you may attempt the following sequence:
    1. Switch the device off (wait while it shuts down completely).
    2. Press and hold the hardware volume down key (on some devices, press and hold the volume up key).
    3. While holding the key, connect the device to your computer via a USB cable.
    4. Wait until the device displays **Download mode** or **Updating firmware 0%**.
    5. Release the key and wait while the drivers are installed.
5. If the device is not switching to the 9006 mode, you can try researching the correct sequence.
6. At this time, Windows will attempt to install the Qualcomm HS-USB 9006 driver. When prompted, choose the correct driver and wait until it finishes installing.
7. Finally, run eMMC RAW Tool, as shown in the following screenshot:

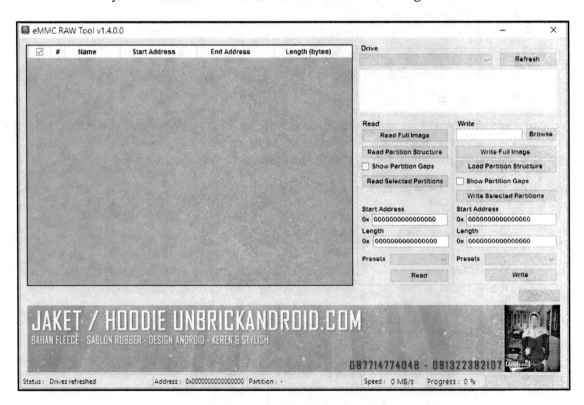

In order to image the device, perform the following steps:

1. Click on **Refresh**.
2. The list of physical drives will appear. Select the appropriate device from the **Drive** box.
3. Click on **Read Partition Structure**. The list of available partitions will appear in the main window.
4. Select all partitions by clicking the check box on the top left-hand side of the window.
5. Click on **Read Selected Partitions**.

Alternatively, you may only select the **USERDATA, DATA,** or **SDCARD** partition during Step 4. This will only read the content of that single partition containing your user data:

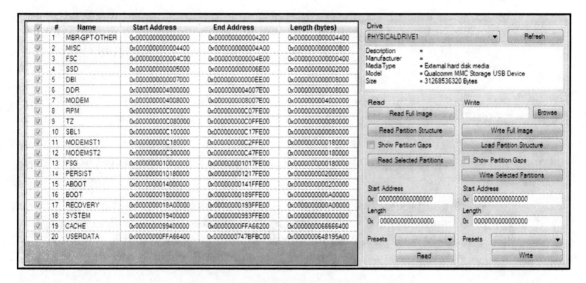

Imaging an Android Smartphone in the Qualcomm 9006 Mode

For example, the **USERDATA** partition in the preceding screenshot (partition number 20) would be the correct partition to image using the **Read Selected Partitions** function. Alternatively, the complete device image can be read by using **Read Full Image**.

That's it, you have successfully imaged the device. You can now proceed to the actual recovery. If, however, this technique did not work for you (for example, your phone does not support the Qualcomm HS-USB 9006 mode), you can try imaging the device using a different method.

Using custom recoveries

There is more than one way of using a custom recovery to image an Android device. The first method is the easiest and involves simply booting into a custom recovery (via `fastboot boot twrp.img` or `fastboot boot cwm.img`) and using on-screen controls to produce a Nandroid backup of the data partition. The second method (via the `dd` command) is more complex and requires opening two separate terminal windows; however, this method returns the full raw image of the data partition. The following is a quick comparison of the two methods:

- **Nandroid backup**: This is quick, easy, and done via graphical user interface (touch-based or controlled with the phone's hardware keys). It only dumps filesystem; no access to unallocated space makes recovering deleted files impossible.
- **Imaging via dd**: This requires extra tools and two terminal windows. It requires a much higher level of expertise to use and returns the complete raw dump of the data partition with full access to unallocated space, making it possible to recover deleted files.

This book is not about rooting Android or installing custom recoveries. Refer to the end of this book for recommended reading on Android forensics.

In this chapter, we'll give a brief overview of what a custom recovery can and cannot do for you and what are the limitations and dangers in imaging the device with a custom recovery.

 Warning: If the device bootloader is locked, unlocking it may (and probably will) cause a full factory reset, which results in complete loss of data. Only proceed if your bootloader is already unlocked or if you know for sure that your device can boot into a custom recovery without wiping data.

Using a custom recovery is risky. The Android platform is highly fragmented. Different manufacturers employ different security policies across the many devices they carry within their range. Booting into a custom recovery can succeed, fail, trigger a full factory reset, or succeed and then trigger a full factory reset. Therefore, using a custom recovery, in general, is not considered a forensically sound way of imaging the device.

Encryption

Custom recoveries may or may not be able to deal with encrypted partitions, even if you know the correct passcode. In addition, if the data partition is captured encrypted, you may or may not be able to decrypt it afterwards—even if you know the passcode.

Just a few examples from some recent cases:

- **Motorola Nexus 6** (and possibly other Nexus devices): Flashing or booting into a custom recovery is possible. However, unlocking bootloader causes factory reset.
- **Motorola Moto X (2014)**: Once the bootloader is unlocked, flashing or booting a custom recovery succeeds (all Android versions from 4.4 to 6.0). Unlocking bootloader causes factory reset.
- **SONY Xperia Z series**: Unlocking bootloader causes factory reset. After that, booting or flashing custom recovery succeeds.
- **ASUS MeMo Pad 7**: Unlocking is not possible. Attempts to boot into custom recovery fail.
- **ASUS ZenPad S 8.0** (all versions): Unlocking bootloader not possible. However, booting into a custom recovery is available via exploit (`http://forum.xda-devel opers.com/android/development/zenpad-s-root-achieved-t316422`) and causes no untoward consequences (tested on all firmware versions up to, and including, the current 4.5.0).
- **ASUS ZenPhone**: Same exploit as for ZenPad S.
- **InFocus M810t**: Unlocking bootloader is possible via exploit; the exploit does not trigger a wipe per se. Booting into custom recovery is possible even while the bootloader is locked. However, booting into custom recovery triggers data wipe on the next reboot. Interestingly, once booted into custom recovery, one can dump partitions before the wipe occurs.

When analyzing the device, you can attempt to install or boot into a custom recovery mode. The two popular custom recoveries are **ClockworkMod (CWM)** (`http://www.clockworkmo d.com/`) and **Team Win Recovery Project (TWRP)** (`http://teamw.in/Devices/`).

 Important: Installing or booting into a custom recovery requires the device bootloader to be fully or partially unlocked. Partially unlocked bootloader may allow booting into a custom recovery; however, the system may wipe data partition afterward. Proceed with extreme caution!

Custom recoveries are nothing but bootable, slimmed-down versions of the Linux OS. Custom recoveries are therefore device-specific, as they need to come with the necessary drivers for each particular device model. As such, custom recoveries can seamlessly bypass Android's standard security measures such as access restrictions (but not data encryption).

Imaging via custom recovery – making a Nandroid backup

Technically, there is nothing preventing custom recoveries from dumping a raw image of the data partition. At this time, neither TWRP nor CWM offer the ability to make raw dumps of the data partition from the user interface (however, boot and system partitions are captured as raw images). As a result, the UI of neither TWRP nor CWM can be used for accessing data stored in unallocated space.

 Important: Making a complete raw dump of the data partition is possible with custom recoveries. However, the process is significantly more complicated compared to making a Nandroid backup. The *Imaging the device* section explains the process of physically imaging Android devices via custom recoveries.

Using a custom recovery UI, however, is a feasible way of making a full backup of the filesystem, including all application data.

If the device being examined has an unlocked bootloader, you can install (or, better yet, boot into) a custom recovery. From there, you can easily back up the entire data partition of the device:

1. If no custom recovery is installed, download the custom recovery image specific to your device from either TWRP or CWM.
2. Boot the device into bootloader (the fastboot mode):
    1. Switch the phone off.
    2. Hold down the volume down key and press the power button.
    3. The phone should boot into bootloader (the fastboot mode). If it does not, determine the correct way of booting into bootloader (fastboot) for your device and follow the instructions specific for that device.
3. Obtain adb and fastboot executables.
4. Place fastboot files and the custom recovery image into a single folder. Open the command line in this folder.
5. Download and install fastboot drivers for the device being investigated (drivers can be manufacturer-specific, device-specific, or chipset-specific, depending on the model).
6. Connect the phone to the PC via a USB cable.
7. Run either the following command:

```
fastboot boot twrp.img
```

Or run the following command:

```
fastboot boot cwm.img
```

Here, `twrp.img` or `cwm.img` are the names of TWRP or CWM recoveries. Use the correct filename or simply rename the downloaded recovery image into a shorter filename.

8. From the custom recovery, back up data partition (only the data partition is needed). Make sure that the destination is either an external SD card or in **on-the-go (OTG)** USB drive. Do not use the phone's internal storage to back up the data.

At this time, you've successfully acquired the complete filesystem of the device in the form of a **Nandroid backup**.

Nandroid backups files created via custom recoveries are usually saved in the form of EXT4, F2FS, or YAFFS TAR images. These are generally easy to extract with a free archive tool such as 7Zip:

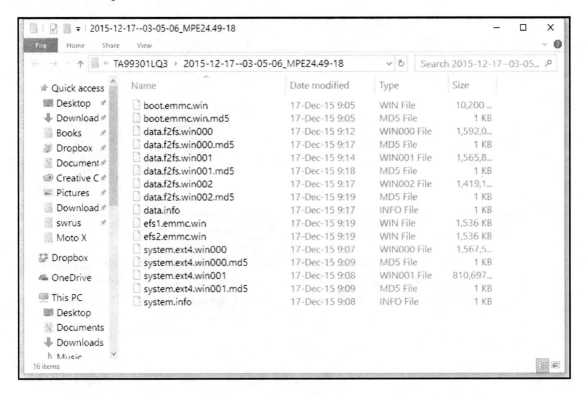

Files produced by TWRP Nandroid backup

7Zip can open multi-volume backups without the need to rename or join files. Simply launch 7Zip and open the `data.f2fs.win000` file (or similar) to extract files from the data partition:

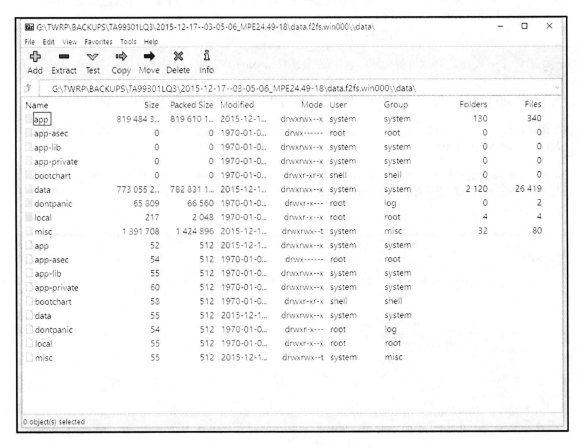

The content of a TWRP backup

TWRP can create YAFFS filesystem images. Extracting files from a TWRP Nandroid backup can be performed with one of the many forensic tools available on the market. There is also an open source utility called **unyaffs**. Its source code is available at `https://code.google.com/p/unyaffs/downloads/list`.

The compiled version of this tool can be used as follows:

```
unyaffs data.img
```

Here, `data.img` is the Nandroid backup file.

Imaging via custom recovery – physical imaging via dd

Acquisition via the user interface of most popular custom recoveries (TWRP and CWM) does not allow for imaging the complete data partition in raw mode. In order to be able to investigate unallocated space, you may want to extract the entire user data partition to a raw image.

In unencrypted Android devices, extracting unallocated areas is only possible by accessing the storage directly. Android built-in security measures prevent such access from within the app framework, making it impossible to scan unallocated areas with any user-level application. Root access is required in order to be able to access storage in low level.

Warning: Rooting the device is unsafe. It may render the device unstable or inaccessible. It may also wipe the device. However, the dd extraction method does not require a rooted device. All you need is a flashed or booted (recommended) custom recovery. A custom recovery is a slimmed down version of this OS that comes with root access by default.

This advanced physical acquisition method uses the dd command to image the device. The dd command allows dumping either the entire physical storage or any number of individual partitions. For the purpose of digital forensics, only the data partition is required.

In order to transfer the data from the Android device to the PC over the USB interface, we'll use the netcat command.

Prerequisites for this include the following:

- **Unlocked or semi-unlocked bootloader (to allow booting into a custom recovery)**: Rooting the device is not required, as custom recoveries come with full root access built in.
- **BusyBox**: This comes pre-installed with custom recoveries (TWRP and CWM). To verify, type any BusyBox command, such as busybox nc, once you're booted into the custom recovery.
- **Android Debug Bridge (ADB)**: This is required to run shell commands on the Android device.
- **Fastboot**: This is part of the ADB package. It should be installed on your PC.
- **ADB drivers**: ADB drivers are device-specific. They must be installed for this acquisition method to work.

Once you have all the required tools installed and configured, perform the following steps:

1. Identify the name of the user data partition on your Android device. If you can't identify the data partition, you will be imaging the entire device (physical storage).

2. Verify that the bootloader is unlocked or semi-unlocked (allowing you to boot into a custom recovery without wiping the data).

3. Boot the phone into the recovery mode. If the device is turned off, do this by holding the volume down key while powering on the device. If the device is turned on, and you have an active ADB connection, use `adb -d reboot recovery` to reboot into recovery.

4. Connect the device to the computer via a USB cable.

5. Ensure that fastboot is operational by running `fastboot devices`. A list of devices should appear. An empty string means something is wrong.

    Note: Some devices require specifying the correct vendor ID in the command line. For example, for booting a Lenovo ZUK into a custom recovery, one would use `fastboot -i 0x2b4c boot recovery.img`. The correct vendor ID can usually be discovered online. In addition, in certain cases `fastboot devices` returns empty while actually booting into a custom recovery works.

6. Boot the device into the custom recovery by using the following command:

```
fastboot boot recovery.img
```

    Here, `recovery.img` is your custom recovery image specific to the device being acquired.

7. Ensure that Netcat is operational in your custom recovery by running the ADB shell (`adb shell`) and executing the `busybox nc` command. You may need to configure your computer's firewall to allow connecting to local ports.

You are now ready to image the device. The following steps describe how to capture an image of the data partition using the `netcat` command. You'll be running two different shell sessions at the same time: one to the device and one to your computer.

Imaging the device

Run `cmd.exe` or use a different terminal (for example, Cygwin). This will be the first shell session that works with the Android device. Run `adb shell`. You will receive the root privileges by default, so running `su` is not needed.

Launch another instance of `cmd.exe` or your favorite terminal. This session opens as a shell on your computer, and will be used to receive the data from the Android device. Navigate to the folder that will receive the user partition (`cd c:\path`). Make sure that you're using an NTFS- or exFAT-formatted hard drive to receive the data; FAT32 volumes will be unable to save images of more than 4 GB, which is less than the typical storage of most phones today. In this shell, run `adb forward tcp:5555 tcp:5555` (you may use a different port number if needed). This command enables ADB to communicate via Netcat on port 5555.

Now, once the connection is established, go back to the first shell that goes to your phone. Type the following command:

```
dd if=/dev/block/mmcblk0 | busybox nc -l -p 5555
```

This command images the contents of `/dev/block/mmcblk0` and writes it via port 5555 across ADB using Netcat.

Alternatively, you may use the following syntax:

```
busybox nc -l -p 5555 -e busybox dd if=/dev/block/mmcblk0p12
```

This command acquires the `mmcblk0p12` data block. Note that you will need to figure out the name of the data block on the device being acquired.

Finally, go back to the second shell (that goes to your computer) and type the following command:

```
nc 127.0.0.1 5555 > image.raw
```

The `nc` (Netcat) command saves the output of the first shell to your computer across port 5555. The file will be stored in the same folder where you launched the second shell from. You can change this folder by navigating to the correct place via `cd disk:\path`. Note that some Windows folders (for example, `C:\Program Files\` and its subfolders) are not write-accessible.

If all goes well, the window will freeze while it's capturing the image. Once the process is finished, you'll be able to mount the newly captured image in a forensic tool of your choice.

 Note: Custom recoveries do not decrypt encrypted devices. As a result, if the data partition was encrypted, you will receive an encrypted image that you may or may not be able to decrypt later on. If the device is encrypted, your only option is performing **live imaging** of the device (refer to the *Live imaging* section for more information), which requires the device to be rooted and have BusyBox installed.

More information on imaging Android devices via custom recoveries:

- Why not load ClockworkMod or TWRP to image a device? Alternate recovery modes are useful, but maybe not for imaging a device (http://freeandroidfore nsics.blogspot.com/215/4/why-not-load-clockworkmod-or-twrp-to.html).

NANDroid backups

This acquisition method is applicable to smartphones and tablets that are either rooted or have a custom recovery installed. It is also applicable to devices with fully or partially unlocked bootloaders (allowing the expert to boot the device into a custom recovery).

If a custom recovery is installed, or can be booted into, a different acquisition method (via the dd command) is available, allowing to capture the complete raw image of the data partition (refer to the *Imaging via custom recovery – physical imaging via dd* section for more information). The dd method returns a full dump of either the entire eMMC storage or just the data partition. A Nandroid backup contains the full filesystem of the data partition; unallocated space is not included, which makes recovering deleted files impossible. This method is relatively easy to use, but requires some technical expertise. Nandroid backups are *not* considered a forensically sound acquisition method; however, a Nandroid backup will still contain significantly more information than available via ADB.

Unlike pretty much every other smartphone OS, Android does not come with the ability to produce full backups of the device. The platform provides no stock tools for making or restoring such backups. Moreover, the platform in its stock state does not even allow third-party developers to make such backup tools as their use would require an elevated level of privileges (*root* rights).

Individual manufacturers implement proprietary tools for making and restoring backups (for example, Sony PC Companion for Xperia phones and tablets). However, these tools are used by relatively few smartphone owners as (again, unlike iOS) they aren't required to perform other routine tasks such as transferring files to and from the device.

The need for creating and restoring full filesystem backups is there, especially among the more active Android users who like to experiment with their devices and want to be able to restore their device to its previous working state, should something go wrong. Full filesystem backup tools are available for these users, but only work on rooted devices, devices with custom recoveries, or devices that can be flashed via fastboot.

Examiners analyzing certain Android devices have yet another venue for extracting the full image of the filesystem (but generally *not* a raw dump of the data partition) by generating a NANDroid backup. NANDroid backups contain the full image of the filesystem for all partitions selected at the time of making the backup. Nandroid backups can be produced by booting the device into a custom recovery, such as CWM or TWRP (by either issuing an ADB command or, if **USB debugging** is not enabled, by holding the volume down and power keys on the device) and selecting the corresponding menu item from the menu.

 Note: The name *NANDroid* is derived from the words *NAND* and *Android*. As such, the correct name is *NANDroid*, which is often written as *Nandroid* for simplicity.

Is unlocked bootloader required?

While most sources say that you need either root privileges or unlocked bootloader (or both) in order to make Nandroid backups, this is not completely true. Technically speaking, all you need to make a Nandroid backup is a custom recovery, such as CWM or TWRP. Granted, many devices require root access for the user to install custom recovery, and the bootloader must be unlocked in order to be able to install the custom recovery. However, the user may safely relock bootloader after installing custom recovery, which will not affect the ability to produce Nandroid backups. In addition, many devices can safely boot into a custom recovery (via `fastboot boot recovery.img`) as opposed to permanently installing one, even if the bootloader is officially locked. For the purpose of mobile forensics, booting into a custom recovery is a much cleaner and more forensically sound method of imaging the device.

Is root access required?

Contrary to popular belief, root access is not an absolute requirement for making Nandroid backups. In order to produce a Nandroid backup, you can either boot into a custom recovery (root status is irrelevant) or use an app (root privileges and BusyBox package required).

Producing a Nandroid backup

The following two ways are available for making Nandroid backups:

- Unlocked or partially unlocked bootloader, custom recovery (for example, CWM or TWRP) specific to the device available: note that unlocked bootloader is normally required in order to install custom recovery. In addition to this, some devices must be rooted in order to install custom recovery. Unlocking bootloader during the investigation is not normally possible as this operation initiates a full wipe of the data partition. However, bootloader may be relocked after having the custom recovery installed, so technically speaking, unlocked bootloader is not required for making Nandroid backups via custom recovery. For the purpose of making Nandroid backups through custom recovery, root status of the device is irrelevant.
- Rooted device, BusyBox installed, a Nandroid backup app is used: You may be able to make a Nandroid backup even if the bootloader is unlocked. For this, you will be using one of the many Nandroid backup apps. You can sideload an app like that onto the phone. Note that you may need to have BusyBox installed (unless the tool uses its own mechanism for imaging the data partition). Root is required to use such apps; however, root is not required if the operation is performed through a custom recovery.

Having a custom recovery, which is basically a standalone version of the OS, helps tremendously in bypassing most security restrictions (except encryption). If you can boot into a custom recovery (or if you can manage to install it without wiping the device), you can easily dump the entire content of the eMMC storage, or just image the data partition onto an external SD card or OTG flash drive (if either device is supported by the phone).

In some situations, you may encounter relocked bootloaders (the user unlocks the bootloader, installs a custom recovery, and then relocks the bootloader). While this, in general, is not an issue, some users may protect access to custom recovery with a password. A combination of a locked bootloader and a password-protected custom recovery is extremely tough to break.

Analyzing Nandroid backups

NANDroid backups are standardized between different recoveries. NANDrpod is a de-facto standard format for storing Android system backups. Nandroid backups can be parsed and analyzed by forensic tools such as Oxygen Forensic Suite (`http://www.oxygen-forensic.com/en/compare`) or Belkasoft Evidence Center (version 7.3 or newer).

In Oxygen Forensic Suite, a Nandroid backup can be imported via **Android backup/image | Android backup**:

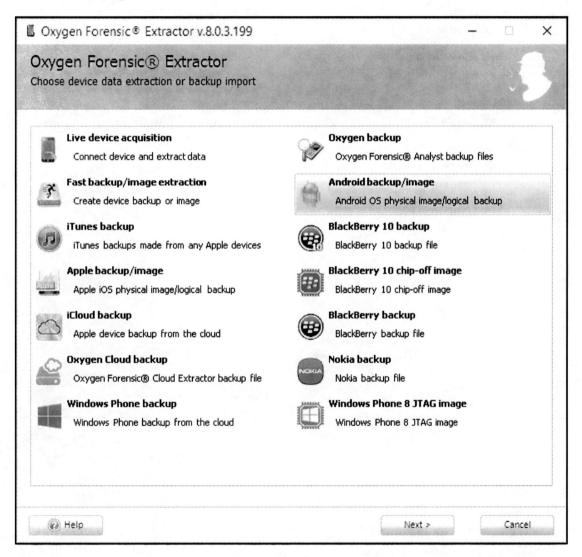

Choose a backup type:

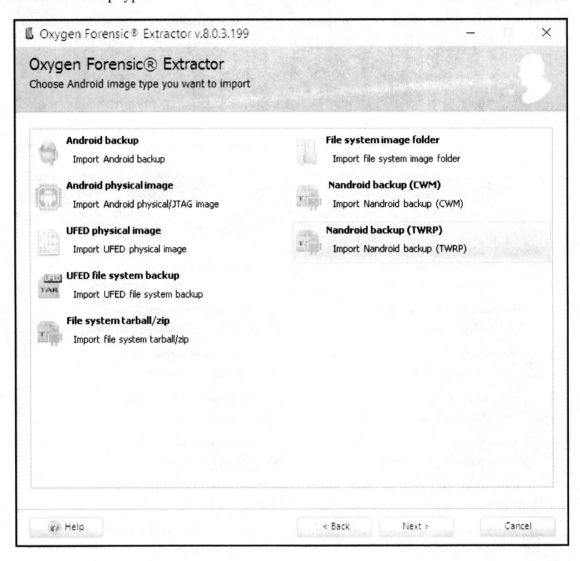

Specify a backup location:

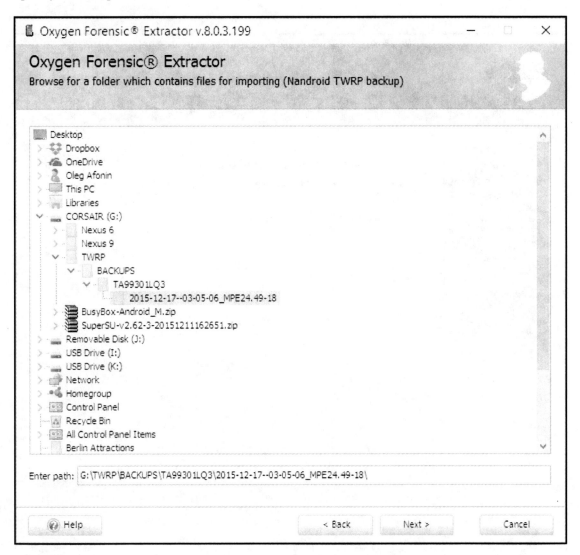

Specify options and click on **Finish**. The data will be processed and imported into the analytic suite:

After the process is finished, you'll be able to access information stored in the backup you have just imported:

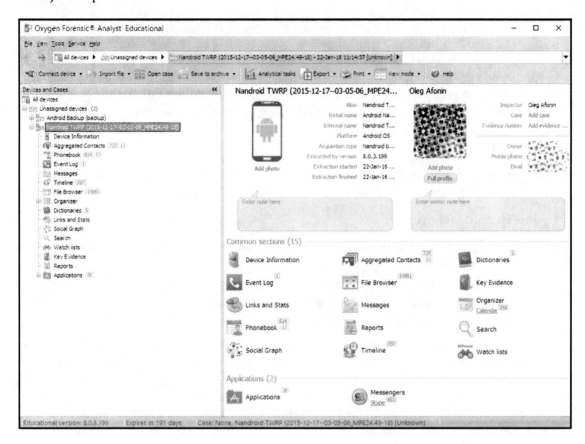

Live imaging

Live imaging may be your last resort when acquiring an encrypted device. Since neither bootloader exploits nor custom recoveries can decrypt encrypted partitions, you may need to start and unlock the device with the correct PIN code in order to gain access to the encrypted data partition.

Live imaging of an Android device is similar to the process described in the *Imaging via custom recovery – physical imaging via dd* section.

Live imaging with root (via dd)

Live imaging is considered to be a less forensically-sound method compared to using a custom recovery or other acquisition methods. This method requires a rooted device with BusyBox installed. Rooting an Android device in general is not always safe or possible. Depending on the version of Android and the method used to obtain root access, rooting may modify the device boot image and/or its system and data partitions. Installing BusyBox may or may not modify the system partition. Rooting and installing BusyBox may also alter the content of the user's data partition. With the recent development of *systemless root*, it is now technically possible to achieve root access and install BusyBox without modifying the system partition.

Instructions on how to root and install BusyBox on Android devices are widely available, so we won't cover them here.

Prerequisites are as follows:

- **Root access**: Your device must be rooted. Unlocked bootloader is not required for this acquisition method.
- **BusyBox**: This must be installed on your Android device.
- **cmd.exe** or another terminal (for example, Cygwin).
- **ADB executable**: Android Debug Bridge (adb.exe) will be required.
- **ADB drivers**: ADB drivers specific to the device being acquired must be installed.
- **USB debugging**: This must be enabled on the Android device in **Developer options**.

Once the device is rooted, you'll be using two shells—one that goes to the Android device and one that goes to your computer:

1. Identify the name of the data partition being acquired. If you can't identify the data partition, you can image the entire device (physical storage).
2. Turn on and unlock the device. If it is locked with a passcode, enter the passcode. If not known, use one of the many passcode recovery techniques to obtain it.
3. In Android **Developer options**, enable **USB debugging**.
4. Connect the device to your computer via a USB cable. Unlock the device.
5. The device will prompt to authorize the debug interface. Tap **OK**.

6. On your computer, open the command line and type `adb devices`. Your device should appear in the list of connected devices. If the returned list is empty, or your phone is listed as offline, troubleshoot the ADB connection.

7. Open the first of the two shells. This will be the connection to the device being imaged. Run `cmd.exe` or open a different shell (for example, Cygwin). Type `adb shell` followed by `su`. On the device, confirm superuser access if prompted.

8. Check whether you successfully received root access by attempting to list `/data`. Type `ls /data`. If you can see the content of this directory, you successfully obtained root access. If not, troubleshoot the root access.

If all goes well, you are ready to image the device.

Launch another instance of `cmd.exe` or your favorite terminal. This session opens as a shell to your computer, and will be used to receive the data from the Android device. Navigate to the folder that will receive the user partition (`cd c:\path`). Make sure that you're using an NTFS- or exFAT-formatted hard drive to receive the data; FAT32 volumes will be unable to save images of more than 4 GB, which is less than the typical storage of most today's phones. In this shell, run `adb forward tcp:5555 tcp:5555` (you may use a different port number if needed). This command enables ADB to communicate via Netcat on port 5555.

Now, once the connection is established, go back to the first shell that goes to your phone. Type the following command:

```
dd if=/dev/block/mmcblk0 | busybox nc -l -p 5555
```

This command images the contents of /dev/block/mmcblk0 and writes it via port 555 across ADB using Netcat.

Alternatively, you may use the following syntax:

```
busybox nc -l -p 5555 -e busybox dd if=/dev/block/mmcblk0p12
```

This command acquires the `mmcblk0p12` data block. Note that you will need to figure out the name of the data block on the device being acquired.

Finally, go back to the second shell (that goes to your computer) and type the following command:

```
nc 127.0.0.1 5555 > image.raw
```

The `nc` (Netcat) command saves the output of the first shell to your computer across port 5555. The file will be stored in the same folder where you launched the second shell from. You can change this folder by navigating to the correct place via `cd disk:\path`. Note that some Windows folders (for example, `C:\Program Files\` and its subfolders) are not write-accessible.

If all goes well, the window will freeze while it's capturing the image. Once the process is finished, you'll be able to mount the newly captured image in a forensic tool of your choice.

 Note: Unlike the previous acquisition method operating via a custom recovery, live imaging of an Android device can successfully acquire encrypted partitions. Encrypted data will be decrypted on-the-fly.

More information on imaging Android devices is available as follows:

- Live imaging an Android device: Not as hard as it sounds if you break it down— `http://freeandroidforensics.blogspot.com/214/8/live-imaging-android -device.html`

Live imaging without root (via ADB backup)

On some devices, root access may not be available. If this is the case, the only remaining imaging option besides **Google Account** acquisition is attempting to make an ADB backup. This method is 100% logical acquisition; we only discuss this here as it is the last acquisition method available if all other methods fail.

It is important to realize the limitations of this method. Unlike Apple iOS or BlackBerry 10, a non-rooted backup on Android devices only extracts a very limited amount of information. Application developers may disable backups in their app's Manifest file; ADB will not back up data from these apps. However, if no other acquisition options are available, an ADB backup may still be better than nothing.

The requirements for this are as follows:

- **USB debugging** enabled, or device unlocked/lock screen bypassed in order to enable **USB debugging**
- If data partition is encrypted, the device must be unlocked (bypassing the lock screen is not enough)
- ADB installed and working

To start imaging the device, turn it on and wait until it is fully booted. Unlock the device (or bypass the screen lock) and make sure that **USB debugging** is enabled in **Developer options**:

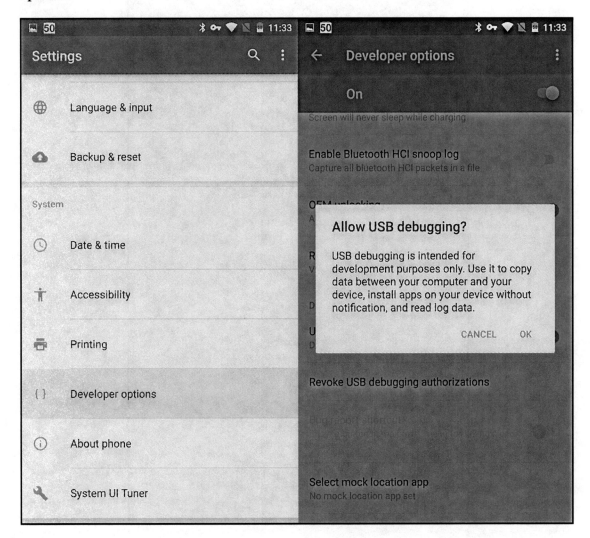

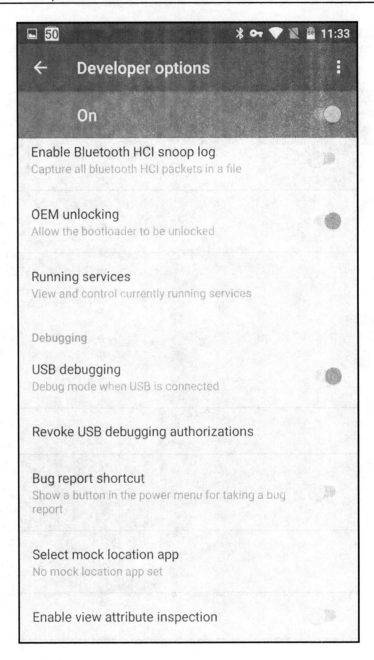

Next, connect the device to the PC via a USB cable. Launch `cmd.exe` in the folder where ADB is installed. Type `adb devices` to verify connectivity. On the phone, you should be prompted to authorize debugging from the connected PC; tap to confirm the prompt. If all goes well, you should see the device listed under the **adb devices** prompt:

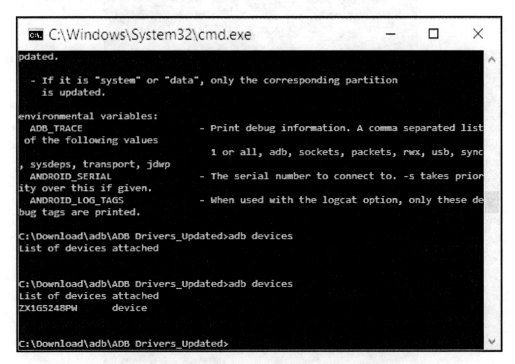

Next, you'll be using the ADB backup command. The command has the following syntax:

```
adb backup [-f <file>] [-apk|-noapk] [-shared|-noshared] [-all] [-
system|nosystem] [<packages...>]
```

If you want to back up the entire content of the device, use the following syntax:

```
adb backup -all -f c:\android\backup.ab
```

On the Android device being imaged, you will see the following prompt:

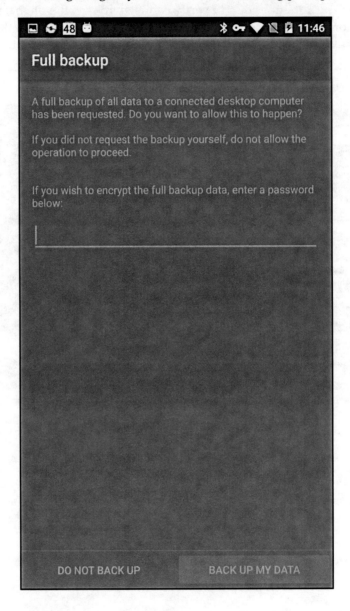

Tap **Back up my data** and wait till the process completes.

> **Note**: On some devices, ADB backup may not work if the data partition is encrypted—even if you unlock the device with the correct passcode. Currently, there is no known workaround.

You can also use Oxygen Forensic Extractor to automatically produce an ADB backup:

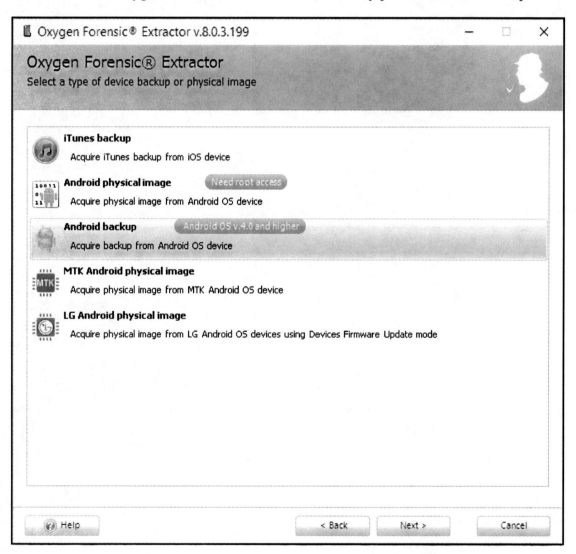

The resulting `backup.ab` file may be opened in one of the many mobile forensic suites on the market. For example, in Oxygen Forensic Suite, use the following sequence to import this backup: **Import File** | **Import Android backup/image** | **Import Android backup…**

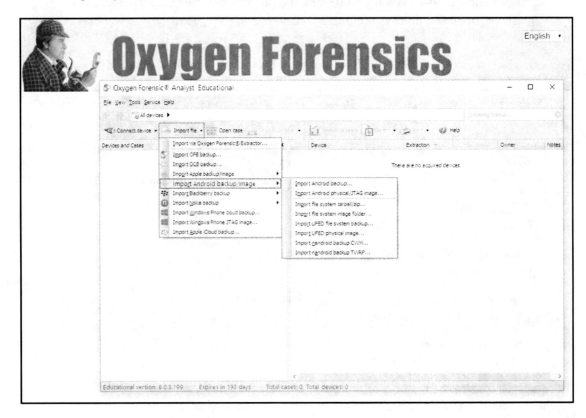

After the import completes, you will see something similar to the following screenshot:

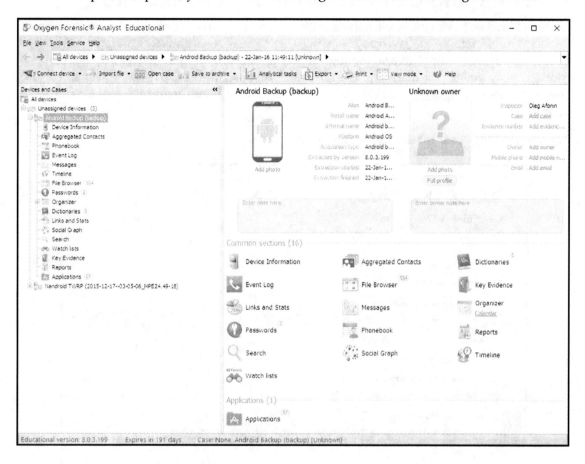

Live imaging using Oxygen Forensic Suite

Oxygen Forensic Suite comes with the ability to live-image many types of Android devices. Its acquisition methods range from manufacturer-specific raw dumps to the physical acquisition of rooted devices and the logical acquisition of Android devices that have no root access available. For many models, Oxygen Forensic Suite can bypass bootloader lock and screen lock completely. For certain devices, the tool can automatically acquire root access.

For live imaging Android devices, you'll be using Oxygen Forensic Extractor:

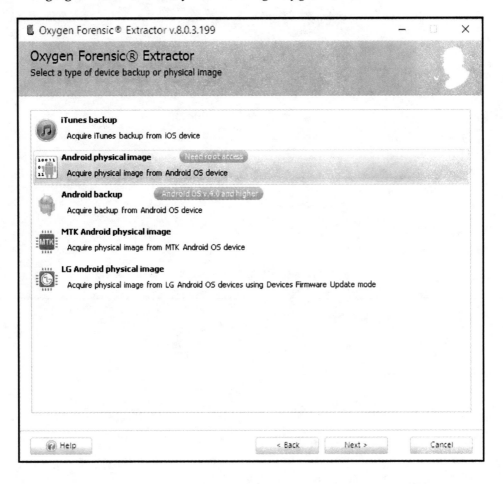

Connect the device via a USB cable. Unlock and ensure that **ADB Debugging** is enabled:

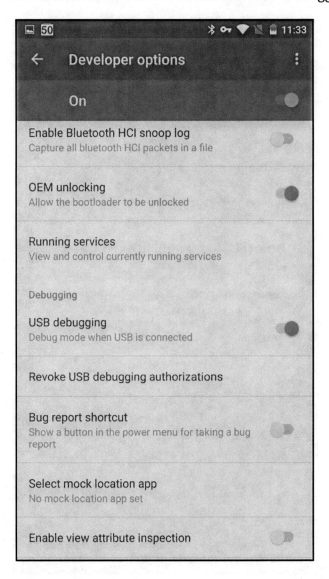

If it is not, enable **USB debugging** in the device's **Developer options**:

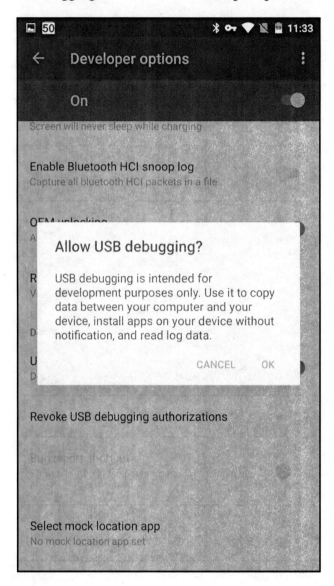

Make sure to authorize **USB debugging** on the device's screen once it's connected to your computer.

If everything goes well, you will see the following screen:

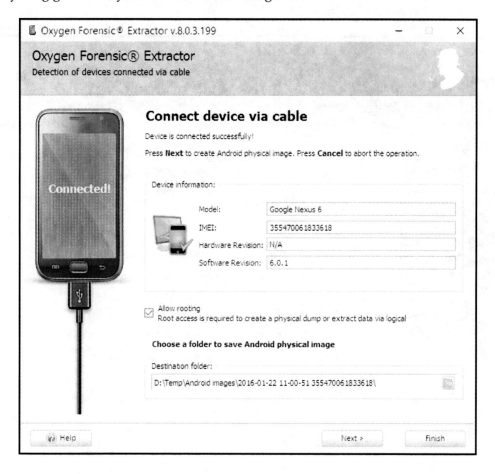

Troubleshooting connectivity: On some occasions, USB debugging will not be available after the device is connected to the PC:

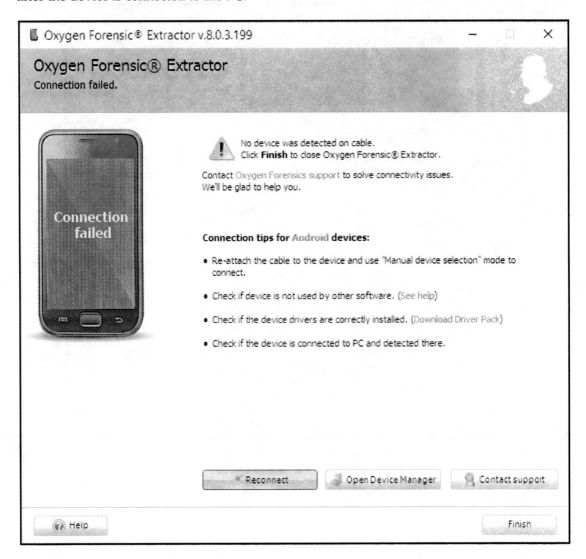

If that's the case, check whether USB connectivity is set to something other than **Charging** by pulling the notification panel from the top of the screen. We recommend that you choose the **Photo transfer (PTP)** option:

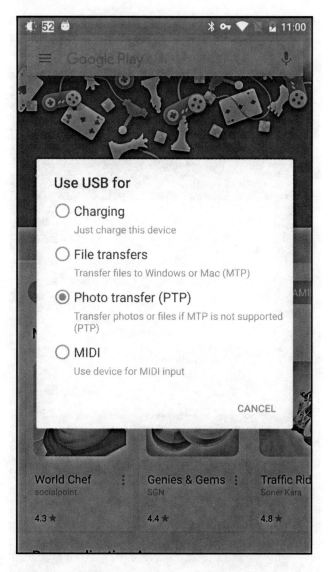

Click on **Reconnect** in Oxygen Forensic Extractor to make another attempt.

After connecting the device, Oxygen Forensic Extractor will probe it for root access. If the Android device is already rooted, the device will prompt you to allow root access. Confirm the prompt:

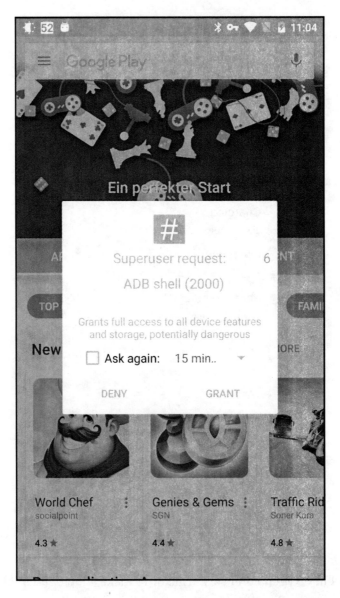

If root was not available on the Android device, Oxygen Forensic Extractor will attempt a range of different exploits to obtain root access:

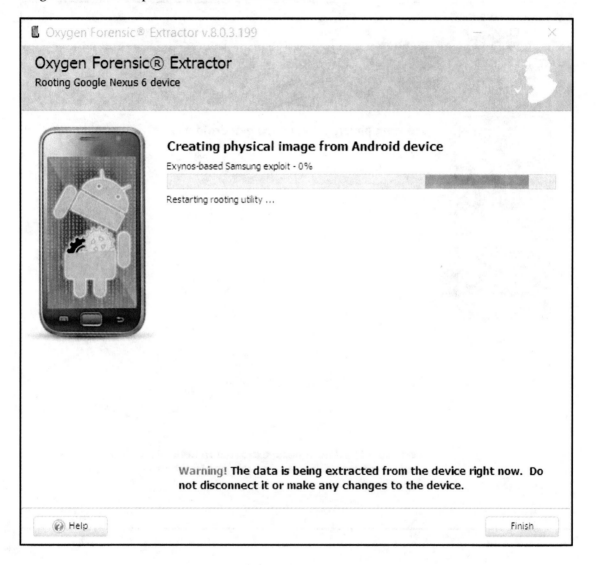

If root access is successfully obtained, the imaging process will begin automatically:

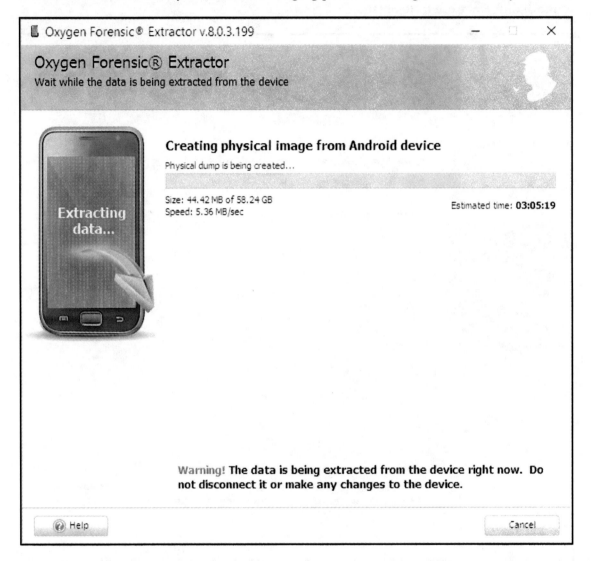

If Oxygen Forensic Extractor is unable to obtain root access, physical extraction will fail. You can attempt a different extraction method, such as over-the-air (refer to the *Google Account acquisition – over-the-air* section for more information) or via ADB backup (refer to the *Live imaging without root (via ADB backup)* section for more information):

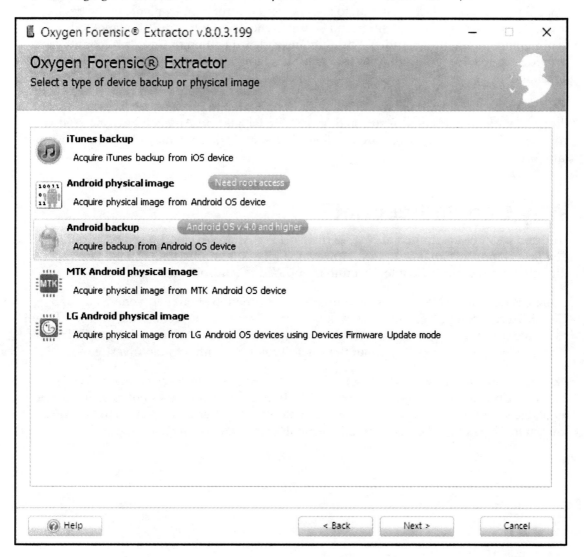

Google Account acquisition – over-the-air

Android is a Google OS. Relying heavily on cloud services, most of which are provided by Google, Android devices inevitably leave traces on Google's servers. Extracting information from Google's servers is a great way to complement information available in the device itself. While over-the-air acquisition can be used when all other acquisition methods fail, it is not limited to acquiring Android devices. Instead, acquisition of Google Accounts can provide a much deeper insight into user activities than what's available in a single Android smartphone.

Note that not all Android devices come with Google Mobile Services; we'll discuss this in detail later on. In particular, Amazon devices (Fire tablets and Amazon Fire Phone) do not come with any Google services preinstalled. However, end users may add Google services later on.

Why Google Account?

Android backups are limited at best. In the world of Android, cloud backups are still new and (as of Android 6.0) incomplete. However, a lot of interesting data can be obtained directly from the user's Google Account as opposed to Android backups.

Google is known to collect massive amounts of information about everyone who has a Google Account. If you are able to log in with the user's Google credentials, you will be able to acquire that data regardless of whether you have the actual Android device available. Knowing what Google knows about the suspect can be essential for an investigation.

Google offers the ability to extract some of this data via its own service, called Google Takeout. Unfortunately, Google Takeout lacks transparency and does not offer full access to available information. The data is stored in a number of different formats, and Google is known for declining requests to help investigators analyze the data.

Google Account – what's inside?

Google provides a diverse range of services, most of which are free of charge. The company offers Google Mail (Gmail), Google Drive, the ubiquitous Google Search, Google Chrome (with cloud sync), Google Maps, and dozens of other services that automatically sync across devices with the help of a single Google Account.

Google Account is a single-stop aggregation of information about the user's online behavior and offline activities. Google analyzes search queries and communications, and recommends places to visit and things to read. Google collects and maintains a comprehensive location history; stores all Google searches performed on registered desktop and mobile devices; syncs Chrome tabs, bookmarks, passwords, and history; keeps notes; annotates pictures; syncs contacts; and does a lot more.

All this data is collected by different services and is stored in different places across Google servers. The data is available in a range of different formats, and requires using vastly different protocols to access. However, the entirety of this data is accessible with a single authentication via Google Account.

What can you expect when extracting data from a Google Account? Nearly everyone has a Gmail account, which means messages and contacts. Google Chrome accounts for nearly half of all Web requests, which means tabs, bookmarks, and search history, as well as Web forms and logins. Google Maps is a major player, and Google Drive offers cloud storage for pretty much everything. Here's what you can expect to see when acquiring data from a Google Account:

- User profile
- Location history (very comprehensive)
- Gmail messages and settings
- Contacts and calendars
- Information about connected devices
- Information about devices, apps, and browsers that requested access
- Google Advertising settings (including age, gender, interests, and so on)
- Google Keep notes
- Google Photos (albums, detected people, EXIF, location data, and so on)
- Hangouts messages
- Google Fit data

The following bits are additionally available from Google Chrome synced data (Google Chrome data may be additionally protected with a password):

- Bookmarks
- Browsing history
- Chrome synced passwords
- Autofill data for Web forms
- Google search queries
- YouTube search queries

Each entry from the search and browsing history contains the following additional information:

- Original IP address
- Browser data
- Page transitions (search results that were opened)
- Actions on ads (tracks clicks and purchases)

Google Takeout does not export the search and browsing history.

A word on Android backups

Cloud backups are new to Android. Automatic backup of third-party application data was only made available in Android 6.0. However, even in earlier versions of Android, some bits of data were still exported into the cloud and restored when the user initialized a new device with their Google credentials. Particularly, we've seen the following data:

- Installed apps (from Google Play only, no data on sideloaded apps)
- Home settings, including wallpaper, folders, and icons
- Google Calendar settings
- List of Wi-Fi networks
- Wi-Fi passwords
- Gmail settings
- Display settings
- Language and input settings, including custom dictionaries for Google Keyboard
- Date and time settings (for example, 12/24 hr, time zone, and so on)

Android 6.0 introduced support for cloud backups, allowing third-party apps to have automatic backup and restore:

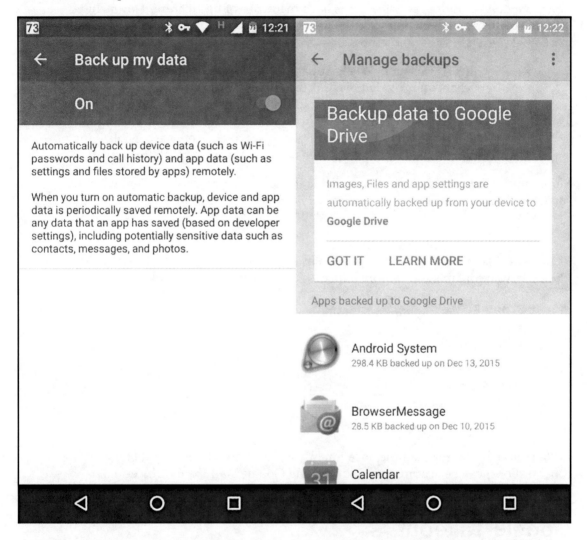

However, Android cloud backups are still severely limited compared to iOS and Windows Phone counterparts. While prerelease versions of Android 6.0 allowed third-party apps to *opt-out* from data backups (the default behavior was *backups enabled for all apps that did not opt out via manifest*), the release version of Android 6.0 did not retain this change.

The final version of Android 6.0 uses the *opt-in* method, allowing application developers to explicitly allow backups for their apps through the manifest file. The default behavior is *no data backups*. As of today, very few apps have made use of this feature. This includes Google's own apps, which don't use the new backup feature of Android 6.0. Instead, they use Google Drive to back up their data.

 Note: At this time, WhatsApp messenger does not use the default backup mechanism provided by Android 6.0. Instead, WhatsApp offers the ability to back up its content directly to Google Drive. WhatsApp backups can be acquired from Google Drive; however, in order to decrypt the backup, one will need to extract the decryption key, which is only accessible if the device is rooted. Oxygen Forensic Suite can accomplish this goal.

More information on this subject is available in the Ars Technica's excellent write-up: *Android 6.0 has a great auto-backup system that no one is using (yet)* (`http://arstechnica.com/gadgets/215/1/android-6-s-auto-backup-for-apps-perfect-data-backup-for-the-1-5/`).

Pictures available in the user's Google Photos space are also stored in the cloud. The Google Photos service contains much more information compared to Google Drive:

- Albums
- Events
- Comments
- Geolocation tags
- Subscriptions
- View counters
- People (faces) tagged on the photos

Certain bits of data (for example, location history, dashboard items, and Hangout conversations) can be acquired without making Google alert the user by e-mail.

Google Takeout

When acquiring information from Google, the first and obvious choice is using Google's own data exporting service, Google Takeout. This service is available at `https://takeout.google.com/settings/takeout`.

Google Takeout allows users to download their data. However, Takeout is not a good forensic solution for several reasons. Takeout uses a plethora of formats such as OPML (RSS), CSV, plain text, JSON (GeoJSON for map data), vCard, PDF, and HTML, as well as several others:

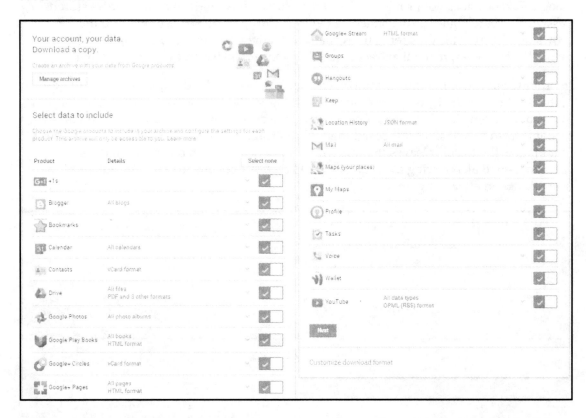

While Google Takeout exports a lot of data, it fails to provide some important bits. Google Takeout leaves traces in the user's account and notifies the user via an e-mail alert that their data was accessed. The resulting file produced by Google Takeout is not immediately usable, as the data is stored in numerous formats and cannot be used for searching and analyzing as-is.

Google Account acquisition and analysis using Elcomsoft Cloud Explorer

Google Takeout does not provide full access to some bits of data, which includes stored passwords, search queries on connected devices, Chrome page transitions, and the browsing history. This data remains available elsewhere in Google and can be extracted manually. However, manual extraction can be labor-intensive and time-consuming.

In order to automate the extraction, you can use Elcomsoft Cloud Explorer. The tool authenticates into the Google Account and automatically downloads all available information from Google servers. The built-in viewer displays information in human-readable form and enables fast searching and filtering. Elcomsoft Cloud Explorer attempts to minimize the traces it leaves in the account being acquired. In particular, it does not cause an e-mail alert during the acquisition. As an example, the tool can display links the user clicked on after firing up a search:

2015-11-25 18:48:44	⊟	ios 9 cydia disable upgrade notification	https://www.google.com/search?q=ios+9+cydia+d.
		Remove OTA update Badge in settings.	
		Top 10 Free Cydia Tweaks for iOS 9 - L.	
		[Discussion] Disable Automatic Softwar..	
2015-11-25 18:23:56	⊟	ipad news settings	https://www.google.com/search?q=ipad+news+s..
		Enable Apple News App In iOS 9 Outsi.	

Elcomsoft Cloud Explorer offers investigators access to Google Accounts and allows downloading all available information. The tool leaves fewer traces compared to Google Takeout while pulling more data than the Google's service:

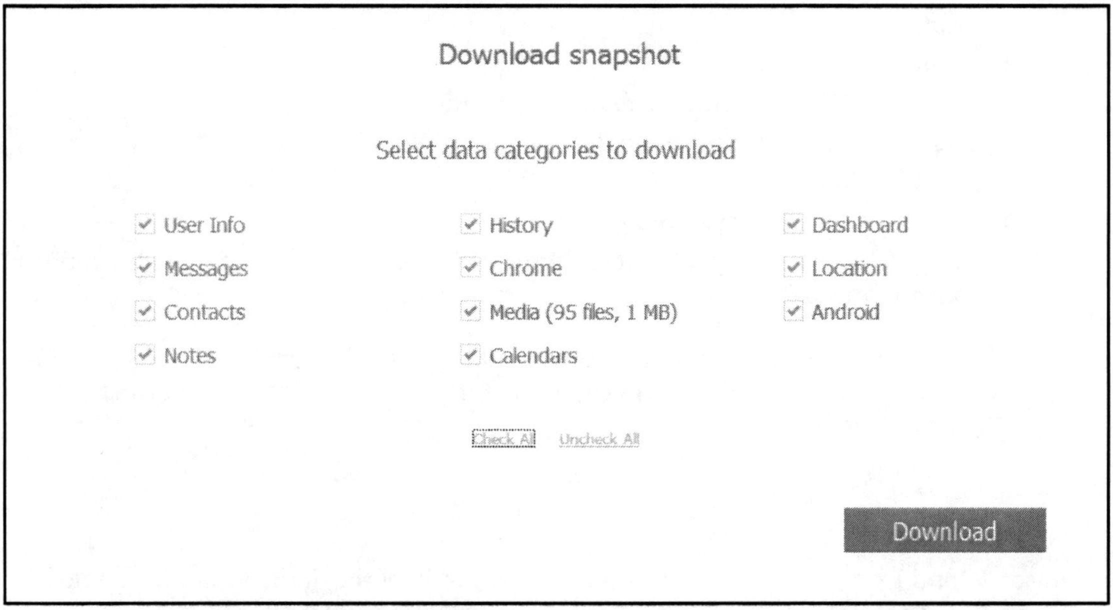

Download snapshot

Select data categories to download

✓ User Info	✓ History	✓ Dashboard
✓ Messages	✓ Chrome	✓ Location
✓ Contacts	✓ Media (95 files, 1 MB)	✓ Android
✓ Notes	✓ Calendars	

Check All   Uncheck All

Download

Note that Google may alert the user once someone accesses the user's Google Account from a different device or IP address. While using Google Takeout is a certain way to trigger such an alert, using Elcomsoft Cloud Explorer reduces (but does not completely eliminate) such probability. At this time, we don't know what types of data might trigger such alerts. Just be aware of the possibility.

You can extract the following:

- User profile
- Dashboard
- Location history
- Hangouts messages
- Contacts (including synced contacts from other devices)
- Google Photos, including EXIF data
- Google Keep notes
- Search history and transitions
- Google Chrome data (bookmarks, forms, stored credentials, and page transitions from all synced devices)

 Chrome synced data may be protected with an additional password. Elcomsoft Cloud Explorer can decrypt the data if you enter the correct password.

- Calendars

Elcomsoft Cloud Explorer includes a built-in viewer for all of the data formats available in the Google Account, including a built-in viewer for synced passwords:

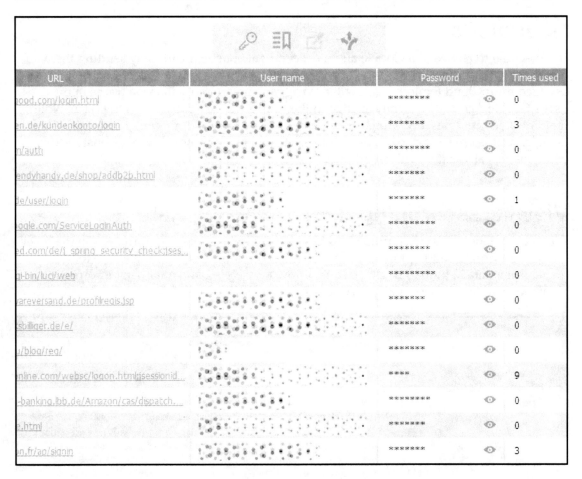

URL	User name	Password		Times used
ood.com/login.html		*******	👁	0
en.de/kundenkonto/login		*******	👁	3
n/auth		********	👁	0
endyhandy.de/shop/addb2b.html		*******	👁	0
de/user/login		******	👁	1
ogle.com/ServiceLoginAuth		*********	👁	0
ed.com/de/j_spring_security_check;jses...		********	👁	0
gi-bin/luci/web		*********	👁	0
areversand.de/profilregis.jsp		*******	👁	0
sbilliger.de/e/		*******	👁	0
u/blog/reg/		*******	👁	0
nline.com/websc/logon.html;jsessionid...		****	👁	9
-banking.lbb.de/Amazon/cas/dispatch...		********	👁	0
a.html		*******	👁	0
n.fr/ap/signin		*******	👁	3

Elcomsoft Phone Viewer: viewing stored passwords

Two-factor authentication

Some Google accounts may be protected with two-factor authentication, requiring experts to provide an extra code in addition to the user's Google ID and password. If you are using Google Takeout or Elcomsoft Cloud Explorer, you will be prompted to enter the additional six-digit code if two-factor authentication is enabled on a given account.

User alerts

It is essential to realize that Google alerts users on Takeout acquisition by sending them an e-mail to their registered address. This only happens when Google Takeout is used. If you use Elcomsoft Cloud Explorer, you will not trigger an alert and will leave traces in the user's Google Account (this may change in the future, but currently this is the case). Note that, in some rare cases, accessing certain types of data may still trigger a notification from Google. At this time, we don't know what exactly triggers this notification. Consider this being the risk associated with cloud acquisition.

Viewing, searching, and analyzing data

When using Google Takeout, prepare to face many cumbersome data formats. On the other hand, Elcomsoft Cloud Explorer automatically decodes these data formats. The tool displays the data in human-readable form, allowing viewing and analyzing information obtained from the suspect's Google Account:

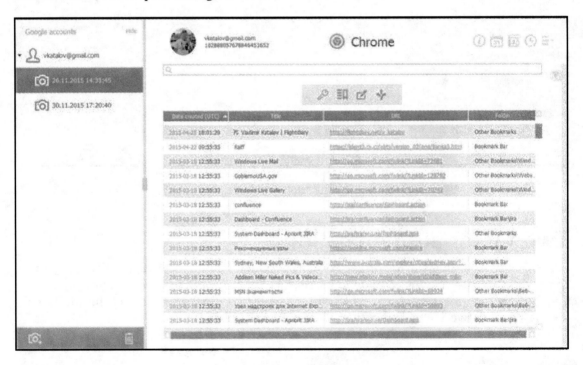

Elcomsoft Phone Viewer: viewing and analyzing information

The built-in viewer recognizes data formats used by Google and is available in the Google Account. The data is parsed and displayed automatically. The viewer offers instant filtering and quick search. Locating contacts, messages, or authentication credentials (login and password) requires typing a part of the word you are looking for into the search box.

Summary

In this chapter, we reviewed the tools, methods, and practical steps to perform the acquisition of various Android devices. We covered low-level acquisition techniques via device service modes, and talked about physical acquisition via root exploits and bootloader-level exploits. We also covered logical acquisition and discussed its limitations on the Android platform. In the next chapter, we'll move over to the other mobile platform, and learn about acquisition techniques applicable to Apple iOS.

5
iOS – Introduction and Physical Acquisition

It was in January 2007 that Apple released the first version of the iPhone. Since then, the global smartphone market has never been the same.

With the advent of Android devices, the relative share of iOS-based mobile phones has been declining steadily over the years. With iPhone accounting for nearly 14% of all smartphones sold in Q2 2015 (according to `http://www.idc.com/prodserv/smartphone-os-market-share.jsp`), the rest of the market is dominated by Android.

In absolute terms, there are still a lot of old iOS devices around. Approximately 74.4 million iPhones were sold during Q1 2015 alone.

In the U.S., iPhones account for 35.58% of the subscriber base in Q3 2015 (source: `http://bgr.com/215/1/1/iphone-market-share-q3-215-android/`). With that many iOS smartphones used throughout the U.S., the need for iOS forensics remains strong.

In this chapter, we will discuss the options available for acquiring information from iOS devices. We will also discuss physical acquisition in detail, discussing the tools and practical steps required to perform physical acquisition. In this chapter, we will cover the following topics:

- Security implications of Apple iOS and how they affect available acquisition options
- Generations of Apple hardware and the difference between legacy, recent 32-bit, and modern 64-bit devices

- The need for jailbreak
- Different iOS acquisition methods and when to use them
- Physical acquisition in detail—tools, techniques, and practical steps

iOS forensics – introduction

Different devices require different acquisition techniques. The different versions of iOS require different acquisition paths, each having its own vector of attack. While in Apple's sector, we don't nearly see such a wide diversity of devices and heavily-customized versions of the operating system (each with its own vulnerabilities), there are still a lot of devices available.

Generations of Apple hardware

iOS is a closed operating system that's only supported on Apple-manufactured hardware. As a result, we don't have to deal with a dozen different manufacturers and thousands of models. By Q2 2015, Apple had released ten iPhone models, five models of iPod Touch, six full-size iPads, and three models of iPad mini.

While general information and up-to-date specifications of Apple hardware can be viewed at https://en.wikipedia.org/wiki/List_of_iOS_devices, there are several things not mentioned in the official specs that can make the device more or less susceptible to physical acquisition.

Early generations of Apple devices had a vulnerability in Trusted Boot, allowing attackers to bypass signature verification while booting in the DFU mode. As the signature-verification code was located in device's read-only memory, Apple was never able to patch this vulnerability in existing devices. This vulnerability allowed mobile forensic specialists to create tools for unconditional, always-working physical acquisition of susceptible iOS devices (for example, Elcomsoft iOS Forensic Toolkit at https://www.elcomsoft.com/eift .html).

Unconditional physical acquisition regardless of iOS version and jailbreak status is available on iPhone 3G, 3GS, and 4; iPod Touch 1st through 4th gen; and the original iPad.

In newer generations of hardware, Apple fixed the vulnerability, making physical acquisition a much more complicated process.

As a result, devices using 32-bit processors, including iPhone 4S, iPhone 5, iPhone 5C, iPad 2+, iPad Mini, and iPod Touch 5th gen can only be acquired if jailbroken (either by the user or by the investigator, if the passcode is known).

What about Apple's newest generation devices using 64-bit chipsets? Physical acquisition is available for all 64-bit Apple devices, such as iPhone 5S, iPhone 6, and iPhone 6 Plus; iPad 2 and newer; iPad Air and Air 2; and iPad Mini 2 and 3, using Elcomsoft iOS Forensic Toolkit. The acquisition process requires a jailbroken device; the passcode must be known and must be removed in the device's **Security** settings prior to the acquisition.

How likely are you to encounter a 32-bit Apple device? While there are no direct statistics about how many devices of each generation are still in active use, we can estimate these numbers by looking at the official iOS version stats. While Apple is known to deliver updates to the latest iOS and even to the old versions of their products, these devices have limited capabilities and timeframe during which they may receive updates. As a result, the latest version of iOS supported on iPhone 4, for example, was iOS 7.1.2; while all newer devices support iOS 8.

By February 2016, Apple claimed (`https://developer.apple.com/support/appstore/`) that around 76% of its users will have already upgraded to iOS 9. Approximately 17% of Apple users use iOS 8, while earlier versions represent only 7% of Apple's user base.

In terms of hardware, this means that early generation devices such as iPhone, iPhone 3G, and 3GS are only marginally represented (2% market share). Since iPhone 4 supports iOS 7.x, it can be counted as part of the 7% group (using iOS 7). Most iPhones, however, are using iOS 9 (76%) or iOS 8 (17%), which means that they are iPhone 4S, 5, 5C, 5S, 6, and 6 Plus.

Is jailbreak required?

As physical acquisition requires low-level access to the data partition, physical acquisition is only possible on jailbroken iOS devices. Other acquisition methods, for example, logical and over-the-air acquisition do not require a jailbreak.

Geolocation information

It's no news that iOS devices equipped with cellular modules periodically collect and store geolocation information. iOS devices are capable of capturing information about nearby cellular towers and Wi-Fi access points in range, even if the device is not connected to them. This information is stored in plain unencrypted form in a `cache_encryptedA.db` file. The file keeps tracking information about cellular towers and Wi-Fi networks in range for up to 45 days. The official Apple statement says:

> *The iPhone is not logging your location. Rather, it's maintaining a database of Wi-Fi hotspots and cell towers around your current location, some of which may be located more than one hundred miles away from your iPhone, to help your iPhone rapidly and accurately calculate its location when requested. Calculating a phone's location using just GPS satellite data can take up to several minutes. iPhone can reduce this time to just a few seconds by using Wi-Fi hotspot and cell tower data to quickly find GPS satellites, and even triangulate its location using just Wi-Fi hotspot and cell tower data when GPS is not available (such as indoors or in basements). These calculations are performed live on the iPhone using a crowd-sourced database of Wi-Fi hotspot and cell tower data that is generated by tens of millions of iPhones sending the geo-tagged locations of nearby Wi-Fi hotspots and cell towers in an anonymous and encrypted form to Apple.*

Notably, the `cache_encryptedA.db` file is not stored in device backups, either cloud or made with iTunes. Since there is no end-user access to system files in Apple iOS, the device must be jailbroken in order to retrieve the file. Naturally, the `cache_encryptedA.db` is always retrieved as part of the physical acquisition process. Mobile forensic tools (for example, Oxygen Forensic Toolkit) can parse the file and display the user's tracking information as shown in the following image:

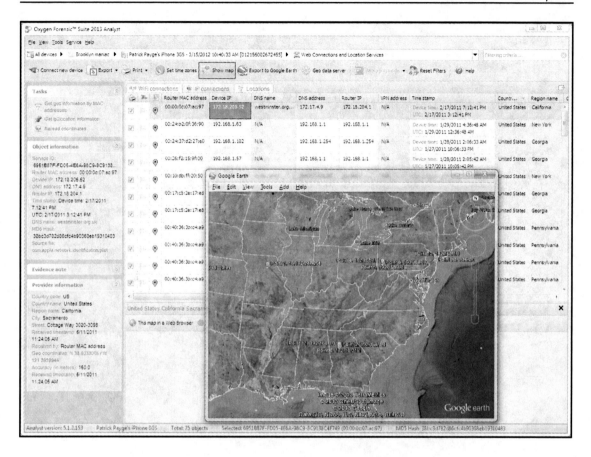

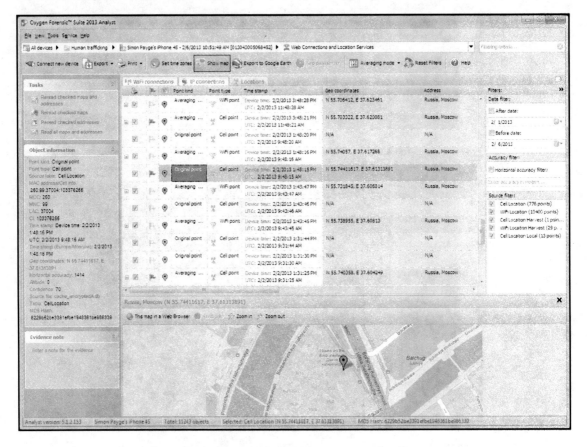

Geolocation information

The ability to extract geolocation information is one of the major benefits of physical acquisition over logical extraction. If physical acquisition is not available for a particular device, attempting a jailbreak and manually pulling `cache_encryptedA.db` will be worth the effort if you need access to the suspect's location history.

Additional sources of geolocation history may also be available, including photo EXIF tags and application data (if geolocation was enabled and allowed by the user).

Where is the information stored?

Obviously, the phone itself is viewed as a primary source of data, and rightfully so. However, what if the phone is locked and the passcode is unknown? Also, what if you don't have the phone?

Information collected by a smartphone is stored in (and can be retrieved from) numerous places. An Apple phone can back up its data to a PC via iTunes or to Apple's own cloud service (iCloud/iCloud Drive) via Wi-Fi. As a result, you may be dealing with a set of backup files (with or without a password), or just have a computer that does not have a single backup file, but was used to sync with iCloud.

Sometimes you'll have it all: a phone, set of offline backups, and computer in sync with iCloud. More often than not, you're going to need information right away, or *the sooner the better*. What is the optimal route for getting as much information as possible in the shortest time? The answer depends on what exactly do you have on your hands.

iOS acquisition methods overview

While different methods exist to help extract the content of mobile devices, the choice of one or another method will usually depend on what you have available. Do you have a working iPhone? You can try physical acquisition, but only if the device falls within the compatibility matrix. Do you have access to the computer that was used to sync with the phone? Search for mobile backups. If you can find an iTunes backup, you can use logical acquisition to break into the backup and extract information. Was that computer used to sync with iCloud? Look for the iCloud authentication token. If found, the token can be used to connect to the user's iCloud account on bypassing the login and password. Do you happen to know the user's Apple ID, BlackBerry ID, or Windows Live account and password? Cloud forensics will help you download data from the cloud.

To choose an acquisition method, refer to the following table:

I have...	Physical acquisition	Logical acquisition (backup analysis)	Cloud forensics
Physical device (iPhone, iPad, or iPod Touch)	YES*	MAYBE	MAYBE
Computer that was synced with (or trusted by) the phone/tablet	N/A	N/A	MAYBE
The iOS device and the computer that it was synced with (or trusted by)	N/A	MAYBE*****	MAYBE
iTunes backup	N/A	YES**	MAYBE
Apple ID login and password	N/A	N/A	YES***
iCloud authentication token	N/A	N/A	YES****

*Physical acquisition is only available for certain devices. Refer to `Chapter 6`, *iOS Logical and Cloud Acquisition* for detailed compatibility matrix.

**Certain backups may be protected with long, complex passwords. There is no guaranteed recovery timeframe or successful password recovery guarantee on password-protected backups.

***Apple's two-factor authentication complicates things a little bit. If two-factor authentication is activated for a certain Apple ID, access to the secondary authentication unit (such as a trusted device, recovery key, or app-specific password) is required. Microsoft takes a similar approach to two-factor authentication. At this time, Elcomsoft products only support two-factor authentication for Apple devices.

****Authentication tokens may have an expiration (depending on the iOS version). Their exact lifespan is currently not known. While we experienced some tokens extracted with the ATEX tool from the **Control Panel** to expire in one hour (iOS 8.x, for cloud backups only), we did not have this experience in other cases. We are continuing extensive testing to find out. Notably, authentication tokens *live* longer for cloud files. iOS 9 moved cloud backups to iCloud Drive; its authentication tokens currently don't have an expiration date (or have a very long lifespan). Finally, authentication tokens are invalidated when the user changes their account password or explicitly logs out from the cloud on a given computer.

*****If you have a computer that was synced with the device and the iOS device itself, you may be able to extract the decryption key and force the device to make a backup, without even knowing the password. However, this is only possible if the iOS device was not rebooted after the last time it synced with the computer. Interestingly, even if automatic synchronization is not enabled on the iOS device, the device prompts whether to trust the computer after you plug it in. If the answer is *yes*, a pair of cryptographic keys will be created (on the device and on the computer).

iOS acquisition methods compared

In an unlikely event, if you possess the physical device, a copy of its offline backup, and the user's Apple ID/password (or a binary authentication token collected from the user's PC), which acquisition method should you choose?

The answer depends on how quickly you need the data, and whether or not you require access to deleted files and the keychain. Physical acquisition is by far the best acquisition method—if your device is supported. Cloud acquisition can return current and past data, while the offline backup can be the easiest (if not password-protected) or the slowest (if password-protected) to recover.

The different acquisition methods offer various benefits over one another.

For iOS devices, physical acquisition is the method of choice if available (refer to the *Compatibility matrix* section in the next chapter). Physical acquisition offers the following benefits:

- Access to complete information stored in the mobile device (if passcode is known or recovered)
- Guaranteed timeframe (if passcode is known or a four-digit passcode is used)
- Extremely high acquisition speed
- Potential access to certain deleted data (for example, contacts and messages) stored in SQLite databases
- Access to keychain information (if passcode is known or can be recovered)
- Access to up to 45 days of geolocation tracking data

Logical acquisition of iOS devices involves the analysis of offline backups produced by Apple iTunes. Logical acquisition offers the following benefits:

- Access to most information stored in the mobile device
- No guaranteed recovery timeframe for password-protected backups
- Potential access to certain deleted data (for example, contacts and messages) stored in SQLite databases
- Access to keychain information is possible (if a decryption key was extracted from the device via physical acquisition)
- Keychain data can be retrieved from password-protected backups
- Long complex password may altogether prevent the recovery

Cloud acquisition is available for mobile devices running Apple iOS, BlackBerry, and Windows Phone 8/8.1. Cloud acquisition offers the following benefits:

- Access to most information stored in the mobile device
- Access to certain files accessed from the device (but not actually stored in the device)
- Recovery time highly dependent on connection speed and available cloud throughput
- Potential access to certain deleted data (for example, contacts and messages) stored in SQLite databases
- iOS: Access to keychain information is possible if a decryption key was extracted from the device via physical acquisition
- iOS: Two-factor authentication may disallow cloud access even if login and password are known (can be bypassed if a valid, non-expired authentication token is available)

Finally, it is possible to perform chip-off acquisition by extracting data directly from the memory chips (special hardware and skills are required). Chip-off acquisition has the following properties:

- On older devices, it is possible to extract all information except encrypted (keychain).
- Recent generation iOS devices rely extensively on encrypted storage. As a result, most user data will remain encrypted with strong, non-extractable encryption keys.

- Guaranteed timeframe, but limited amount of accessible data.
- Extremely high acquisition speed.
- No access to keychain information or historical location data.

The following table summarizes the possible outcome of the various acquisition methods:

	Physical acquisition	Logical acquisition	Cloud forensics	Chip-off
Approximate timeframe	35-50 minutes (depending on device model)	• Instant (unprotected backups) • Unknown (password-protected)	0-4 hours (depending on connection speed and data volume)	1-4 hours (depending on skill level)
Keychain recovery	Yes	• No (unprotected backups), unless **securityd** is available • Yes (password-protected)	No (unless securityd is available)	No
Access to deleted files	No*	No	No	No
Access to deleted SQLite records	Yes	Yes	Yes	Yes
Up to 45 days of geolocation tracking data	Yes	No	No	Yes

Possible issues	Last-generation devices must be jailbroken (refer to *Compatibility matrix*)	Long and complex passwords may prevent the recovery	• Apple ID/password or authentication token required • Two-factor authentication • Notification e-mail	• Only for iOS 1 through 4 • Recent devices use complete hardware encryption • Encrypted data non-recoverable and non-decryptable • Chip-off acquisition is *not available* for recent iOS devices

*Accessing deleted files is possible for iOS 1.x through 3.x. However, the chances of encountering an iOS version that old are close to none.

iOS advanced logical acquisition

A while ago, a so-called advanced logical acquisition method was introduced by Jonathan Zdziarski. It was a very popular acquisition method while it lasted. The examiner still had to possess an unlocked device, but if this was the case, it was possible to obtain more information compared to pure logical acquisition (backup analysis).

Compared to pure logical acquisition, advanced logical acquisition offered the following benefits:

- iTunes backup password could not stop accessing personal data such as contacts or text messages that were not protected with any password
- More application data, including log files, could be extracted

The method was short-lived as Apple patched the vulnerability used by this acquisition method by hiding the corresponding service. Since iOS 8, only app-shared documents (for example, documents edited by an office app or videos watched with a media player) can be extracted with this method.

iOS physical acquisition

Physical acquisition is the most comprehensive acquisition method available for iOS devices. Other platforms (for example, Android, BlackBerry OS, BlackBerry 10, and Windows-based devices) can be acquired by one of the lower-level techniques, such as JTAG, ISP, or chip-off. These acquisition techniques are not available for iOS devices due to mandatory full-disk encryption that is enforced out of the box, regardless of whether the user sets up additional security. Physical acquisition returns significantly more information compared to any other method, such as logical acquisition or backup analysis. Data stored in Apple's protected storage, the keychain, is exclusively available via the physical process.

Physical acquisition is very decisive: it either works or it doesn't. If it works, you can expect to image the entire device in under 40 minutes, even a 32-GB iPhone 4, which is among the slowest. Devices with larger storage can take longer; however, there is no uncertainty as in attempting to attack backup passwords. ElcomSoft developed a physical acquisition toolkit for iOS devices:

Starting with the release of iPhone 4S, featuring stronger security compared to all legacy devices, physical acquisition became increasingly difficult for each new generation of iOS devices. Up to this day, physical acquisition support of newer iOS devices is only available in Elcomsoft iOS Forensic Toolkit.

It is important to note that unrestricted, unlimited, and guaranteed physical acquisition is only available for older Apple devices (refer to the *Compatibility matrix* section in the following chapter). Starting with iPhone 4S (or iPad 2), a successful physical acquisition requires the examiner to either know the user's original passcode (in order to install jailbreak) or have a jailbroken device. If a device is locked with a passcode, installing jailbreak is not possible, and the device cannot be acquired. In addition to jailbreak, an OpenSSH tool from Cydia must be installed.

On jailbroken devices, Elcomsoft iOS Forensic Toolkit can break the original passcode with brute force or dictionary attack. Passcode recovery speed on jailbroken iPhone 5 and 5C devices is approximately 15.5 passcodes per second, allowing iOS Forensic Toolkit to break typical four-digit passcodes in about 10 minutes. However, one can easily dump the device even without the passcode; as a result, downloaded mail and keychain data will remain encrypted.

On iOS devices equipped with a 64-bit platform and Secure Enclave, physical acquisition is even more limited. On such devices, one must know the passcode and be able to remove it from device settings (that's in addition to jailbreaking the device). Even then, keychain can be extracted, but it cannot be decrypted on 64-bit devices.

Physical acquisition benefits

Physical acquisition offers numerous benefits over other acquisition methods. Fixed timeframe and guaranteed delivery are just a few things to be mentioned.

Physical acquisition offers the following benefits:

- Acquires complete bit-precise device images
- Unallocated space is extracted, but cannot be decrypted on recent versions of iOS
- Decrypts keychain items and extracts device keys

- Guaranteed timeframe: 20 to 50 minutes for 32 GB models
- Zero footprint
- Passcode not required (for older devices or if jailbreak is installed)
- Simple four-digit passcodes recovered in 10-40 minutes (for older or jailbroken devices)

Physical is the only acquisition method that can extract the following information:

- **Cached (downloaded) mail**: Regardless of the type of e-mail account, cached mail is not available in offline or online backups. Downloaded mail can be also acquired via so-called *advanced logical acquisition*, which exploits some undocumented iOS services and requires either a passcode or a pairing record from a trusted computer. Additionally, cached mail can be obtained via the 64-bit physical acquisition process.
- **Geolocation data**: While iTunes and iCloud backups contain only limited geolocation data (for example, extracted from geotagged images), physical acquisition can extract significantly more detail about the user's location. This includes frequent locations and location data requested by applications and system services on the device. Location data is requested (and stored) on certain events, such as using maps, calibrating the compass, ad tracking, browsing web pages, requesting the user's location, looking up wireless networks, and so on. By extracting location data with physical acquisition, one can reconstruct the suspect's whereabouts with a great deal of precision.
- **System logs and crash logs**: This shows the applications launched or installed.
- **Cached application data**: This provides cached web pages, typed addresses, and any Web data that is cached by third-party apps. Many iOS apps are Web-based, so the amount of cached data available via physical acquisition can be overwhelming.
- **Certain types of deleted data**: This includes deleted contacts, text messages, and iMessages (can be also extracted from SQLite databases with logical acquisition).
- **Keychain**: In Apple devices, this protected storage is used to store highly sensitive information, such as passwords to websites and online accounts, financial information, and any data written to protected storage by third-party applications. With different classes of protection, only some keychain items can be decrypted when processing a backup. Physical acquisition allows decrypting the entire keychain, extracting all available information.

- **Extended keychain acquisition**: Apple changed the keychain format in iOS 7. In iOS 8, Apple moved a lot more data into the keychain. Since iOS 7, devices registered to a certain Apple ID may contain a cached copy of the iCloud keychain for that Apple account (subject to user authorization). If iCloud keychain is available, its extraction may enable access to passwords and credit card information stored in other Apple devices sharing the same Apple ID.

What's unique about physical acquisition?

Is physical acquisition still worth the effort? Jailbroken iOS devices are rare in the wild. However, the possibility to jailbreak iOS devices is still there, especially considering the number of devices that have been collected as evidence are waiting for a long time. We still believe that physical is the way to go if it's available for a given device. Here are the reasons why:

- Apple has a new policy to **turn down** government information requests for devices running iOS 8 or 9, Secure Enclave or not. Apple fiercely defends its policy. Handing over the device to Apple will no longer result in receiving its full image if the device is running iOS 8 and newer, even if Apple faces legal action (h ttps://www.apple.com/privacy/government-information-requests/)
- In some regions, Apple runs certified refurbished programs, still selling refurbished 32-bit phones at a cheaper price. For example, refurbished iPhone 4S and 5 units accounted for as much as 46% of all iPhones sold through retail channels in Russia in Q1 2015.
- Physical acquisition still returns significantly more information compared to any other acquisition method (remember, chip-off is not available for Apple devices). E-mail messages, application data, logs, location, and a lot of other data never makes it into backups.
- Full keychain extraction is exclusive to physical acquisition (32-bit devices only). Decrypting the keychain is only possible on devices without Secure Enclave. This includes records encrypted with device-specific keys. While some keychain items can be extracted from password-protected iTunes backups, many items cannot be decrypted without a device-specific key.
- Physical acquisition (32-bit process) can help extract the securityd (0x835) key from the device. This key can be used for complete keychain decryption. Additionally, this very key can be used to decrypt keychain items from iCloud backups and local iTunes backups that are not encrypted with a password.

- Physical acquisition of 32-bit devices returns a standard DMG disk image (HFS+ filesystem), while the same process on 64-bit devices returns a TAR archive that contains the complete directory structure of the device.

As far as we know, Elcomsoft iOS Forensic Toolkit is the only non-Apple tool that can do physical acquisition of iPhone 4S, 5, and 5C, and especially the newer 64-bit devices.

The future of physical acquisition

Unconditional physical acquisition is only supported for legacy devices. With every new iteration of iOS, and with every new hardware revision starting with iPhone 4S, Apple has been improving security, making physical acquisition increasingly difficult.

The release of iOS 8 was an important benchmark, making physical acquisition even tougher. The following two major things have changed with iOS 8:

- All user data is now stored in a container encrypted with passcode-dependent keys
- A hardware-level five-second delay is added for passcode attempts (newer hardware only)

iOS 8 moved most user data under the stricter controls. Messages, photos, contacts, call logs, and many other things are now stored inside a passcode-protected container. Once the phone is rebooted, the decryption key is lost, and the data becomes unavailable until the user enters the correct passcode. However, if the device is unlocked at least once, most data (except for the keychain) is decrypted and remains decrypted until the device is powered off. This is exactly what's used by the 64-bit acquisition process.

What about brute forcing the passcode? With A7- and A8-based devices (iPhone 5S, 6, and 6 Plus), Apple introduced a hardware-level five-second delay for passcode attempts. Here's what Apple has to say:

> *On a device with an A7 processor, the key operations are performed by the Secure Enclave, which also enforces a 5-second delay between repeated failed unlocking requests. This provides a governor against brute-force attacks in addition to safeguards enforced by iOS. (Source:* `https://www.apple.com/br/ipad/business/docs/iOS_Security_EN_Feb14.pdf`*.)*

While it is not exactly known whether the delay is hardcoded or can be disabled with software, third-party acquisition tools can no longer try more than one passcode every five seconds. This means that there are about 14 hours to try all possible combinations of a four-digit passcode. With longer and stronger numeric or alphanumeric passcodes, brute-force attacks are no longer feasible.

At this time, physical acquisition is available for all existing devices equipped with 32-bit and 64-bit chipsets. A working jailbreak is mandatory to perform physical acquisition. Additionally, the passcode must be known (and removed for 64-bit devices) in order to acquire the maximum amount of information.

Physical acquisition compatibility matrix

Physical acquisition is a great technique. Unfortunately, at this time, physical acquisition has limited availability. Newer Apple devices (starting with iPhone 4S and iPad 2) have stronger security, which limits our ability to perform physical acquisition. Today, the following devices can be acquired with this method:

- iPhone 3G, 3GS, and 4 (GSM and CDMA models)
- iPhone 4S, 5, and 5C***
- iPod Touch (1st through 4th generations)
- iPod Touch 5th gen ***
- iPad (1st generation only)
- iPad 2***
- iPad with Retina display (3rd and 4th generations)***
- iPad Mini***

These devices can run any of the following operating systems:

- iOS 1 through 3 (up to 3.1.3)
- iOS 4.x—up to iOS 4.3.5 (up to iOS 4.2.10 for iPhone 4 CDMA)
- iOS 5.x
- iOS 6.x
- iOS 7.0
- iOS 7.1 (with Pangu 1.2+ jailbreak)
- iOS 8.x and 9.x****

	iPhone 3G iPod Touch 1/2		iPhone 3GS, iPod Touch 3rd gen, iPad 1		iPhone 4 iPod Touch 4th gen iPod Touch 5th gen (***) iPad 2+, iPad Mini (***) iPhone 4S/5/5C (***)	iPhone 5S/6/6S/Plus, iPad Mini 2-4, iPad Air/Air2, iPad Pro, iPod Touch 6th gen
	iOS 1..3	iOS 4.x	iOS 3	iOS 4/5	iOS 4-9	iOS 6-9
Physical imaging	✓	✓	✓	✓	✓	✓*****
Passcode recovery	Instant	✓	Instant	✓	✓	N/A
Keychain decryption	✓	✓	✓	✓	✓	✓
Disk decryption(*)	N/A*	N/A**	N/A*	✓**	✓	✓

*Devices running iOS versions prior to 3.0 do not have Data Protection enabled, and their user partition is not encrypted.

Devices originally shipped with iOS 3.x, including those running iOS 4/5 that were upgraded from iOS 3.x without performing erase install (that is, using the **Update option in iTunes as opposed to **Restore**), do not have Data Protection enabled, and user partitions are not encrypted. Therefore, the decryption is not required.

***iPhone 4S, iPhone 5, iPhone 5C, iPad 2+, iPad Mini, and iPod Touch 5th gen can be recovered if the passcode is known or if the device is jailbroken (iOS 5 through 9).

****Physical acquisition of newer devices (iPhone 4S and newer) remains subject to jailbreak availability. Jailbreaking the device and recovering (and in some cases, removing) the passcode is mandatory as all user data is now encrypted with passcode-dependent keys (as a comparison, iOS 7 used encryption this strong exclusively for keychain and mail protection).

*****Physical acquisition for 64-bit models (iPhone 5S/6/6S/Plus, iPad mini 2/3/4, iPad Air / Air 2, and iPad Pro) is available via a different acquisition process referred to specifically as **physical acquisition for 64-bit devices**. Jailbreaking the device and removing passcode protection in iOS settings is mandatory. Acquisition of 64-bit iOS devices is covered in a separate chapter.

Unallocated space – unavailable since iOS 4

Unallocated space is only available via physical acquisition if you are acquiring a device running iOS 3.x or older. Since these are very old versions of iOS, you are extremely unlikely to ever encounter one in real life. If you do, you'll be able to use Elcomsoft iOS Forensic Toolkit to bypass passcode protection and extract the complete image of the device along with unallocated space.

Since iOS 4, Apple uses passcode-dependent encryption of the filesystem. iOS does not keep encryption keys to areas that are not occupied by files. After a file is deleted, the system destroys encryption keys for corresponding data blocks. As a result, decrypting these unallocated areas is not possible at the time of physical acquisition. In the case of in-house physical acquisition performed with Elcomsoft iOS Forensic Toolkit or any other third-party tool, unallocated disk space will be extracted, but not decrypted.

What *can* be recovered is SQLite records that contain deleted text messages, call log, and chat entries. However, the process is far from simple and requires the use of specialized software or SQLite-specific expertise.

Sending device to Apple

In its privacy policy (`https://www.apple.com/privacy/government-information-reque sts/`), Apple clearly states the following:

> *On devices running iOS 8, your personal data such as photos, messages (including attachments), email, contacts, call history, iTunes content, notes, and reminders is placed under the protection of your passcode. Unlike our competitors, Apple cannot bypass your passcode and therefore cannot access this data. So it's not technically feasible for us to respond to government warrants for the extraction of this data from devices in their possession running iOS 8.*

Analyzing the way the system works on newer 64-bit devices, we tend to believe that the preceding statement is true.

While it is not currently possible to request a decrypted device image from Apple due to their new policy based on the technical features of iOS 8, law enforcement agencies can still send Apple devices running an older version of iOS in order to obtain their unencrypted images. In such cases, Apple provides a full decrypted image of the device (with keychains being a possible exception if the passcode is not known).

The role of passcode

Passcode is key to iOS security. Even if it's just a simple PIN number consisting of only four digits, in reality, a passcode is key to some of the strongest security models in the mobile world. This passcode, combined with a unique and very long string of binary data (hardware encryption key), is used to generate a unique and extremely strong encryption key. The device then encrypts the device's sensitive data, including text messages, e-mail, photos, and so on, using this encryption key and a government-standard AES encryption algorithm.

It is important to note that it is impossible to generate the encryption key without having access to the device's hardware encryption key, and it is impossible to get access to that hardware encryption key even after disassembling the device to small bits. Without the correct passcode, passcode-encrypted data will remain encrypted, even if the complete image is extracted.

In other words, some parts of the iOS device are likely to remain encrypted unless the original passcode is known (this is especially true with the latest iOS releases). Recovering the original passcode is only possible on the device itself.

Older versions of iOS did not encrypt all user data using the passcode. We could break into those devices and retrieve almost everything even without a passcode. This is no longer the case with iOS 8.

The following chart summarizes whether you require a passcode for successful acquisition:

- **iOS 1.x through 3.x**: Here, the passcode is not required. All data is accessible. The passcode is instantly recovered and displayed.
- **iOS 4.0 through 7.x**: The passcode is not required, but highly recommended. Some data is protected with passcode-dependent keys:
    - E-mail messages
    - Keychain items
    - Certain third-party application data if the app requested secure access
- **iOS 8 and 9**: The passcode is mandatory for successful acquisition. Most user information is protected with passcode-based keys.

Physical acquisition of iOS 8 and 9

iOS 9 is the latest and most secure version of Apple's mobile operating system. According to Apple, by February 2016, approximately 76% of Apple customers already upgraded to the latest iOS, while 17% of users still used iOS 8. Only 7% of devices were running iOS 7 or earlier (source: `https://developer.apple.com/support/app-store/`).

In iOS 8, Apple further strengthened the security of iOS devices. The 8th and 9th generations of Apple's mobile operating system encrypt more information than ever. Data encryption is not new on Apple devices. It's been in place for a number of years. What is new is the amount of data the phone will store in the encrypted form. In iOS 8, Apple moved things such as e-mails, messages, photos, and videos into the encrypted part of the phone. Once again, a lot of information that was previously accessible (and highly valuable for investigations) is moved into passcode-protected part of the phone, making physical acquisition of a device without knowing the correct passcode nearly useless. Apple claims iOS 8 and newer to be so secure that the company is to deny government requests to extract information even if provided with a working device (source: `https://www.apple.com/privacy/government-information-requests/`).

From a practical standpoint, this means that you must break a passcode in order to properly image a device running iOS 8 or 9. In order to break a passcode on one of the newer devices (iPhone 4S, iPad 2, and their newer generations), you'll need to have the device jailbroken or unlocked. Breaking a passcode is still possible on non-jailbroken devices earlier than iPhone 4S and on the original iPad. At this time (February 2016), the only forensic tool providing physical acquisition support for iOS 8 and 9 devices is Elcomsoft iOS Forensic Toolkit. The tool supports 32-bit and 64-bit devices that are either jailbroken or can be jailbroken by the investigator. Without a jailbreak (and not knowing the passcode), the ONLY information that remains accessible via physical acquisition is call log and text message history. In addition, when performing physical acquisition of 64-bit devices, the passcode must be removed in device Security settings prior to acquisition.

More information on how Apple encrypts information and what's changed in iOS 8 is available at the following URLs:

- `http://www.slate.com/articles/technology/future_tense/214/9/ios_8_encryption_why_apple_won_t_unlock_your_iphone_for_the_police.html`
- `http://blog.cryptographyengineering.com/214/1/why-cant-apple-decrypt-your-iphone.html?m=1`

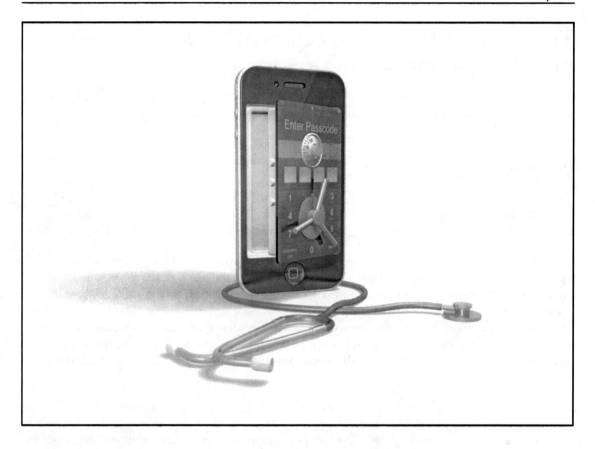

Tools for iOS physical acquisition

Physical acquisition of iOS devices requires the use of a dedicated acquisition tool. Elcomsoft offers iOS Forensic Toolkit (http://www.elcomsoft.com/eift.html), a tool offering physical-acquisition support for more models than any competing product.

Note that the following page contains videos demonstrating how to use the toolkit to acquire an iPhone:

http://www.elcomsoft.com/ios_forensic_toolkit_video.html

Tutorial – physical acquisition with Elcomsoft iOS Forensic Toolkit

Let's use iOS Forensic Toolkit to extract the content of an iPhone. However, first let's take a look at what actually happens at the time the tool performs physical acquisition.

What the does the tool do?

The first step of the acquisition process involves putting the device into a so-called **DFU** mode (**Debug and Firmware Upgrade**) with a combination of Home and Power buttons. Elcomsoft iOS Forensic Toolkit displays tips on how to put the device to this mode.

Once the device is in its DFU mode, we can use its *F* function, emulating a firmware upgrade. However, instead of Apple's original firmware, the Toolkit attempts to load an altered one. The device will verify the new firmware by checking its digital signature via bootrom functions (these are read-only and can't be switched off). Now, if we're acquiring an iPhone 4 or earlier, the Toolkit can use a bootrom exploit that allows skipping the check and sideloading the altered firmware into device volatile memory (RAM). In this case, device storage remains unaltered as all operations are performed exclusively in the device's volatile memory.

If we are acquiring an iPhone 4S, the bootrom exploit that we could use with earlier iPhones is not available. As a result, the Toolkit uses a different method that only works if the device is jailbroken. With this method, the Toolkit connects to the device via OpenSSH and installs and launches acquisition tools. This method alters the content of the device by installing acquisition tools. This must be taken into account and documented appropriately in order to keep the process forensically sound.

Prerequisites

You'll need a working iOS device, a compatible cable to connect it to your computer, and a copy of Elcomsoft iOS Forensic Toolkit (which requires a USB dongle to operate).

Please note the following:

- The imaging tool must be installed in order to acquire the device
- If no jailbreak is installed, you'll have to enter the device into the DFU mode (Device Firmware Upgrade mode) with a combination of Home and Power keys
- Physical acquisition for Apple's 64-bit devices is available via a separate process (refer to *Acquiring 64-bit Apple devices*)
- Passcodes can only be recovered in the DFU mode

Step 0 – connecting the device: Connect the Apple device to your computer using the appropriate USB cable. Launch iOS Forensic Toolkit.

Step 1 – entering the DFU mode: If you are imaging a device for which there is a known way to enter the DFU mode, consider it luck. In iOS Forensic Toolkit, enter 1, as shown in the following screenshot:

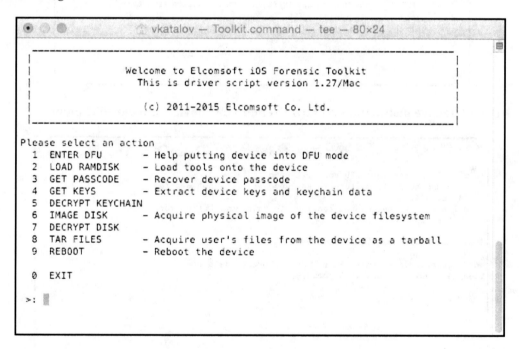

If you are imaging a newer device, such as iPhone 4S, iPhone 5, iPhone 5C, iPad 2, iPad 3, iPad 4, and newer), physical acquisition will only be available if you either know the correct passcode or if the device is jailbroken. To acquire such a device, skip directly to step 3:

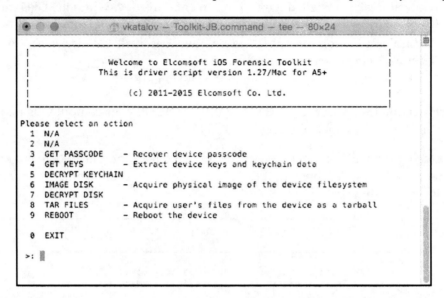

You'll see interactive instructions on how to enter your device into the DFU mode:

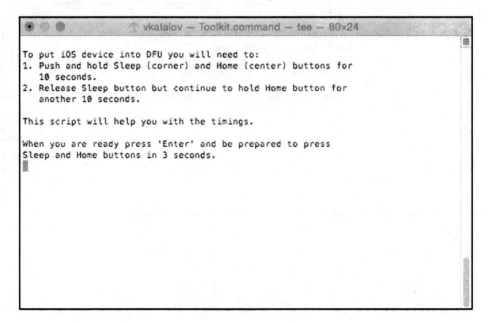

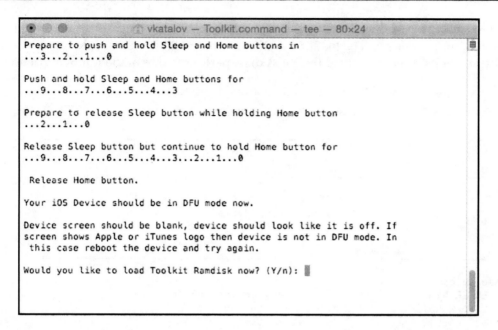

It's a bit tricky to master this in the first try. Take your time and make several attempts until you succeed. When you have your device in the DFU mode, go to step 2.

Note that having the device in the DFU mode or having a jailbroken/unlocked unit is essential to recover the original passcode.

Step 2 – loading RAM disk: During this step, you'll be loading the acquisition code into the Apple device. The code will be loaded into the device's volatile memory (RAM) and will not modify any of its content. To load the RAM disk, perform either of the following actions:

- Agree to load RAM disk when prompted
- Press 2 on the main screen and follow the instructions:

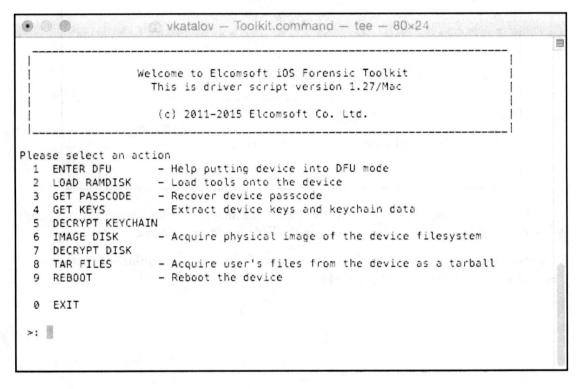

The device will display the Elcomsoft logo when RAM disk is loaded.

Note that, starting with iOS 4, loading RAM disk is a mandatory prerequisite for recovering the passcode.

Step 3 – recovering the passcode: This step used to be optional a year ago. Today, making an attempt to recover a passcode is mandatory to obtain any meaningful information. If you already have the correct passcode, skip to the next step.

Whether you need to recover the passcode to acquire the user data depends on the version of iOS used in the device:

- **iOS 1.x through 3.x**: The passcode is not required. All data is accessible. The passcode is instantly recovered and displayed.
- **iOS 4.0 through 7.x**: The passcode is not required, but highly recommended. Some data is protected with passcode-dependent keys:
  - E-mail messages
  - Keychain items
  - Certain third-party application data if the app requested secure access
- **iOS 8 and 9**: The passcode is mandatory for successful acquisition. Most user information is protected with passcode-based keys.

If you read the earlier chapters, you will know that the passcode is key to Apple's security. In older devices and early versions of iOS, the passcode was used to generate a secure encryption key protecting the information stored in Apple's secure storage, the keychain. Even in older devices and early releases of iOS, protected data included bits such as account passwords, credit card data, Wi-Fi passwords, and a lot of other information essential to an investigation.

With the release of iOS 7 and subsequent upgrade to iOS 8 (and iOS 9 later on), the role of the passcode has increased dramatically. In modern devices running iOS 8 or 9, passcode-protected partition now stores more information than ever. In fact, pretty much everything of interest is now stored on a passcode-protected disk. E-mail and text messages, passwords, picture and video captures with the phone's camera, and a lot of other information is now encrypted. As a result, imaging the device without having a passcode today will return much less information than it did a year ago. In order to decrypt information stored in the protected area, one must first recover the passcode.

Due to the way Apple has designed and implemented its security model, recovering passcodes is only possible using the original device. While using a computer or a cluster of GPU-accelerated workstations to recover passcodes sounds tempting, it is impossible even in theory.

Apple devices can use standard numeric (four-digit PIN), long numeric, and full alphanumeric passcodes. These types of passcodes can be recovered with iOS Forensic Toolkit by either brute forcing or using a dictionary attack (if breaking an alphanumeric passcode).

Note that you'll need to load the RAM disk first (as described in the previous step) to recover passcodes for devices running iOS 4 or later.

Another thing to note is the speed of breaking the passcode. Passcode recovery is slow! It's slow on purpose, by design. Apple carefully balanced algorithms used in its various devices, apparently targeting the time required to verify a passcode at approximately 80 ms per passcode. As a result, recovering a four-digit passcode may take around 35 minutes; brute forcing will take a little longer, and alphanumeric passcode may take forever.

With iOS Forensic Toolkit, recovering a passcode is engaged by entering the 3 (**Get Passcode**) command on the home screen. You'll see the following window:

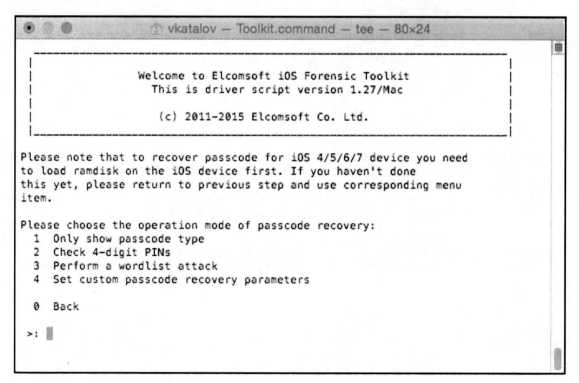

You'll have the option to **(1)** view the type of passcode (numeric four-digit, numeric long, alphanumeric), **(2)** brute force a four-digit PIN, **(3)** perform a dictionary attack on an alphanumeric passcode, or **(4)** use the fully manual option.

While we've seen some limited success in recovering longer alphanumeric passcodes, majority of iPhone users opt for simple four-digit passcodes. Brute forcing such passcodes by enumerating all of the possible combinations takes approximately 35 minutes on iPhone 4S. After entering 2, you'll see the progress report window. The currently tried passcode will be displayed:

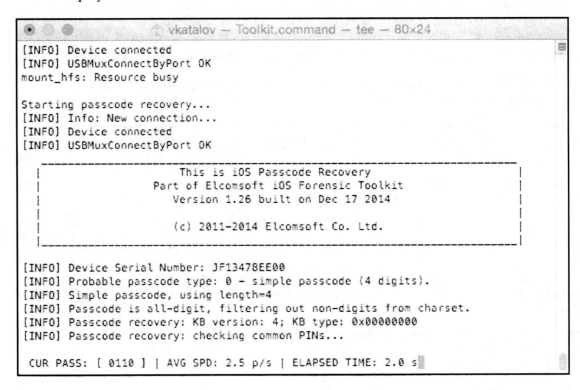

```
● ◉ ●                    vkatalov — Toolkit.command — tee — 80×24
[INFO] Device connected
[INFO] USBMuxConnectByPort OK
mount_hfs: Resource busy

Starting passcode recovery...
[INFO] Info: New connection...
[INFO] Device connected
[INFO] USBMuxConnectByPort OK

   _____
  |                    This is iOS Passcode Recovery               |
  |              Part of Elcomsoft iOS Forensic Toolkit             |
  |                  Version 1.26 built on Dec 17 2014             |
  |                                                                |
  |                  (c) 2011-2014 Elcomsoft Co. Ltd.             |
  |_____|

[INFO] Device Serial Number: JF13478EE00
[INFO] Probable passcode type: 0 - simple passcode (4 digits).
[INFO] Simple passcode, using length=4
[INFO] Passcode is all-digit, filtering out non-digits from charset.
[INFO] Passcode recovery: KB version: 4; KB type: 0x00000000
[INFO] Passcode recovery: checking common PINs...

CUR PASS: [ 0110 ] | AVG SPD: 2.5 p/s | ELAPSED TIME: 2.0 s
```

Once the correct passcode is discovered, it will be displayed. Write it down and press *Enter* to continue to extract device keys:

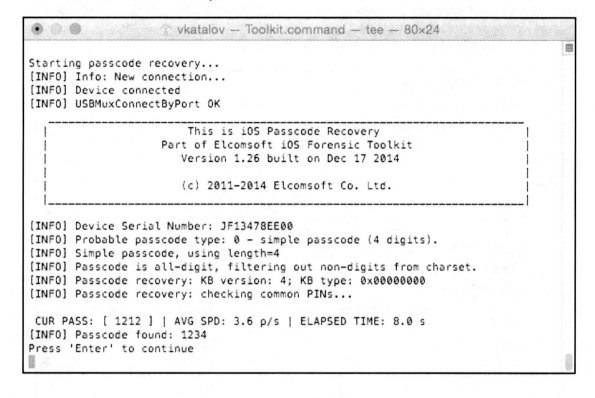

Step 4 – extracting device keys: In order to be able to decrypt information stored on the encrypted partition (as a reminder, this includes user passwords, e-mail, messages, and so on), you will need to obtain device keys and keychain data. In iOS Forensic Toolkit, use the 4 (GET KEYS) command. This action is mandatory, you cannot skip it. Without the keys, neither the keychain nor the device image can be decrypted:

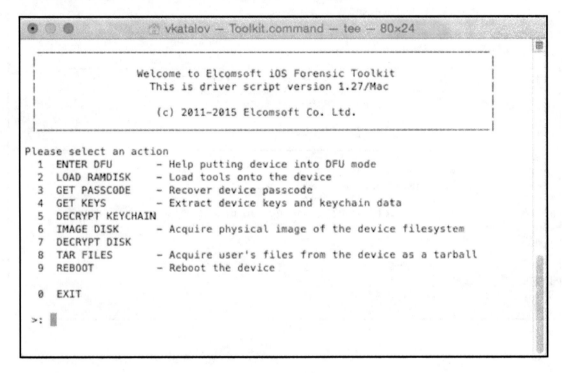

To obtain device keys and keychain, enter 4.

In order to successfully obtain device keys and keychain data, you will need to provide the device passcode (if non-empty):

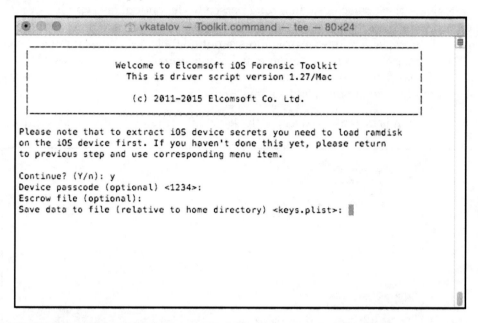

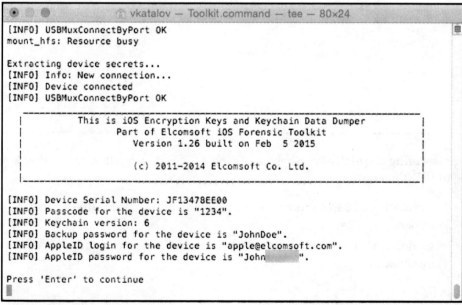

Step 5 – decrypting keychain items: Some of the most valuable information stored in the iPhone, iPod Touch, or iPad is kept in the system's protected storage called keychain. Secured information is protected with strong passcode-dependent encryption keys (that's why you need to recover the passcode in order to obtain these keys and decrypt the keychain). With every iOS release, Apple moves more data to keychain storage. Depending on the iOS version, protected information may include e-mail account passwords, messages, Wi-Fi passwords, passwords entered into websites and certain third-party apps, financial information, documents, and so on.

Keychain decryption is instant. To decrypt the keychain, enter 5 on the tools' main screen:

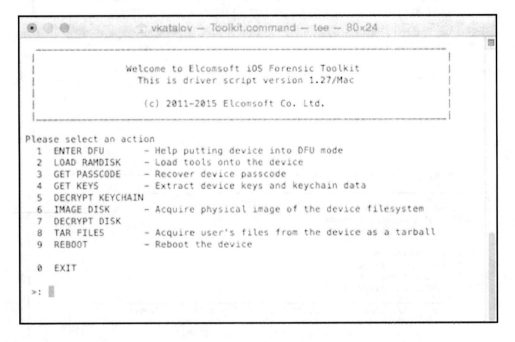

Step 6 – performing acquisition: When capturing an iOS device via a physical link, you will have two distinct options:

- In option 1, you can capture the entire image of the device (the IMAGE DISK command, 6)
- In option 2, you can download user's files as a UNIX-style tarball (the TAR FILES command, 8)

The option to download individual files is sometimes referred to as **logical acquisition**, yet we prefer using that term for the acquisition method involving the analysis of offline backup produced with Apple iTunes. Downloading individual files is a faster option with on-the-fly decryption. However, if you opt to download the files, you'll be missing any information that might be stored in unallocated disk space.

On the other hand, the IMAGE DISK command performs the complete physical imaging of the device. When we talk about *physical acquisition*, we usually mean this option. With disk imaging, you'll be downloading a bit-precise copy of the device; no on-the-fly decryption is performed. As a result, you'll need to decrypt the disk later by using the DECRYPT DISK tool (command 7).

Let's see what happens when you enter 6 (IMAGE DISK). First, you'll see the list of available partitions. Typically, you'll see the **System** partition (which is normally unencrypted, and contains system files and applications) and the **User** partition (which would be normally encrypted). To select a partition to image, enter its number in the prompt:

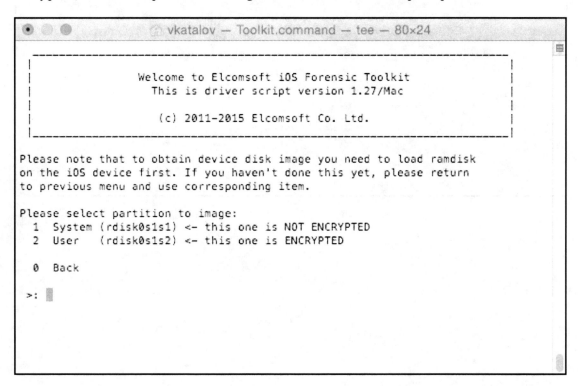

After you've selected a partition to image, the acquisition process will begin immediately. It may take around 35 to 90 minutes to image the device, depending on the model and storage capacity. If you opt for filesystem-level acquisition as in the 8 command, the time required to acquire the device will depend on the amount of user data actually stored in the device. If the user does not have a lot of data, the acquisition in that mode can be really fast:

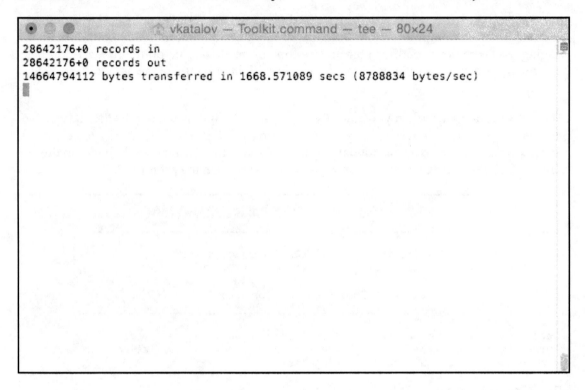

Step 7 – decrypting the disk: After acquiring the disk image in the previous step, you'll end up with one unencrypted (system) and most probably an encrypted (user) partition. In order to be able to analyze user data, you'll need to decrypt the partition first. The decryption is performed by choosing the 7 command (DECRYPT DISK) from the main window:

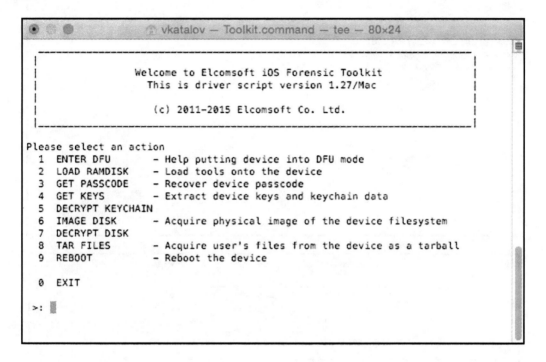

```
  ● ● ●                 vkatalov — Toolkit.command — tee — 80×24

  ┌─────────────────────────────────────────────────────────────────────┐
  │                                                                       │
  │              Welcome to Elcomsoft iOS Forensic Toolkit                │
  │               This is driver script version 1.27/Mac                  │
  │                                                                       │
  │                  (c) 2011-2015 Elcomsoft Co. Ltd.                     │
  └─────────────────────────────────────────────────────────────────────┘

  Please select an action
     1   ENTER DFU        - Help putting device into DFU mode
     2   LOAD RAMDISK     - Load tools onto the device
     3   GET PASSCODE     - Recover device passcode
     4   GET KEYS         - Extract device keys and keychain data
     5   DECRYPT KEYCHAIN
     6   IMAGE DISK       - Acquire physical image of the device filesystem
     7   DECRYPT DISK
     8   TAR FILES        - Acquire user's files from the device as a tarball
     9   REBOOT           - Reboot the device

     0   EXIT

  >: █
```

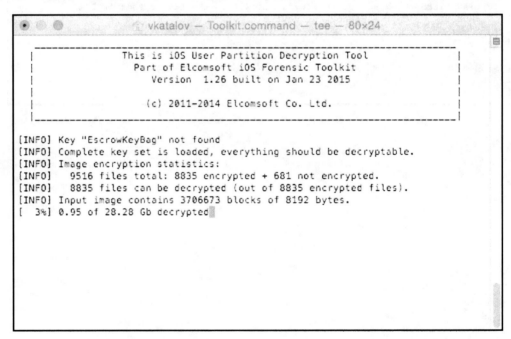

```
●  ●  ●          vkatalov — Toolkit.command — tee — 80×24

   ┌─────────────────────────────────────────────────────────────────┐
   |             Welcome to Elcomsoft iOS Forensic Toolkit             |
   |              This is driver script version 1.27/Mac              |
   |                                                                   |
   |             (c) 2011-2015 Elcomsoft Co. Ltd.                     |
   └─────────────────────────────────────────────────────────────────┘

Encrypted image file <user.dmg>:
Device keys file <keys.plist>:
Write decrypted image to file <user-decrypted.dmg>: █
```

```
●  ●  ●          vkatalov — Toolkit.command — tee — 80×24

   ┌─────────────────────────────────────────────────────────────────┐
   |            This is iOS User Partition Decryption Tool             |
   |                Part of Elcomsoft iOS Forensic Toolkit            |
   |                 Version  1.26 built on Jan 23 2015               |
   |                                                                   |
   |             (c) 2011-2014 Elcomsoft Co. Ltd.                     |
   └─────────────────────────────────────────────────────────────────┘

[INFO] Key "EscrowKeyBag" not found
[INFO] Complete key set is loaded, everything should be decryptable.
[INFO] Image encryption statistics:
[INFO]   9516 files total: 8835 encrypted + 681 not encrypted.
[INFO]   8835 files can be decrypted (out of 8835 encrypted files).
[INFO] Input image contains 3706673 blocks of 8192 bytes.
[  3%] 0.95 of 28.28 Gb decrypted█
```

That's it! You just acquired an iOS device and have the data ready for analysis. The data is saved in a standard DMG image. To analyze information, you can use one of the many third-party forensic tools. If you are using a Mac PC, in order to manually access information contained in the DMG image, you can simply mount the image into the system (read-only). If you are using a Windows PC, you will need to install an HFS+ driver, such as Paragon HFS+, available at `http://www.paragon-software.com/home/hfs-windows/`. Either way, after mounting the image, you will be able to access the individual files and databases available in the device.

Acquiring 64-bit Apple devices

Elcomsoft iOS Forensic Toolkit is the only tool on the market (as of December 2015) that allows physical acquisition of Apple's 64-bit devices. The tool comes with the ability of acquiring information from jailbroken 64-bit iPhones, such as Apple iPhone 5S, 6/6S/Plus, and 64-bit iPads, including iPad mini 2-4, iPad Air/Air2, and iPad Pro.

The 64-bit acquisition process differs significantly from the old methods that were used to extract data from 32-bit devices. The new method is backward compatible with 32-bit iPhones and iPads; however, if you have a choice, we recommend sticking with the old and proven acquisition routine if you've got a 32-bit iPhone to extract.

Note that a working jailbreak is absolutely mandatory for the new acquisition process to work.

If you don't want to read the theory, you can skip directly to the *Performing physical acquisition on a 64-bit iOS device* section.

Comparing 64-bit process and traditional physical acquisition

In order to successfully operate on Apple's 64-bit devices, the new acquisition process must work within the limits of the target platform. Apple's 64-bit platform implements much stricter security compared to legacy devices based on older hardware; as a result, there are certain limitations to 64-bit acquisition that one never has to deal with when acquiring 32-bit hardware.

The first difference between the two acquisition methods lies in the output data format. The 32-bit physical acquisition process returns the complete bit-precise image of the device by accessing the data in raw mode. The 64-bit platform implements stronger protection, making it possible to dump a disk image, but it never releases the encryption keys required to decrypt files. For this reason, the 64-bit acquisition process is limited to using higher-level access for capturing the filesystem in the form of a Unix-style TAR archive. Mind you, the archive contains the same data as a raw dump produced by the traditional process. However, keychain items cannot be decrypted. Analyzing the filesystem image is also a bit more complicated compared to processing the full DMG image, as DMG images are supported by virtually all mobile forensic tools, while filesystem dumps are not as widely supported.

Here comes the second difference between the two acquisition methods. The 64-bit process can *extract* the keychain database from the device. However, with no access to the securityd device key, the new process cannot *decrypt* the keychain. Therefore, stored Web forms and passwords, as well as other data put into keychain, will remain inaccessible (at least for the time being).

Finally, you must unlock the device with the correct passcode and remove passcode protection in iOS settings before the extraction.

Finally, the 64-bit acquisition process is significantly more invasive, compared to the old 32-bit process. This means that every step of the acquisition process and every modification done to the content of the device must be carefully documented; otherwise, extracted evidence may not be admissible.

To sum it up, the 64-bit process has the following limitations compared to physical acquisition for 32-bit devices:

- Keychain extracted, but *not* decrypted
- HFS+ filesystem image (64-bit) versus bit-precise image (32-bit)
- Passcode must be removed in iOS settings prior to acquisition (64-bit)
- Highly invasive, requires careful documentation for evidence to remain admissible

Supported devices and iOS versions

Hardware wise, the 64-bit acquisition process supports all of the following devices regardless of the version of iOS they are running (assuming that a working jailbreak exists for this version of iOS):

- iPhone 5S, 6, 6 Plus, 6S, and 6S Plus
- iPad Air, Air 2, and Pro
- iPad mini Retina and iPad mini 3 and 4
- iPod Touch 6th gen

The new acquisition process requires unrestricted access to the filesystem, and therefore, it relies heavily on a device being jailbroken. Since new versions of iOS are a constant challenge for jailbreakers, you may be out of luck (at least for a while) if you encounter a device running the latest version of iOS that does not have a jailbreak so far. At this time (December 2015), iOS 9.1 and 9.2 Beta still don't have a working jailbreak, so you will be unable to use the new acquisition process on any of these devices.

Performing physical acquisition on a 64-bit iOS device

The internals of the 64-bit acquisition process differ significantly from how it works on 32-bit devices. As a result, an extra step is required to perform physical acquisition on an iPhone 5S, 6/6S, or any of the Plus versions.

Step 1 – on your iOS device:

1. **Ensure that the device is jailbroken**: Physical acquisition for 64-bit devices is exclusive to jailbroken iPhones, iPads, and iPods. If it is not jailbroken, proceed to *Install jailbreak*.
2. If OpenSSH is not installed, install it from Cydia (`https://cydia.saurik.com/openssh.html`) or by following the instructions at `http://www.cydiaos.com/install-openssh-on-iphone-ipod-without-cydia/`.
3. Unlock the device by supplying the correct passcode.
4. If the passcode is empty, go to iOS Forensic Toolkit.

5. Disable passcode protection in iOS Settings.

iOS 8 (no Touch ID): **Settings** | **Passcode Lock** | **Turn Passcode Off**:

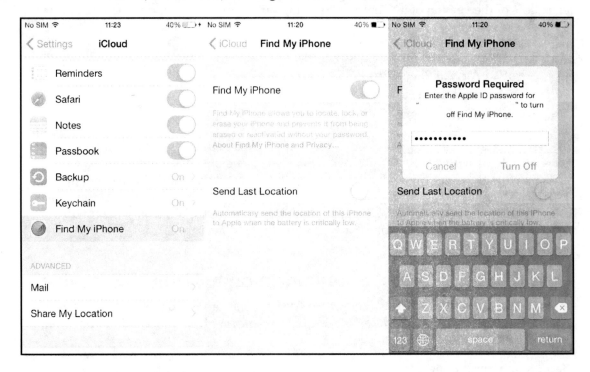

Step 2 – install jailbreak

Jailbreaking iOS 8 and 9 is a cumbersome process without guaranteed outcome. Depending on the version of iOS, you may need to follow different steps and use different tools to jailbreak.

For example, installing a Pangu jailbreak on iOS 9.0.1-9.0.2 may get stuck at 85% with an error message. If that happens, you will need to open the Photos app after the first reboot (and before putting the device into the **Airplane mode**) to ensure that at least one photo exists on the device. Opening (and leaving) the Photos app may be enough to carry on; however, there can be other numerous obstacles in installing jailbreak.

What you need to know

In order to jailbreak an iOS device, you'll need to disable several protection layers. In order to do this, you may need to specify the correct Apple ID password and enter the correct passcode (if either or both protection layers are enabled).

Preparing for jailbreak

- Before jailbreaking, you will need to unlock the iOS device using the correct passcode
- Check whether **Find My Phone** is enabled. If it is, in iOS Settings, disable **Find My Phone** (Apple ID password required):

TaiG and Pangu jailbreaks require disabling Touch ID and passcode protection. If you haven't disabled them during the previous step, do it now. Check whether passcode protection is enabled (if you had to enter a passcode in order to unlock the device, it is.) If enabled, disable **Touch ID** and **Passcode** in iOS **Settings** (original passcode required):

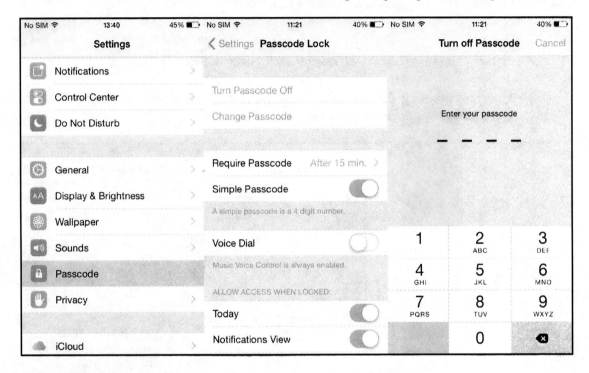

Install jailbreak

For iOS 8.x (all versions), use TaiG jailbreak and follow the instructions at `http://www.taig.com/en/`.

For iOS 9 through 9.0.2, use Pangu jailbreak and follow the instructions at `http://en.pangu.io/`.

For iOS 9.1 and 9.2, at this time, no jailbreak is available (may change in the future).

Step 3 – connect the device

Once your device is jailbroken, you may connect it to your computer via the Lightning cable. Launch iOS Forensic Toolkit. The majority of options are unavailable for 64-bit devices. The 64-bit acquisition process is available under the TAR FILES command.

Step 4 – use iOS Forensic Toolkit:

1. **Launch the Toolkit:**

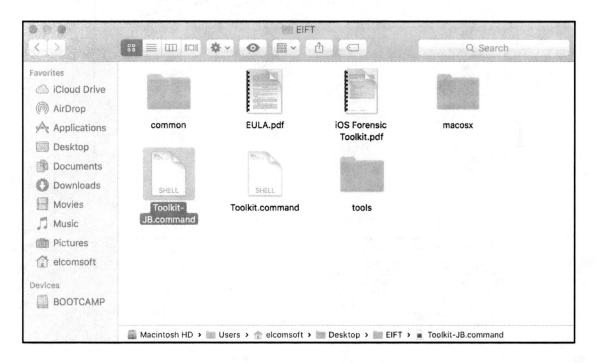

2. **Use the TAR FILES command (item 8) from the main menu**: This will return a Unix-style TAR archive of the filesystem, complete with all application data. The keychain database will also be extracted; however, it won't be decrypted as keychain decryption keys are not accessible on 64-bit devices:

```
●  ○  ○        elcomsoft — Toolkit-JB.command — tee • Toolkit-JB.command — 80×24

  _____
 |                                                                      |
 |            Welcome to Elcomsoft iOS Forensic Toolkit                 |
 |           This is driver script version 2.0/Mac for A5+              |
 |                                                                      |
 |                 (c) 2011-2015 Elcomsoft Co. Ltd.                     |
 |_____|

Please select an action
   1  N/A
   2  N/A
   3  GET PASSCODE     - Recover device passcode
   4  GET KEYS         - Extract device keys and keychain data
   5  DECRYPT KEYCHAIN
   6  IMAGE DISK       - Acquire physical image of the device filesystem
   7  DECRYPT DISK
   8  TAR FILES        - Acquire user's files from the device as a tarball
   9  REBOOT           - Reboot the device

   0  EXIT

  >:
```

```
●  ○  ○        elcomsoft — Toolkit-JB.command — tee • Toolkit-JB.command — 80×24
establishing ssh trust between the device and the computer...
setting permissions...
cheking ssh directory...
[INFO] Info: New connection...
[INFO] Device connected
[INFO] USBMuxConnectByPort OK
root@localhost's password:
```

If prompted, enter the root password. By default, the root password is alpine. You will need to enter the password twice.

Re-enter the root password:

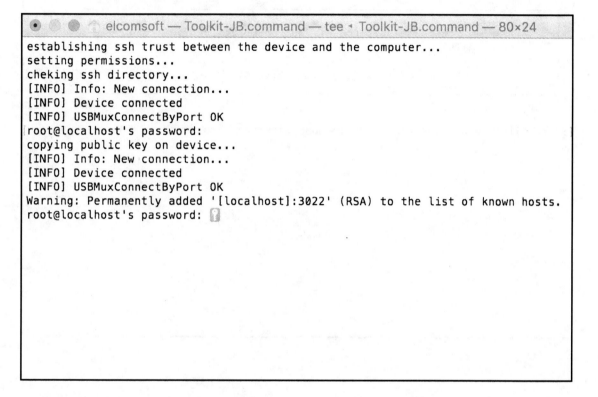

```
establishing ssh trust between the device and the computer...
setting permissions...
cheking ssh directory...
[INFO] Info: New connection...
[INFO] Device connected
[INFO] USBMuxConnectByPort OK
root@localhost's password:
copying public key on device...
[INFO] Info: New connection...
[INFO] Device connected
[INFO] USBMuxConnectByPort OK
Warning: Permanently added '[localhost]:3022' (RSA) to the list of known hosts.
root@localhost's password:
```

3. **Specify the file name**: The path is relative to the home directory:

```
●  ●  ●  ⇧  elcomsoft — Toolkit-JB.command — tee ‹ Toolkit-JB.command — 80×24

   |                                                                        |
   |              Welcome to Elcomsoft iOS Forensic Toolkit                 |
   |            This is driver script version 2.0/Mac for A5+               |
   |                                                                        |
   |                (c) 2011–2015 Elcomsoft Co. Ltd.                        |
   |_____|


Store files to archive (relative to home directory) <user.tar>: ▌
```

4. **Wait while the filesystem is being extracted**: This can be a lengthy process, especially when acquiring devices with a large amount of data (in our lab, it took us about 10 minutes to pull 7.5 GB of data):

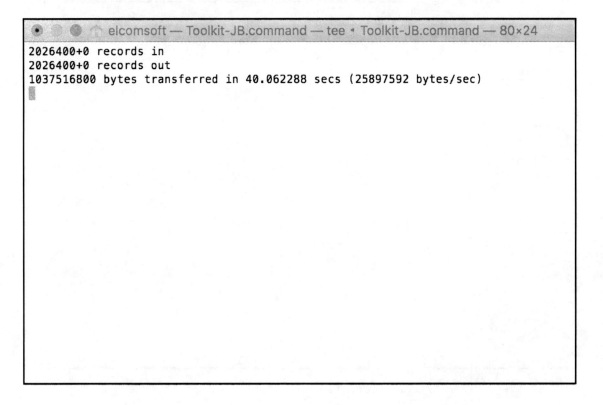

5. **When the process is finished, disconnect the device and proceed to analyze the data:**

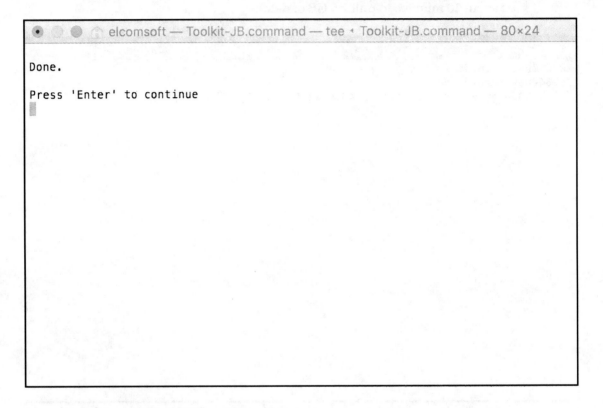

What is available via 64-bit physical acquisition

The 64-bit acquisition process returns the full filesystem of the device, including the keychain (which, unfortunately, cannot be decrypted). We were able to access all the following data that is *not* available in either iTunes or iCloud backups:

- Location data (`/private/var/root/Library/Caches/locationd`)
- Downloaded mail (`/private/var/mobile/Library/Mail`)
- Health data (`/private/var/mobile/Library/Health`)
- Music (`/private/var/mobile/Media/iTunes_Control/Music`)
- Detailed battery usage (`/private/var/mobile/Library/BatteryLife`)

- Application data and caches
  (`/private/var/mobile/Containers/Data/Application/<application
  id>`, `/private/var/mobile/Library/Caches`)
- Mobile Safari cache—history, recent searches, and more
  (`/private/var/mobile/Containers/Data/Application/4FF7BF97-4B3B-
  4964-ACD8-974AADB8D4F8/Library/Safari`)
- Lockdown certificate info (`/private/var/root/Library/Lockdown`)
- CPU usage data (`/private/var/mobile/Library/CoreDuet`)
- Push notifications (`/private/var/mobile/Library/ApplePushService`)
- Battery usage (`/private/var/mobile/Library/BatteryLife`)
- Configuration files (`/private/var/mobile/Library/Preferences`)
- Network and data usage (`/private/var/networkd`,
  `/private/var/wireless/Library/Databases`)
- Various log files (`/private/var/log`, `/private/var/logs`,
  `/private/var/wireless/Library/Logs`,
  `/private/var/mobile/Library/Logs`)
- SHM and WAL files for all SQLite databases (delayed transactions)
- Applications activity
  (`/private/var/mobile/Library/AggregateDictionary`)
- Spotlight data (`/private/var/mobile/Library/Spotlight`)
- Keyboard cache (`/private/var/mobile/Library/Keyboard`)

The logs include information on application install/uninstall, restoring from backup, syncing and pairing, application crashes, GSM network connections, iCloud access (by app), iOS updates, application crash logs, info on device on/off, diagnostics and security logs, and more.

Caches include a lot more than just the application cache. In addition to this, you'll get cache of the data downloaded over the Internet, screenshots of applications' recent state (at the time they were suspended), information stored in the clipboard of the device, and much more.

There is quite more data to analyze, especially in the `/private/var/mobile/Library` folder.

Interestingly, some of this data is also available when performing acquisition of a locked device, even if you don't know the passcode.

Locked device with unknown passcode

The new acquisition process can be used to pull some information from 32-bit and 64-bit devices that are locked with an unknown passcode (jailbreak required). This includes devices that were powered on (or rebooted) and never unlocked. Jailbreak is absolutely mandatory; we cannot pull anything from a non-jailbroken device with an unknown passcode!

The amount of information that can be extracted varies depending on whether the device was unlocked at least once after it powered on or rebooted. If the device was never unlocked after a reboot, only a very limited dataset is available. However, if the user entered the correct passcode at least once, a lot of information (such as the SMS database, contacts database, Wi-Fi password, and so on) is decrypted and can be extracted later on, even after the device is subsequently locked.

The following data can be pulled from jailbroken, passcode-locked devices:

- Some geolocation data (cellular tower and compass calibration data, including coordinates)
- Incoming calls (numbers only) and text messages
- App and system logs (installs and updates, net access logs, and so on)
- SQLite temp files, including **write-ahead logs** (WAL)

What exactly may or may not be available from a locked device depends, in particular, on whether or not the device was unlocked at least once after booting up. For example, incoming text messages will be placed in a temporary, unencrypted database if the device was never unlocked after booting up. However, if the device was unlocked at least once, all text messages will be transferred into the encrypted database even if they were received while the device was subsequently locked. As a result, if a device was unlocked at least once and it has a jailbreak installed, it may be possible to pull a lot more data compared to devices that were never unlocked after the boot. This is one of the reasons why you should do your best to prevent seized devices from switching off (using the Faraday bag and charger routine).

Viewing and analyzing the image

The 64-bit acquisition process returns an archived (.TAR) image of the device's filesystem. If you are using Windows, simply extracting the files and folders from the TAR archive may not return the complete content of the archive as some files and folders may contain characters that are not allowed in NTFS or exFAT. You can either allow the archiver to rename these files or extract information onto a mounted HFS/HFS+ volume:

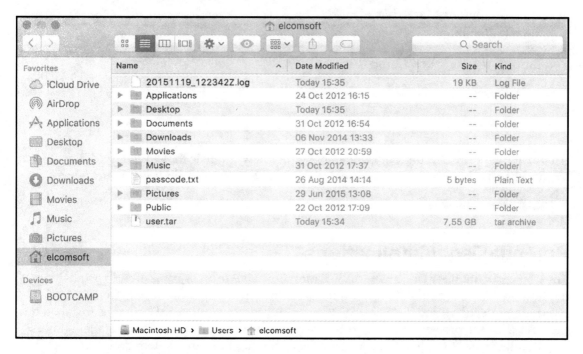

If you are using a macOS X computer, you could simply mount the DMG image (extracted via the 32-bit process) as a virtual disk. However, the 64-bit process does not return a DMG image, meaning that you'll have to manually extract the filesystem from the TAR archive and analyze the files individually. Converting a TAR image of the filesystem into a mountable DMG image is possible; we are currently working on a tool to perform the conversion on-the-fly during acquisition. Stay tuned for iOS Forensic Toolkit 2.1!

If you are using a Windows PC to analyze the extracted dataset, you may need to install a third-party tool in order to mount the HFS+ volume. We assembled the following list of tools to help you mount the HFS+ volume on a Windows PC:

- **HFSExplorer**: `http://www.catacombae.org/hfsexplorer/` (free)
- **Paragon HFS+ for Windows**: `https://www.paragon-software.com/home/hfs-windows/` (free or $19.95)
- **Mediafour MacDrive**: `http://www.mediafour.com/software/macdrive/` ($49.99)

You can also try using BootCamp drivers:

- `http://forums.macrumors.com/threads/apple-hfs-windows-driver-download.13681/`
- `http://lpmv.epfl.ch/page-19141-en.html`

Analyzing the extracted dataset is available with many forensic tools. We found BlackLight by BlackBag Technologies to work great on both macOS X and Windows platforms:

`https://www.blackbagtech.com/software-products/blacklight.html`

Potential legal implications

Physical acquisition for 64-bit devices is a more invasive process compared to acquisition methods available for old hardware. It involves modifying system settings (removing passcode protection), and it does write files onto the phone (OpenSSH must be installed on the device for the process to work). If the device does not have a jailbreak installed, it must be jailbroken prior to acquisition, which once again, modifies the system and data partitions.

With all that in mind, evidence obtained with the new extraction process may not be admissible in court unless every step is properly documented. Producing and obtaining device backups (making the device produce an offline backup via iTunes or an online one via iCloud) prior to attempting physical acquisition is highly recommended. You can use Elcomsoft Phone Breaker (`https://www.elcomsoft.com/eppb.html`) to decrypt the local backup or download one from iCloud.

Summary

This chapter introduced iOS forensics, detailing available acquisition options for different generations of Apple iOS devices. We reviewed the various acquisition options and learned how to perform physical acquisition of an iOS device using Elcomsoft iOS Forensic Toolkit. We also took a brief look at other acquisition techniques, which will be detailed in the next chapter.

6
iOS Logical and Cloud Acquisition

In this chapter, we'll refer to logical acquisition in the sense of acquiring and analyzing iTunes backups. Every time an iPhone user syncs their device with a PC (Windows or macOS X), iTunes creates a local copy of all user data stored in the device (unless the user opts for cloud backups, which will be covered in the next chapter). While it is arguable whether automated backups with no user intervention are a good thing or a bad thing, unless a *cloud* option is selected, users end up having backup copies of their device contents on every computer they sync with.

As a result, the chance of encountering a local copy of an iPhone on the user's PC is not insignificant. By default, iTunes stores offline backups in the following folders on the user's computer:

- **macOS X**: `~/Library/Application Support/MobileSync/Backup/`
- **Windows XP**: `Documents and Settings\(username)\Application Data\Apple Computer\MobileSyncBackup`
- **Windows Vista, Windows 7, 8, and 8.1, Windows 10**: `Users\(username)\AppData\Roaming\Apple Computer\MobileSyncBackup`

While these locations can be changed, having a large set of files stored in one of the above folders is a good indication of a local backup being present.

Compared to the device itself, local backups contain somewhat less information. However, even that is a lot of data. According to Apple, an offline backup may contain:

- Address Book and Address Book favorites
- App Store Application data

- Application settings, preferences, and data
- Autofill for web pages
- CalDAV and subscribed calendar accounts
- Calendar accounts
- Calendar events
- Call history
- Camera Roll
- In-app purchases
- Keychain (encrypted with a strong hardware-dependent encryption key in non-password backups, but encrypted with a backup password if one is present)
- List of External Sync Sources (Mobile Me, Exchange, ActiveSync)
- Location service preferences for apps and websites you have allowed to use your location
- Mail accounts
- Managed Configurations/Profiles
- Map bookmarks, recent searches, and the current location displayed in Maps
- Microsoft Exchange account configurations
- Network settings (saved Wi-Fi hotspots, VPN settings, network preferences)
- Nike + iPod saved workouts and settings
- Notes
- Offline web application cache/database
- Paired Bluetooth devices (which can only be used if restored to the same phone that made the backup)
- Safari bookmarks, cookies, history, offline data, and currently open pages
- Saved suggested corrections (these are saved automatically as one rejects suggested corrections)
- SMS and MMS (pictures and video) messages
- Trusted hosts that have certificates that cannot be verified
- Voice memos
- Voicemail token
- Wallpapers
- Web clips
- YouTube bookmarks and history

An iTunes backup is not made as a single file. Instead, Apple produces a large number of randomly named files containing various bits of information. The names of the files are probably not completely random; our guess is that the filenames are hash sums of full paths to those same files when stored inside the device.

According to unofficial iOS Forensics blog, *the filenames produced by the backup through iTunes result from iTunes computing a SHA1 hash value of the file's path and name appended to the iOS domain via a hyphen (that is, iOSDomain-FilePath/FileName).*

Interestingly, these files are in fact SQLite database files. In the case of an unprotected backup, they can be read and analyzed with pretty much any forensic tool supporting the SQLite format.

Understanding backups – local, cloud, encrypted and unencrypted

Apple offers its users the choice of three different backup methods, allowing to be created, plain and password-protected local backups via iTunes, or making over-the-air iCloud backups. The following table plots major differences between the three types of backups:

	iTunes, plain (unencrypted)	iTunes password-protected (encrypted)	iCloud
Keychain encrypted with	**securityd** (*)	Password (same as the rest of the backup); some keychain items with a higher protection class are still protected with hardware-backed securityd key	securityd (*)
Amount of data	Full (but keychain data may remain inaccessible unless securityd is extracted out of the physical device)	Limited (some keychain data unavailable)	Limited (for example, no IMEI and other hardware-specific data)
Type of recovery	Most information available instantly	Must recover original password	Must know Apple ID/password, or must have non-expired authentication token

Keychain recovery possible?	Keychain recovery unavailable (unless securityd is available)	Keychain decrypted with other data (if password recovered). Only some keychain data can be recovered.	Keychain recovery unavailable (unless securityd is available) **

* iCloud backups as well as iTunes offline backups saved without a password do not expose keychain information in plain text. Instead, keychain data is encrypted by using a hardware-specific key called securityd.

** In addition to the regular keychain, the iCloud account also contains a so-called *iCloud Keychain*. iCloud Keychain is maintained independently of backup keychains, and is synchronized automatically between all devices that are configured accordingly, even including Mac desktop PCs and even if cloud backups are disabled. The purpose of iCloud Keychain is keeping and synchronizing online form data, such as logins and passwords to websites between devices. Information contained in iCloud Keychain is maintained independently of regular keychains maintained in cloud backups; however, iCloud Keychain contains a subset of data available in regular keychains. Extracting iCloud Keychain is significantly more difficult compared to extracting the iCloud backup due to forced two-factor authentication involving the use of a trusted device, a special access code that may or may not match the device password, or a recovery key. iCloud Keychain recovery is currently not available with any commercial tools. ElcomSoft made a proof-of-concept tool for internal testing purposes. There will be more on iCloud Keychain in the next chapter.

The great thing about the securityd key is that it remains constant for the lifetime of the device. This key is what allows iOS users to access all of their past, current, and future iOS keychains restored from the unencrypted backups. Unfortunately, extracting securityd is only possible via physical acquisition. As a result, if all you have is an unencrypted backup, and you don't have access to a physical device matching the compatibility matrix for physical acquisition, you will be unable to access keychain data. If, however, you have extracted the securityd key from the device, you will be able to use it to decrypt all current, as well as all future, backups made with that device.

You can read more about securityd in the following article:

- **Improved iOS Keychain Explorer**: `http://blog.crackpassword.com/212/4/ne` `w-features-in-eppb/`

Encrypted versus unencrypted iTunes backups

If all you have is an iTunes backup, understanding your options is essential for a successful investigation.

When configuring a backup policy, iOS users have a choice between creating non-encrypted and password-protected backups. Here's what Apple has to say:

In the iTunes **Summary** screen, select **Encrypt iPhone backup** if you want to encrypt the information stored on your computer when iTunes makes a backup. Encrypted backups are indicated by a padlock icon (as visible below in the **Deleting a Backup** section), and a password is required to restore the information to iPhone. You may want to write down the password for your backup and store it in a safe place. If you use a Mac, when you set a password you can select to store the password in the keychain. With iOS 4 and later, you can transfer most of your keychain items to a new device if you encrypt the backup.

Warning

If you encrypt an iPhone backup in iTunes and then forget your password, you will not be able to restore from the backup and your data will be unrecoverable. If you forget the password, you can continue to do backups and use the device; however, you will not be able to restore the encrypted backup to any device without the password. You do not need to enter the password for your backup each time you back up or sync.

If you cannot remember the password and want to start again, you will have to do a full software restore and when prompted by iTunes to select the backup to restore from, choose **Set up as a new device**.

If you read the earlier paragraphs, you may get a sense that password-protected backups allow extracting more information compared to their non-encrypted counterparts. This is true. In a password-protected backup, the keychain (containing a lot of sensitive information such as mail, passwords, account data, and so on) is encrypted with the same password as the rest of the data. In non-encrypted backups, the keychain is encrypted with a hardware-specific key that cannot be broken from the outside.

Consequentially, users who protect their backups with a password can have them restored to any Apple device complete with all secured items stored in the keychain. Users who opted for non-protected backups can still restore a backup on any Apple device, but will be unable to restore/access any data stored in the keychain. Apple confirms this impression with the following statement:

"If you encrypt the backup with iOS 4 and later, the keychain information is transferred to the new device. With an unencrypted backup, the keychain can only be restored to the same iPhone or iPod touch. If you are restoring to a new device with an unencrypted backup, you will need to enter these passwords again."

With Apple pushing more and more stuff into the keychain, protecting backups with a password becomes more convenient for the user than ever, while allowing investigators to access secured information stored in the keychain... if they can break the password.

Breaking backup passwords

If you encounter a password-protected backup, you'll need to recover (or break) the original password in order to decrypt its content. There is no way around the password. Apple's backup encryption is pretty strong by today's standards, which makes it easier to attack the original password rather than attacking the binary encryption key. The password can only be recovered via the usual means (brute force and dictionary or hybrid attacks).

In order to break the password, we'll use in-house Elcomsoft Phone Breaker (formerly Phone Password Breaker). This tool was originally designed to do exactly that: breaking iOS backup passwords. Elcomsoft Phone Breaker will attempt to *guess* the password by performing several kinds of attacks. How much time it will need to recover the password, and whether or not it'll be able to recover the password at all, depends on how strong the original password was. Short, simple passwords (for example, 4-digit PIN) can be broken extremely fast, while long, complex alphanumeric passwords can take forever to recover. Unlike the passcode, Apple backup passwords are used infrequently; therefore, users tend to select longer passwords containing letters, numbers, and special characters.

Breaking the password – how long will it take?

How fast exactly can you break the password? Unfortunately, unlike physical acquisition, there is **no fixed timeframe** and **no guarantee** for breaking backup passwords. The following factors affect password recovery speeds:

- The speed of your computer's CPU and its graphics card (the latter is way more important than the former)
- The length and complexity of the password (which is a big unknown)
- Any information you know about the password (for example, user's other passwords and any patterns derived from their password-related habits)

A fast CPU and a faster video card

The urge to have a fast CPU is self-explanatory, but why do we need a fast graphics card? And why do we state that having a fast video card is way more important than having a fast CPU?

The reason for that is GPU acceleration. Today's video cards are extremely fast. Just consider how much computational power is needed to support modern 3D games in high resolutions and 60 frames-per-second, and you'll realize it takes a lot of processing power.

Using that power to break passwords can give a significant boost to the speed of recovery. By offloading computation-intensive parts of the process to the massively parallel array of graphical processing units (GPUs) of a typical gaming board costing no more than $200-300, one can increase the speed of recovering iTunes passwords 10 to 20 fold. By using an even faster video card, or by utilizing two or more cards, one can boost speeds 30 to 50 fold compared to using a high-end quad-core CPU. Interestingly, ElcomSoft Phone Breaker can utilize all video cards installed in the system even if no SLI/Cross Fire mode is configured.

There is no limit to how many video cards can be used.

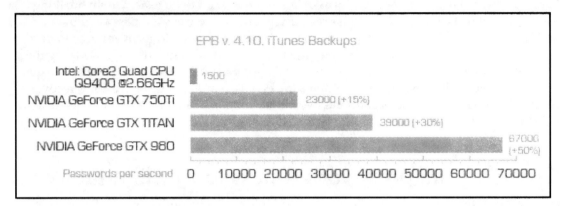

Elcomsoft Phone Breaker includes a smart solution to lengthy attacks. The tool can dramatically increase the speed of attacks by utilizing the sheer computational power of consumer or gaming video cards. The tool uses a patented GPU acceleration algorithm to greatly reduce the time required to recover iPhone/iPad/iPod and BlackBerry backup passwords. The latest generation of ElcomSoft GPU acceleration technology supports unlimited numbers of AMD or NVIDIA boards such as NVIDIA GeForce 400, 500, 600, 700, 800, and 900-series and AMD Radeon HD 5000, 6000, 7000, R7, and R9 series. ElcomSoft GPU acceleration provides true supercomputer performance at consumer prices.

Breaking complex passwords

It is obvious that long and complex passwords take more time to break. The password breaking tool will have to try more possible combinations to discover a long alphanumeric password compared to breaking a simple 4-digit PIN.

If a password only contains numbers, the use of each additional character makes the password 10 times stronger, which means that breaking the password takes 10 times longer with every additional number. A password that consists entirely of small Latin characters gets 26 times stronger with each extra letter. If the password contains numbers and both small and capital letters, it gets 62 times stronger with every additional character.

Briefly, the total number of combinations to try is calculated as follows:

(number of different characters the password may contain) in a power of (password length)

For example, a rather simple password that consists of only six characters and contains numbers, small and capital Latin letters has $62^6 = 56,800,235,584$ (56+ billion) possible combinations. If you don't have any information about the password and just know the length and the fact that it is alphanumeric, the password recovery tool will try them all until it finds the one that matches (unless a more advanced attack such as a wordlist or dictionary attack is successful).

Knowing the user helps breaking the password

Some passwords are protected stronger than others. In fact, in our daily life we routinely use passwords that are weakly protected or not protected at all. Instant messenger passwords? Stored in Windows Registry or configuration files in plain text or barely scrambled. Website passwords? Depending on the Web browser, these are extracted instantly or in a matter of seconds. E-mail passwords in popular applications such as Outlook Express, Windows Mail, Windows Live! Mail, or Thunderbird? Displayed instantly with a simple free tool. Older Office documents, third-party office applications, and many other sources may contain passwords that are more easily accessible compared to passwords protecting Apple backups.

It is a good idea to spend some time extracting the easily recoverable passwords stored elsewhere. Add those passwords to the top of the wordlist file used for a dictionary attack, and in some cases, you won't have to deal with lengthy attacks at all.

Even if none of the other passwords work on an iTunes backup, you didn't spend time for nothing. Look at those passwords. Do you see a common pattern? If passwords chosen by the user are not completely random, more often than not they'll all follow a common pattern. Maybe one or more commonly used words, a phone number, pet name, football team, or just *god, sex,* or *topsecret*. Maybe they all start with one capital letter and end with a number. Maybe they have something else in common that you can use to create a common pattern and use that pattern in Elcomsoft Phone Breaker to reduce the number of possible password combinations and speed up the recovery significantly.

Elcomsoft Phone Breaker also includes a so-called *wordlist* with the most commonly used passwords used by users speaking English, German, and Russian. There are plenty of other lists with commonly used passwords available on the Internet. It's definitely worth downloading some of those lists, as many users are likely to have one of the passwords that are already there. Finally, special options in the product, which allow you to check variations of the words from the wordlist; we call them *smart mutations*.

What if the user selects a completely random password for every purpose? Complex random passwords, sometimes generated with special software, are not the best security choice. While it is possible for an ordinary person to memorize one or two passwords like that, it is unlikely that such passwords are ever changed. If more than a handful of random passwords are encountered, there is a good chance they are all written down somewhere. Maybe it's a small sheet of paper, and maybe it's a password manager (password keeper) application, either online or installed on the computer. Breaking a master password to that application reveals all of the other passwords, no matter how long or complex they might be.

Tutorial – logical acquisition with Elcomsoft Phone Breaker

Enough theory! Let's go ahead and do the acquisition.

First and foremost: Elcomsoft Phone Breaker should be used offline, on your own computer, and never on the suspect's PC. The tool allows decrypting an encrypted backup that is accessible from the computer where you have Elcomsoft Phone Breaker installed. You can mount a disk image or use a network disk; there will be no performance penalty when breaking the password.

Breaking the password

Before accessing information stored in the backup, you'll need to decrypt the data. In order to decrypt the data, you'll require the original plain-text password. If you don't know the password, Elcomsoft Phone Breaker will perform an attack in order to recover it.

In order to recover the password, you will not need to have the complete backup sitting on your computer. In fact, a single tiny file named `Manifest.plist` is all that you need to start breaking the password (if you are working with a BlackBerry backup, please refer to online documentation for more information).

Elcomsoft Phone Breaker recovers the password by *attacking* the backup. You can specify one or more different attacks, for example, wordlist (known password attack), dictionary, brute force, and so on. A combination of attacks makes up a recovery pipeline.

To recover the password in Elcomsoft Phone Breaker, do the following:

1. Open the **Password Recovery Wizard** page.

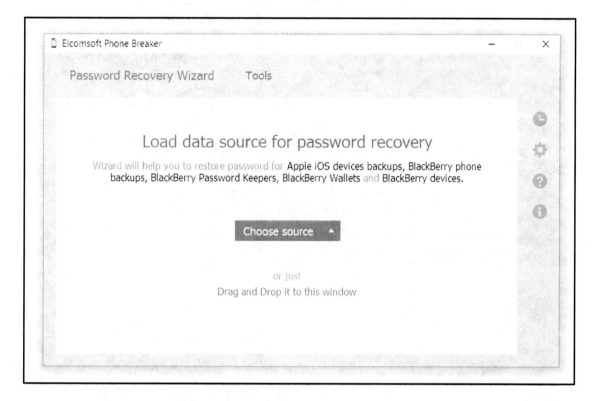

2. Specify the backup file by either selecting the file with the **Choose source** command or by dragging and dropping the `Manifest.plist` onto the **Password Recovery Wizard** window.

   - By default, the tool will list all locally available backups. If you are recovering a backup located on the suspect's hard drive, external device, or mounted forensic disk image, you will need to manually specify the location of iTunes backups. For the purpose of breaking the password, the tool will only need a single file named `manifest.plist` (the full set of backup files will be required for the decryption).

   - If you are specifying the location manually, here are the default paths used by iTunes on the different operating systems:

     - **Windows XP:** `\Documents and Settings\(username)\Application Data\Apple Computer\MobileSync\Backup\`

     - **Windows Vista, 7 and 8:** `\Users\username\AppData\Roaming\Apple Computer\MobileSync\Backup\`

     - **macOS X (all versions):** `~/Library/Application Support/MobileSync/Backup/`

3. After specifying the backup file, you will need to define the attacks that will be used to break the password.

4. Click on the plus + sign to add various attacks for breaking the password. By default, **Dictionary** and **Brute-Force** attacks are added automatically. For more information about attacks and their settings, see the password recovery attacks topic in the online manual.

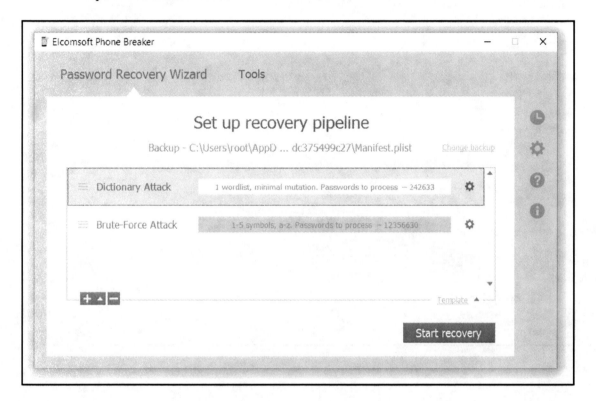

5. You can optionally configure both the **Dictionary attack** and **Brute-Force** by clicking on the gear icon to the right of each method.

6. You can use the default dictionary of English words (supplied with Elcomsoft Phone Breaker) or choose any number of custom dictionaries in plain text format (each word or phrase must be on a separate line). A high-quality custom dictionary is essential for breaking the password. If at all possible, try building a custom dictionary containing the user's other passwords.

7. Click **Start recovery**. Elcomsoft Phone Breaker will begin attacking the password. The estimated time left as well as the currently processed word will be displayed. You can click More Info next to the name of the attack to see additional information, such as the number of attempted passwords and the average attack speed.

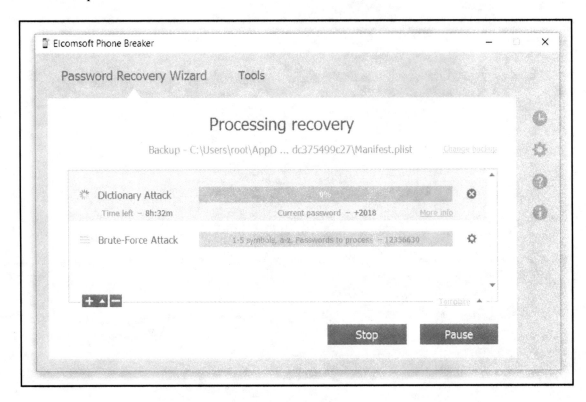

8. If the attack is successful, the discovered password will be displayed in the **Recovery results** window.

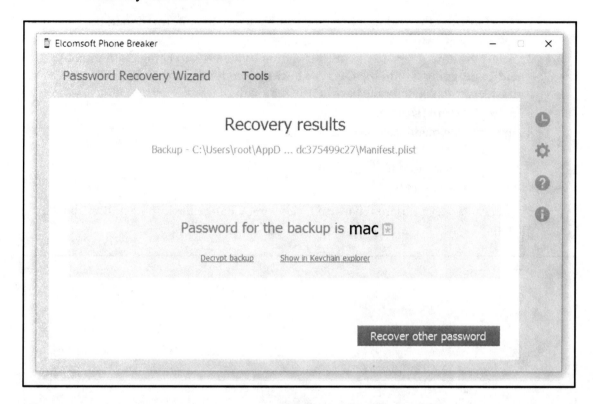

That's it, we have successfully recovered a password. This password can now be used to decrypt the backup. In addition, you can view information stored in the keychain by using**Keychain explorer**.

Decrypting the backup

You can only decrypt the backup if you already know or have already recovered the original plain-text password. If you don't have the password, please recover the password first.

Launch Elcomsoft Phone Breaker. Assuming that you do know the password, do the following to decrypt a backup:

1. After loading the backup file, you'll be able to see the information in the following screenshot:
2. Select the `Manifest.plist` file belonging to the backup being decrypted by either dragging it onto the **Decrypt backup** window, or by clicking **Choose backup** to navigate to the backup file manually.
3. Select **Decrypt backup**.
4. In the **Tools** menu, select the **Apple** tab.
    *   Serial number
    *   Backup date
    *   Product type
5. You can select a different backup by clicking **Change backup** next to the backup name.

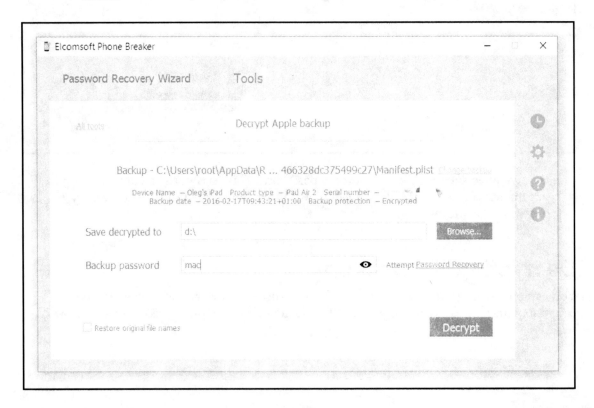

6. Define backup decryption options:
    - **Save decrypted to**: Select the location for saving the decrypted backup.
    - **Backup password**: Enter the password for the backup. Toggle the

        View ( ) button to display the password as characters or in asterisks (*). Click **Restore password** if you have not recovered the password to the backup yet.
    - **Restore original file names**: Renames files to match the way they appear on the device. If you uncheck this option, the files will still be available after decryption; however, their names will remain unmodified.

> If you are using a third-party mobile forensic tool to analyze the backup, *do not* restore original filenames as this will confuse the analysis tool. Only choose this option if you are viewing files manually.

7. Click **Decrypt**.
8. The decryption process starts. You can view the number of processed files and the number of errors received during decryption.

9. When decryption is finished, you can view the backup in the location on the local computer to which it was saved by clicking the **View** (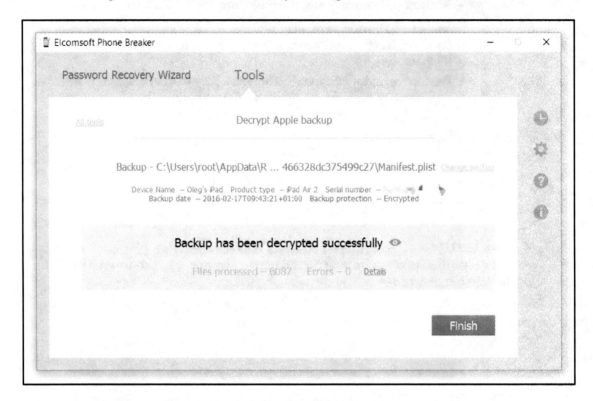) button.

10. To view a detailed report about decrypted files and errors that occurred during decryption, click **Details**.
11. Click **Finish** to close the **Decrypt backup** window.

The backup is now available on your computer for further analysis. You can use Elcomsoft Phone Viewer to browse and view the content of the backup.

Dealing with long and complex passwords

However simple we made it sound; attacking Apple backup passwords is a slow and technically complex process. The recovery speed will depend on available hardware (your computer's CPU and video card), the type of attack, and any information you know about the password. To learn how to speed up the recovery, please read all of the following pages:

- **General password recovery walkthrough**: `http://www.elcomsoft.com/help/en/eppb/recovering_passwords.html`
- **Decrypting the backup**: `http://www.elcomsoft.com/help/en/eppb/decrypting_iphone_backup.html`
- **Types of attacks available in Phone Password Breaker**: `http://www.elcomsoft.com/help/en/eppb/password_recovery_attacks.html`
- **Options for breaking the password**: `http://www.elcomsoft.com/help/en/eppb/password_breaking_options.html`
- **Options for brute force attack**: `http://www.elcomsoft.com/help/en/eppb/brute-force_attack_options.html`

Specifically, the two last links explain how to specify information you know about the password in order to speed up the recovery.

But what if the password is long and complex, or what if you don't know much about the password, and the recovery takes ages of fruitless attacks? If this is the case, you may explore other acquisition options. Particularly, information can be downloaded from the cloud without attacking the password.

Elcomsoft Phone Breaker on a Mac, inside a virtual PC, or via RDP

Many customers are using computers running macOS X. Elcomsoft Phone Breaker is native Windows software. For this reason, some users run Elcomsoft Phone Breaker in a virtual machine (Windows box) on their Mac. However, there are certain limitations in this setup. One major disadvantage of running Elcomsoft Phone Breaker in a Windows box in a virtual machine is lack of speed. At the time of writing there are no drivers allowing for proper implementation of GPU acceleration in any virtual machine. As a result, attempting to brute-force passwords in a virtual machine will inevitably lead to a severe drop in performance. If your computer is equipped with a mid-range video card, by running password recovery in a virtual box you'll be making the recovery 20 to 50 times slower compared to running the same tool on a physical computer.

A workaround exists. You can set up a Windows computer on your network, and connect to that computer remotely from your Mac. Note, however, that using the RDP protocol will cause the same slowdown as using a virtual machine. In order to unleash the full potential of GPU acceleration, we recommend connecting via an alternative interface such as TeamViewer.

iOS Cloud forensics – over-the-air acquisition

Sometimes, accessing information stored in the user's iPhone is possible remotely, even without accessing the original device. Such access is made possible by the fact that iCloud had more than 250 million users last year; this number is steadily growing.

Meet iCloud forensics: acquiring user data with no lengthy attacks and no physical access to an iPhone device. With recent developments, you don't even need the user's Apple ID and password to access their cloud data. Sounds too good to be true? Let's see what the catch is.

About Apple iCloud

Apple iCloud is a popular service providing Apple users with 5 GB of free online storage space. This storage can be used to back up the content of Apple devices, and to store additional information such as documents, pictures, and music. Last year, more than 300 million Apple customers were actively using iCloud. The numbers are constantly growing.

iCloud offers great convenience to its users. If, for example, one loses their iPhone during an overseas trip, one can simply buy a replacement device from a local Apple Store, enter their iCloud credentials and have all of their data restored to the new device completely automatically. The same goes for switching or upgrading devices.

iCloud backups are completely automatic. However, they only occur if certain conditions are met:

- The user has enabled iCloud backups in their device
- The device is docked or connected to a charger
- A Wi-Fi connection is present

While iCloud backups are incremental and only sync whatever has changed in the device, restoring a backup takes just one go when initializing a new Apple device. However, with larger amounts of data to be transferred, an expert may want a faster acquisition. With Elcomsoft Phone Breaker, one can selectively download certain types of data in order to be able to begin the investigation sooner.

More information about Apple iCloud is available from Apple:

- **iCloud**: *Store and back up your content in iCloud*
- **Creating an iCloud account**: *Frequently Asked Questions*
- **iCloud**: *Backup and restore overview*

Getting started with iCloud Keychain

Starting with an intermediary release of iOS 7 (version 7.0.3), iCloud also contains keychain data. iCloud Keychain was added as a feature allowing Apple users to sync their account names and passwords across Apple devices. Data stored in iCloud Keychain syncs automatically between all authorized iOS 7 devices and OS X Mavericks sharing the same Apple ID.

While iCloud Keychain is not automatically enabled, Apple makes it easy to set it up. When initializing a new iOS 7 (or later) device, or immediately after upgrading iOS to the latest version, users are prompted to enable iCloud Keychain. If they decline the choice, it can still be enabled later at **Settings** | **iCloud** | **iCloud Keychain**.

As an additional security measure, Apple wants users to set up an iCloud Security Code to protect their most sensitive keychain data. This code can be a 4-digit PIN or a more complex passcode. iCloud Security Code is used to authorize any additional devices to access iCloud Keychain. In addition, this passcode is used when recovering iCloud Keychain if the user upgrades or loses a device.

iCloud Keychain is protected with mandatory two-factor authentication. At this time, there are no commercially available third-party tools allowing the decryption of iCloud Keychain. Technically, iCloud Keychain can be accessed with a third-party product if one has access to a recovery key or a trusted device. ElcomSoft has a proof-of-concept utility allowing us to do just that; however, it has not made it into a commercial product as of yet.

Another way of accessing data stored in the iCloud Keychain is enabling iCloud Keychain on the Apple device, synchronizing the device, extracting the data from the local keychain, and decrypting it with Elcomsoft Keychain Explorer. This method requires having an unlocked, trusted iOS device.

Interestingly, the iCloud Keychain (as well as the local keychain of a recently synced device) contains a backup password as well as an Apple ID and password, which may come in handy if one was accessing iCloud by using the authentication token. A password protecting the backup is stored in the regular keychain, and has the strongest protection class. As a result, this password can only be decrypted via physical acquisition.

More on iCloud Keychain:

- **General information**: https://www.apple.com/support/icloud/keychain/
- **iCloud Keychain FAQ**: http://support.apple.com/kb/HT5813

Getting started with iCloud Drive

iOS 8 introduced the ability to save information other than device backups into the cloud. Apple named the new service the iCloud Drive. In addition to backups, applications were allowed to store data in the cloud; one notable example of such an application is WhatsApp, which maintains its backups separately from iCloud backups. iCloud Drive is aimed to compete with established cloud storage providers such as Box, Dropbox, Google Drive, and Microsoft OneDrive. Users can store just about any type of file in iCloud Drive, while accessing the data from any Apple device as well as from Windows PCs.

In order to enable iCloud Drive, Apple users must explicitly upgrade their accounts. While Apple users can upgrade their iCloud account to use iCloud Drive at any time, iOS 8 or later is required to access iCloud Drive from iPhones and iPads. iOS 9 makes a much wider use of iCloud Drive, storing cloud backups in the new system and migrating away from the classic iCloud.

By February 2016, 76% of Apple users had already upgraded to iOS 9, and have their cloud backups stored in iCloud Drive by default. 17% of devices were still running iOS 8 by the time, meaning that cloud backups were stored in the "normal" iCloud, while app-specific backups and other files could also be kept in iCloud Drive. The rest (7%) did not have access to iCloud Drive by February 2016.

The new iCloud Drive may be used to store all types of user data, including but not limited to the following:

- iWork documents (if configured to be stored in the cloud) such as Pages, Numbers, Keynote
- Third-party app data (for example, WhatsApp backups, 1Password password databases, and so on)
- Certain system files that are synced across devices (for example, user dictionaries that may contain words and phrases entered by users that are not part of a common dictionary)

iCloud Drive uses a different protocol compared to Apple iCloud. As a result, all cloud forensic tools require explicit support for iCloud Drive in order to be able to access information stored in the cloud service. At this time, Elcomsoft Phone Breaker remains the only tool fully supporting both iCloud and iCloud Drive.

Understanding iCloud forensics

iCloud forensics offers experts yet another way of obtaining important evidence. The pros of cloud forensics are obvious: no access to physical device is required, and there is no need (nor possibility) for lengthy password attacks. Potential issues include: you must either know the user's Apple ID and password, or have a recent (non-expired) authentication token obtained from the user's PC.

With cloud forensics, you only have two options. First, you could use a new (or factory-reset) Apple device to restore the data to, then make a backup of that data. This is a long and complicated process. Alternatively, you can use Elcomsoft Phone Breaker, which is the only cloud forensic tool currently available as Apple does not provide means for downloading iCloud information to a PC. If a user owns more than one device, and those devices are registered with the same Apple ID, their online backups can be seamlessly recovered from iCloud with no extra effort.

Tutorial – cloud acquisition with Elcomsoft Phone Breaker

At the time of writing, there is only one tool on the market that can perform the complete over-the-air acquisition of iOS devices, including accounts upgraded to iCloud Drive. Elcomsoft Phone Breaker (previously Elcomsoft Phone Password Breaker) was the first and remains the only third-party forensic tool that can retrieve and decrypt backups stored in iCloud and download files stored in the subject's iCloud Drive with or without the original Apple ID and password. Notably, Apple does not provide means for downloading iCloud information to a PC, so Elcomsoft Phone Breaker remains the only tool available for that purpose.

In order to be able to access the backup, you will need to supply a valid authentication credential to the Apple iCloud server. Until recently, the only way to authenticate when downloading from the cloud was via login (the user's Apple ID) and password. However, it was recently discovered that under certain conditions, a binary authentication token is created and stored on the user's computer, allowing forensic experts to access information from the cloud without knowing the original login and password.

Depending on whether you know the original Apple ID and password, if you have access to the actual physical device or information obtained from the user's computer, you may choose one of the several acquisition paths.

Downloading iCloud backups – using Apple ID and password

If you know the person's Apple ID and password, you may use Elcomsoft Phone Breaker to download information from their iCloud account. The tool will download the backup from iCloud, decrypt data, and convert it into an iTunes backup so that you can use pretty much any mobile forensic tool to analyze its content. Note, however, that we do not recommend restoring the device using the converted copy of the backup.

To download an iCloud backup, launch Elcomsoft Phone Breaker and do the following:

1. In the **Tools** menu, select the **Apple** tab.
2. Select **Download backup from iCloud**.
3. On the **Download backup from iCloud** page, define the authentication type as **Password**:

   - **Password**: To use your Apple credentials (Apple ID and password).
   - **Token**: To use the Authentication token extracted from iCloud using Elcomsoft Apple Token Extractor. For more information about extracting the token, see the *Extracting authentication* token topic.

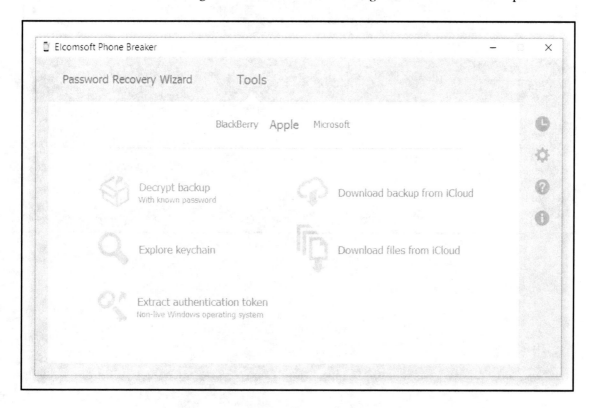

- Enter the **Apple ID** and Password into the corresponding fields, and click **Sign in** to enter iCloud.

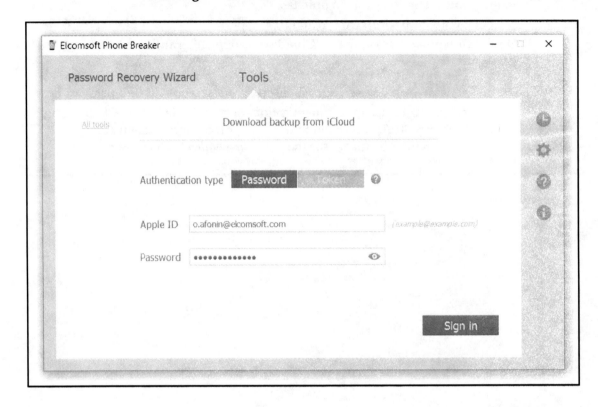

4. Once Elcomsoft Phone Breaker successfully signs into iCloud (assuming no additional authentication steps), it will display the list of devices associated with that specific Apple ID. Note that you will see all devices registered with that Apple ID, including those that are not part of the investigation. The iCloud backup storage opens:

You can view a username, user ID, and Apple ID of the iCloud user, as well as a list of backups belonging to that user. By default, three latest backups are displayed. Hover the mouse over the green (**i**) icon to view storage capacity and occupied size.

To select backups saved by another iCloud user, click **Change user**.

If a certain device is busy saving a new backup, and the backup is still in progress, that device will not be listed as available for downloading.

5. For every device, the following information is displayed:
   - **Device name**
   - **Model**
   - **Serial number**
   - **Unique device ID**
   - **Date and time when the latest backup was made**: The time is displayed in the time zone that is local for the acquiring PC; this is essential if the device being analyzed belongs to a different time zone
   - **Size of backup**

6. Select the device(s) whose backups you would like to download by selecting the checkboxes on the left.

7. Define the options for downloading backups. Click **Info** to view hints for each option.

   - **Restore original file names**: If selected, this allows saving all backup files with the same filenames as in the iOS operating system, including the full path. For example, messages (SMS and iMessage) are saved as `\HomeDomain\Library\SMS\sms.db` (SQLite format). If this option is not selected, the backup will be saved in the iTunes format (the same format is used for local backups).

If you are using a third-party mobile forensic product, make sure to disable the **Restore original file names** option. If you disable this option, the backup will be saved in the iTunes format supported by virtually all mobile forensic tools on the market.
The option for restoring original filenames is automatically enabled for **Download only specific data** mode, as follows:

   - **Download only specific data**: By specifying this option, you can speed up the investigation by quickly downloading the most important data first. Please note that this option is not a replacement for full iCloud backup analysis. Instead, it is more of a *quick peek* of the most essential data.

8. After defining all the options, click **Download**.

9. Specify the location on your local computer where the downloaded files will be stored by using**Select Folder**.

10. The download begins.

> Attempts to download partial (in-progress) backups will fail.

11. The tool puts a check mark next to the downloaded backup once the download is complete. Click **Finish** to exit the downloading wizard.

The downloaded backup is now available on your computer for further analysis. You can use http://www.elcomsoft.com/epv.html to browse and view the content of the backup.

Downloading iCloud/iCloud Drive backups – using authentication tokens

It is natural to expect that one needs the original login credentials (Apple ID and password) to access information stored in the cloud. What happens if you don't know the user's Apple ID and password, but have access to their computer that was used to sync with iCloud (or iCloud Drive)? If this is the case, you may attempt connecting to iCloud using a binary authentication token extracted from the user's computer.

The use of a binary authentication token provides the ability to bypass the login and password authentication of Apple iCloud. As an added benefit, using an authentication token bypasses any two-factor authentication specified by the user.

Technically speaking, authentication tokens are small binary files created by iCloud Control Panel to spare the user from entering their login and password every time they sync with the cloud. The token can be extracted from the user's computer if iCloud Control Panel (or iCloud for Windows) is installed and if the user was logged into the Panel on that computer at the time of token acquisition. If the user logs out of iCloud Control Panel, the token is deleted and invalidated, meaning it can no longer be used to access iCloud data even if carved from the hard disk.

 Authentication tokens do not contain a password to the user's Apple account. They don't contain a hash of the password either. You cannot use an authentication token to brute-force the original plain-text password.

The iCloud Control Panel is an integral part of macOS systems. Windows systems can use iCloud for Windows. For convenience, users stay logged in to their iCloud Control Panel for seamlessly syncing contacts, passwords (iCloud Keychain), photos, and other types of data. This means it is highly likely to be able to obtain authentication tokens from computers where iCloud Control Panel (iCloud for Windows) is installed.

Downloading an iCloud backup using an authentication token works similarly to using an Apple ID and password, except that you will need to supply an authentication token instead of the user's Apple ID and password on the following screen:

Please note that you will need to copy the complete authentication token string from the text file extracted with the appropriate command-line tool. In the following screenshot, the entire second line of the text file represents the authentication token:

Extracting authentication tokens

A valid authentication token can only be extracted from a system if all of the following are true (in this case, we're discussing a Windows PC):

- The user has iCloud for Windows installed
- The user logged in to iCloud for Windows and did not sign out by the time of acquisition
- The user did not change their Apple ID password by the time of acquisition

 Connection to a physical iOS device is not required at any stage.

Elcomsoft Phone Breaker offers two different methods for extracting tokens. When extracting a binary authentication token from the currently logged in user on a live system, investigators can use the supplied command-line tool (`atex.exe`). In all other cases, Elcomsoft Phone Breaker offers a convenient user interface.

The authentication token must be extracted from the user's computer, hard drive, or forensic disk image before it can be used. Elcomsoft Phone Breaker comes with tools allowing locating, extracting, and decrypting of binary authentication tokens. The tools can extract authentication tokens for all users of that computer including domain users (providing that their system login passwords are known). In addition, authentication tokens can be extracted offline from the user's hard drive or forensic disk image. Command-line tools are available for both Windows and macOS X.

Let us see how extracting authentication tokens works in Windows. For instructions on how to extract authentication tokens in macOS X, visit
`http://www.elcomsoft.com/help/en/eppb/extracting_authentication_mac.html`.

The authentication token can be extracted for the current iCloud Control Panel user as well as for all other users in the system providing that the correct account password (or the administrative password) is known. In addition, one can extract authentication tokens from binary files m, stored on virtual disks or forensic disk images. For the sake of simplicity, let's extract an authentication token for the current user of iCloud Control Panel.

To extract the authentication token for the current iCloud for Windows user on a Windows PC, do the following:

1. Launch `atex.exe`. A file named `icloud_token_<timestamp>.txt` will be created in the same folder where you launch the tool from (or in the `C:\Users\<user name>\AppData\Local\Temp` folder, if you don't have enough permissions for writing files to the folder where `atex.exe` was launched from).

2. The full path to the extracted file will be displayed in the console window:

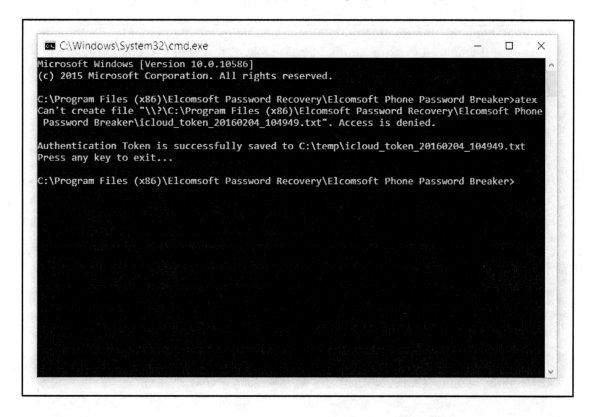

3. The resulting file with a `.txt` extension contains the Apple ID of the current iCloud Control Panel user and its authentication token.

If you need to extract authentication tokens for other Windows users, or if you are working with a forensic disk image, you can use the token extraction wizard.

4. Launch Elcomsoft Phone Breaker and select **Extract authentication token**.

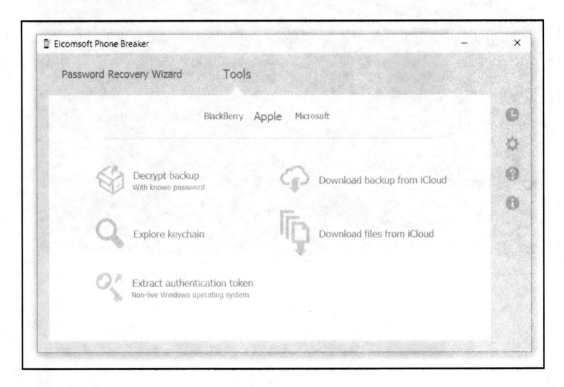

5. Specify the path to the token file (usually `%appdata%\Apple Computer\Preferences\`).

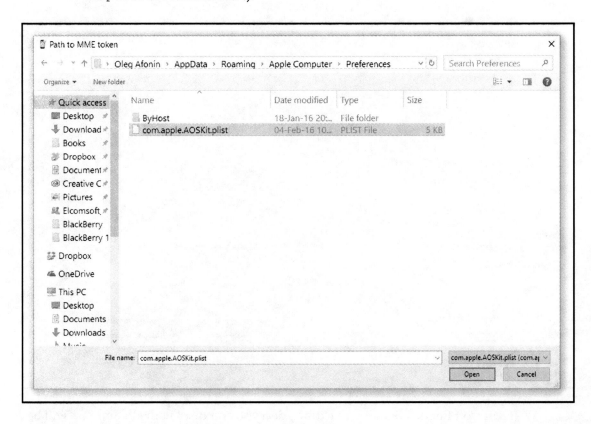

6. Specify the path to the master key (required to decrypt the token) and click **Extract**. This key is used to decrypt the authentication token.

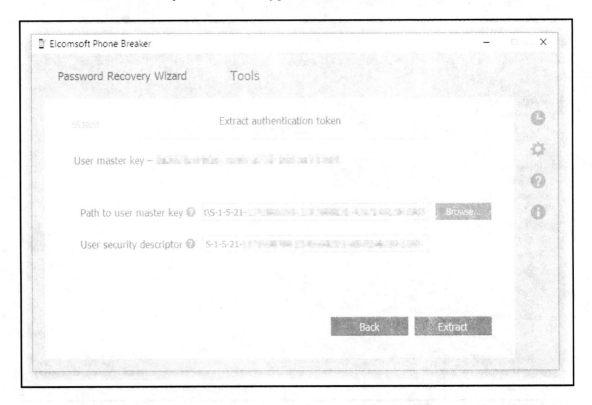

7. Elcomsoft Phone Breaker will extract, decrypt, and display the token. You will be able to export the token into a file. You can now use this token to log into iCloud and download backup from iCloud.

Once again, if you are using a macOS X computer, read the following document for step-by-step instructions:

```
http://www.elcomsoft.com/help/en/eppb/extracting_authentication_mac.html
```

Up to date information on extracting authentication tokens is available at
```
https://www.elcomsoft.com/help/en/eppb/index.html?extracting_token_on_non-live_
w.html.
```

iCloud authentication tokens (iOS 6 through 9) – limitations

So are these binary authentication tokens (ATEX) a silver bullet of iOS forensics? We thought so for a few months after discovering this acquisition method. However, Apple has implemented some changes, making iCloud acquisition via binary authentication tokens a somewhat less attractive proposition.

 Depending on iOS version, ATEX tokens extracted from iCloud Control Panel may have limited usability. While one can still use the token to log in to iCloud and view the list of devices and their corresponding backups, on some rare occasions the token may be only valid for one hour for the purpose of downloading iCloud backups. This applies to iOS 8.x.

The validity period of iCloud authentication tokens was severely reduced by Apple in response to the celebrity photos hack. However, as new authentication methods became available (which includes two-step verification, later superseded by two-factor authentication), Apple relaxed the rules again.

 The quick token expiration does *not* apply to the new Apple iCloud Drive. While "classic" iCloud tokens apparently expire after one hour, these same tokens when used to authenticate into iCloud Drive (which is used to extract data including cloud backups from devices running iOS 9 and newer) do not appear to have such a short lifespan. We couldn't determine exactly how long the tokens are valid for this purpose, but the lifespan is certainly much longer than that of the *classic* iCloud.

The following table explains what ATEX tokens for the *classic* Apple iCloud (iOS 6 through 8) are good for:

	Within one hour of iCloud Control Panel login	After one hour and until expiry
List of devices	Yes	Yes
List of iCloud backups	Yes	Yes
Downloading iCloud backups	Yes	• No (iOS 8.x) • Yes (iOS 9.x)
Downloading files stored in iCloud Drive	Yes	Yes

iCloud Drive authentication tokens (iOS 9 and newer) – a different beast altogether

Since iOS 9, Apple keeps cloud backups in iCloud Drive instead of the *classic* iCloud. iCloud Drive tokens are governed by different rules, and do not appear to have such a short lifespan as iCloud tokens.

That being said, we were unable to determine the exact validity period of iCloud Drive tokens. It's definitely much longer than that of the "classic" iCloud ATEX tokens, and it's definitely longer than a few days. As a result, cloud extraction of iOS 9 and newer devices has more chances to succeed compared to iOS 8.

Quick start – selective downloading

Apple iCloud is not exactly the fastest cloud on the planet. In fact, it can be pretty slow at times. Much slower than the speed the average broadband connections. In reality, this means that downloading of full iCloud backup may take several hours, or even overnight in some cases.

However, you may not even need the full dataset of iOS devices. The user's call history, messages, browsing data, notes, contacts, social communications, and some other types of data are extremely important for an investigation, yet they take very little space in the phone. Considering the speed of Apple iCloud, you may choose to spend a few minutes downloading some selected types of data before obtaining the full backup.

If you need some data right away to start your investigation, you may use the **Download only specific data** option available in Elcomsoft Phone Breaker.

Next, you'll need to click Customize to specify the types of data to download.

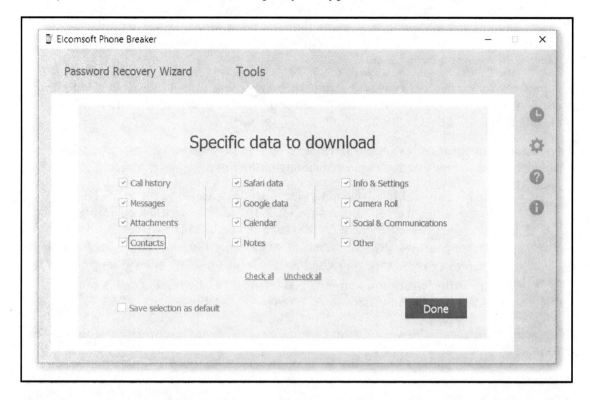

Do realize that this option is not a proper substitute for full iCloud backup analysis. Its intended purpose is to provide a *quick peek* at the most essential data, allowing you to start your investigation while the full backup is still being downloaded.

More information on the types of data available for selective download is available at `http://www.elcomsoft.com/help/en/eppb/downloading_specific_data.html`.

Two-factor authentication

The world of IT security is constantly changing. Recent security outbreaks made Apple implement additional security measures. These increased security measures include the expansion of two-factor authentication and the delivery of notifications to users when information stored in their cloud account is being accessed from a new device. Two-factor authentication is now available (yet still remains optional) for cloud backups.

Apple has also announced an additional two-factor authentication method. In addition to existing authentication methods that include a verification code on the trusted device and recovery key, the app-specific password method has been added. However, app-specific passwords have little to do with forensic acquisition as they are not related to either backups or files stored in the cloud.

The pressure for extra security was so strong that Apple was forced to tighten iCloud security ahead of the iOS 8 release. This put an end to using many third-party tools for accessing the cloud if two-factor authentication was enabled.

Two-factor authentication (as well as the older two-step verification) is still optional. If enabled, experts can only access cloud data if any of the following is available:

- **Security code sent to a trusted device** must have access to the trusted device or SIM card with a trusted phone number. A trusted device must be unlocked in order to see the security code. A SIM card can be used to receive a verification text message in any device; there is no need to use the original iPhone for that.
- **Recovery key** created during the time the two-step verification is set.
- **Binary authentication token** obtained from one of the trusted devices or extracted from a computer

Two-factor authentication covers iCloud backups as well as other information stored in the cloud.

Two-factor authentication is optional

As of today (May 2016), Apple does not enforce two-factor authentication on its customers. Enforcing the extra authentication takes its toll on the ease of use and convenience Apple users are accustomed to. The extra authentication step could lead some users to abandon the idea of cloud backups. As a result, Apple still tries to find a balance by trial and error.

Apple does not disclose the number of users who have two-factor authentication enabled. Two-factor authentication and two-step authentication are still not completely transparent. In the real world, we don't see many Apple users enabling two-factor authentication. We expect the two-factor authentication acceptance rate to grow slowly but steadily in the foreseeable future.

Two-factor authentication versus two-step verification – understanding the differences

Two-step verification and two-factor authentication are two distinctly different yet confusingly similar processes aiming to secure access to Apple ID and associated services. Both methods add a secondary authentication factor in addition to the already used Apple ID and password, verifying *something you have* in addition to *something you know*.

Unlike other companies (for example, Google), Apple does not use a single two-factor authentication solution. Instead, the company had to use two different processes with similar user experience, slightly different names, and completely different technical implementation. What was the reason behind using two different processes? The reality is, **two-step verification** was a rushed afterthought. Apple had to act quickly during the scandal with the celebrity photos leak, implementing tighter security to users of existing (and legacy) versions of iOS. On the other hand, **two-factor authentication** (aren't you already confused?) appeared in iOS 9 and macOS El Capitan, and is available exclusively to users of the latest iOS versions. So what are the differences between the two verification processes, and what is their effect on mobile forensics? Let's try to find out.

Apple official documentation about the two verification methods.
Two-step verification:

- **Two-step verification (2SV)**: https://support.apple.com/en-us/HT24152
- **App-specific passwords**: https://support.apple.com/en-us/HT24397

Two-factor authentication:

- **Two-factor authentication (2FA)**: https://support.apple.com/en-us/HT24915
- **Getting verification codes with 2FA**: https://support.apple.com/en-us/HT24974

Two-step verification

Two-step verification (2SV) was introduced in 2013 as a rushed response to the iCloud celebrity hack. It was released ahead of iOS 8 to protect access to certain activities with users' Apple ID. 2SV adds an extra verification step when logging in to Apple ID services. The secondary verification step is mandatory when signing into Apple ID or iCloud or making a purchase from a new device (please refer to the earlier Apple links for more information).

For the purpose of digital forensics, the important part is how Apple delivers codes that serve as the secondary authentication factor.

There are four different methods in which users can receive codes for two-step verification.

Delivering secondary verification codes:

- Push notification to a trusted device
- Text message or phone call to a trusted phone number
- Recovery key (offline)
- App-specific password

Enabling two-step verification:

- From an Apple device
- Online via My Apple ID

Two-factor authentication

Unlike two-step verification,which was a rushed afterthought, two-factor authentication (first released in 2015 with iOS 9) is a real technological improvement over the previous scheme. The new and improved security method requires built-in OS support, and only works in iOS 9 and later or OS X El Capitan and later. Importantly, two-factor authentication (2FA) cannot be used with devices running older versions of iOS. Availability of two-factor authentication is currently limited to some regions. 2FA will roll out slowly to all regions.

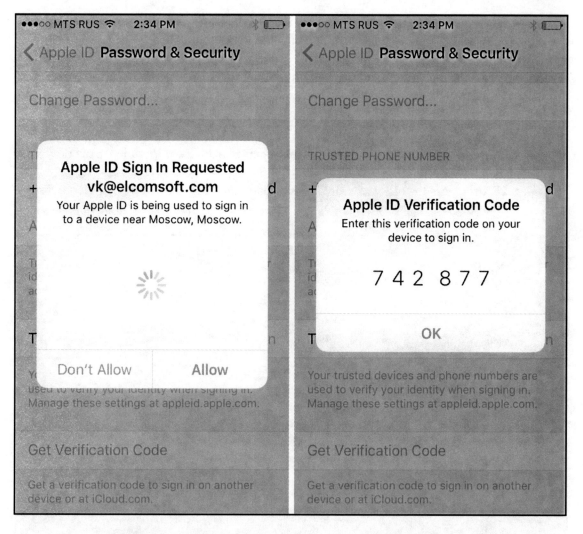

Two-factor authentication lost offline recovery keys and app-specific passwords.

Delivering secondary authentication codes:

- Push notification to a trusted device (interactive prompt appears on all trusted devices; device must be unlocked to allow access and to see the code).
- Text message or phone call to a registered number (using the **Did not get a verification code?** link).

- **New**: No application-specific passwords. Appending a 6-digit authentication code to the original password can be used to authenticate apps not supporting two-factor authentication.
- **New**: Offline authentication via a time-dependent code generated from the settings of a trusted device.

Enabling two-factor authentication:

- One can only enable two-factor authentication from a compatible Apple device (iOS 9, El Capitan). No Web-based online activation possible.
- 2FA replaces the older 2SV. If 2SV is already enabled, it must be disabled before enabling two-factor authentication.

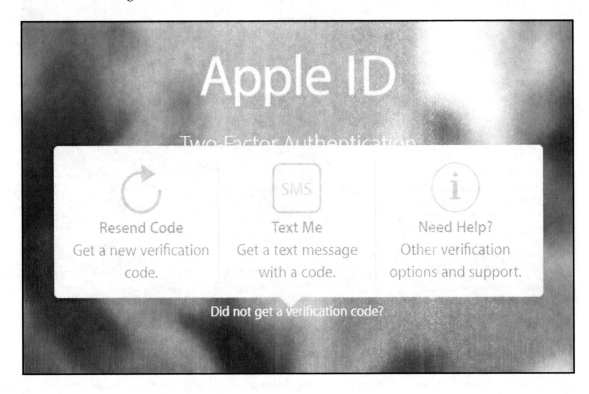

A major advance in two-factor authentication is the ability to generate (and use) authentication codes offline by requesting them from a trusted device.

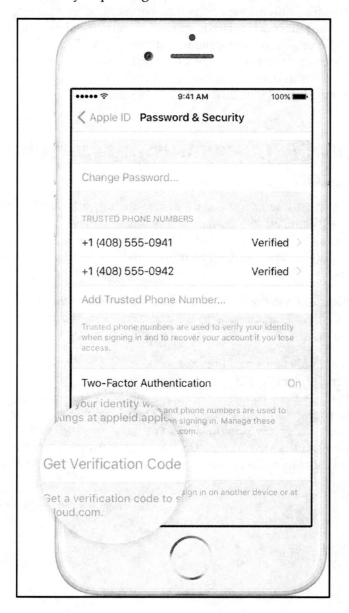

These new offline authentication codes work similar to Google's and Microsoft's implementations. A new code is generated every 30 seconds. There is a difference to Google's and Microsoft's authenticator apps though. Apple uses a unique seed for each trusted device, meaning that each trusted device generates a unique authentication code, while Google and Microsoft only allow maintaining a single seed for all authenticator apps. This means that Apple users can revoke 2FA authorization from each individual device, while Google and Microsoft users revoking 2FA authentication would immediately invalidate all authenticator apps installed on all trusted devices.

No app-specific passwords in two-factor authentication

There are no more app-specific passwords available to support apps that don't recognize Apple's two-factor authentication scheme. Also gone are Recovery Keys. When accessing a device or service protected with two-factor authentication, users who have at least one device without support for 2FA (such as an iPhone with iOS 8 or older) will see the following prompt:

Some of your devices are not ready for two-factor authentication. If you continue you will have to add a six-digit verification code to the end of your password any time you enter password on an old device

Apple seems to have made steps making this not as inconvenient as it could be. The first time one attempts making an App Store purchase from an iOS 8.3 device (no 2FA support), one is prompted to enter the password with a 6-digit code appended at the end. A trusted device displays the prompt and the code. Interestingly, in a test we've carried out the next day, the regular Apple ID password worked. To reiterate, we did not have to attach the 6-digit code when we used the same device the next day. However, our trusted device (running iOS 9) still displayed the prompt and the code—yet we didn't have to use it. This is rather confusing.

What if you don't have access to the secondary authentication factor? No trusted device and no access to a registered phone number.

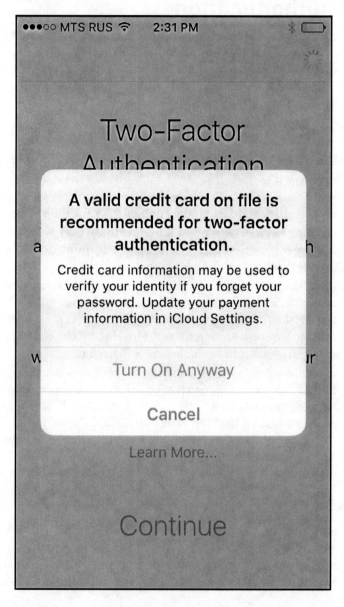

In this case, the official path is submitting a request to Apple to regain access to Apple ID with two-factor authentication account recovery
https://support.apple.com/en-us/HT204921.

Cloud acquisition with two-step verification and two-factor authentication

If you're using Elcomsoft Phone Breaker for cloud acquisition, and if an Apple ID is protected with either 2SV or 2FA, you will need that secondary authentication factor in order to be able to authenticate and access the backups. If two-step verification is enabled on the Apple ID, Elcomsoft Phone Breaker will automatically prompt to enter the secondary authentication code.

Please note the following:

- App-specific passwords cannot be used to download iCloud backups.
- If the device runs iOS 8.x or earlier, it can only use two-step verification (and not two-factor authentication). However, if the user has at least one device supporting 2FA, they may still have enabled 2FA for their Apple ID regardless.
- One option to proceed if two-factor authentication is enabled for a given Apple ID is generating (or receiving) a 6-digit authentication code. *When authenticating Elcomsoft Phone Breaker, you can append that six-digit code to the end of the password.*
- If you're acquiring a backup from an Apple account that uses two-factor authentication (iOS 9 and newer) and you are using an offline 2FA code generated from the trusted device's settings, note that such codes are short-lived. You can only authenticate using these codes during the first 30 minutes after they've been generated, after which they will expire.
- If you don't have access to the secondary authentication factor, you may try using a binary authentication token. Such tokens can be acquired from a computer with iCloud Control Panel (iCloud for Windows) installed. These tokens don't seem to expire for iOS 9 backups that are stored in iCloud Drive, but are known to expire quickly for iOS 8.x and earlier backups located in the *classic* iCloud.

What next?

Acquiring information from an iOS device is one of the first steps. The next step is viewing the data, then discovering and analyzing evidence. There are many excellent forensic tools available for analyzing information extracted from all types of mobile devices. These tools range from extremely simple to large all-in-one packages allowing you to cross-analyze multiple data sources at once.

If you don't have experience with any of these tools, you may want to start with something light and simple—like, for example, Elcomsoft Phone Viewer.

Elcomsoft Phone Viewer is a small, lightweight tool one can use to view information extracted from mobile backups. The tool can display contacts, messages, call logs, notes, calendar data, as well as many other types of data. It is also possible to view deleted SMS and iMessages stored in iOS backups.

Summary

In this chapter, we've covered the two most commonly used iOS acquisition methods: logical acquisition and cloud extraction. We discussed backup encryption and password protection and learned about cloud backups and iCloud authentication. We covered the differences between Apple's two-step verification and two-factor authentication, and provided comprehensive step-by-step tutorials covering logical acquisition and cloud extraction. In the next chapter, we'll move from Apple's platform to Microsoft's, and discuss available acquisition options for Windows Phone 8/8.1 and Windows 10 Mobile.

7
Acquisition – Approaching Windows Phone and Windows 10 Mobile

Windows Phone is a newcomer in the mobile market. Microsoft is playing aggressively, selling large numbers of low-cost devices through many wireless carriers. The operating system is optimized to run perfectly even on low-end hardware and it offers a much smoother user experience on cheap phones, compared to the bulkier and heavier Android.

According to IDC (`http://www.idc.com/prodserv/smartphone-os-market-share.jsp`), Windows Phone accounts for some 2.6% market share (Q2 2015). 8.8 million units were sold in Q2 of 2015.

Unlike BlackBerry, whose market share has been dropping year over year, Microsoft manages to grow its user base by selling millions of inexpensive devices in emerging markets, such as India. Windows Phone is a strong third after Google Android and Apple iOS, while BlackBerry barely makes it into the **Others** chart.

According to Kantar (`http://www.kantarworldpanel.com/smartphone-os-market-share/intro`), in December 2015 Windows Phone devices accounted for 6.4% of all smartphone sales in Germany (compared to the 20.2% market share of Apple iPhone). In the U.S., Windows Phone accounts for 1.6% of smartphone sales, while iOS enjoys a healthy market share of 39.1%.

In general, Windows Phone becomes a popular choice in Europe (9.2% in Great Britain and 8.1% in Italy). The Microsoft mobile operating system is uncommon in Asia (1.2% in China and nearly absent in Japan):

Smartphone OS Sales Share (%)

Germany	3 m/e Sep 2013	3 m/e Sep 2014	% pt. Change	USA	3 m/e Sep 2013	3 m/e Sep 2014	% pt. Change
Android	77.9	79.2	1.3	Android	57.3	61.8	4.5
iOS	10.7	11.8	1.1	iOS	35.9	32.6	-3.3
Windows	8.5	7.1	-1.4	Windows	4.6	4.3	-0.3
Other	2.9	1.8	-1.1	Other	2.1	1.2	-0.9
GB	3 m/e Sep 2013	3 m/e Sep 2014	% pt. Change	**China**	3 m/e Sep 2013	3 m/e Sep 2014	% pt. Change
Android	55.5	58.2	2.7	Android	80.4	83.4	3.0
iOS	29.3	31.0	1.7	iOS	13.8	15.2	1.4
Windows	10.0	9.6	-0.4	Windows	3.2	0.4	-2.8
Other	5.2	1.2	-4.0	Other	2.6	1.0	-1.6
France	3 m/e Sep 2013	3 m/e Sep 2014	% pt. Change	Australia	3 m/e Sep 2013	3 m/e Sep 2014	% pt. Change
Android	68.2	72.7	4.5	Android	55.6	58.1	2.5
iOS	15.0	15.4	0.4	iOS	32.6	34.7	2.1
Windows	10.7	10.6	-0.1	Windows	9.3	6.2	-3.1
Other	6.1	1.2	-4.9	Other	2.5	1.0	-1.5
Italy	3 m/e Sep 2013	3 m/e Sep 2014	% pt. Change	Japan	3 m/e Sep 2013	3 m/e Sep 2014	% pt. Change
Android	71.6	71.8	0.2	Android	50.0	64.5	14.5
iOS	10.2	10.4	0.2	iOS	47.2	31.3	-15.9
Windows	13.7	15.2	1.5	Windows	0.7	0.9	0.2
Other	4.6	2.6	-2.0	Other	2.1	3.2	1.1
Spain	3 m/e Sep 2013	3 m/e Sep 2014	% pt. Change	EU5	3 m/e Sep 2013	3 m/e Sep 2014	% pt. Change
Android	89.5	90.4	0.9	Android	72.5	73.9	1.4
iOS	4.8	6.3	1.5	iOS	13.9	15.4	1.5
Windows	3.8	3.0	-0.8	Windows	9.4	9.2	-0.3
Other	1.9	0.3	-1.6	Other	4.2	1.5	-2.7

Source: http://wp7forum.ru/kantar-worldpanel-otchet-po-dole-rynka-mobilnyx-operacionnyx-sistem-za-sentyabr-2014-goda/

Windows Phone security model

A comprehensive whitepaper on the Windows Phone 8 security model is available from Microsoft at `http://download.microsoft.com/download/B/9/A/B9A269-28D5-4ACA-9E8E -E2E722B35A7D/Windows-Phone-8-1-Security-Overview.pdf`.

Windows Phone physical acquisition

Apparently, Microsoft did a great job protecting Windows Phone devices. Indeed, Microsoft has full control over the platform (Qualcomm) that is used by the different manufacturers of Windows Phone devices, so unlike Android there can be no sub-standard implementations here. As a result, all Windows Phone devices are roughly equivalent in terms of security. Until very recently, JTAG and chipoff acquisitions were the only methods to acquire most Windows Phones. However, in January 2015, Cellebrite implemented an acquisition module enabling investigators to perform physical acquisition of a lot of Lumia devices. The technology is still at an early stage. There's still a lot to do in parsing the contents. However, the filesystem is NTFS, and the OS is very similar to Windows, so eventually, this will be done.

Since then, yet another development emerged. **Windows Phone Internals** (`http://www.wpi nternals.net/`) developed a bootloader unlock method for Lumia 520, 521, 525, 620, 625, 720, 820, 920, 925, 928, 1020, and 1320. Devices with unlocked bootloaders can be used to boot unsigned code which, in turn, can be used for the purpose of physical acquisition.

JTAG forensics on Windows Phone 8.x and Windows 10 Mobile

Similar to Android, most Windows Phone 7.x, 8.x, and Windows 10 Mobile devices can be successfully acquired via the process of JTAG forensics. The process is very similar to that of acquiring Android devices, so refer to JTAG acquisition in the following chapter, JTAG Forensics [p.42].

The chances of successfully JTAGging a Windows smartphone are very high compared to Android devices. However, things happen to change with regard to JTAG acquisition as Windows Phone 8.x devices upgrade to Windows 10 Mobile.

Windows Phone 8.x device encryption

Windows Phone 8 and 8.1 do not offer a user-configurable setting for encrypting the data partition. According to the official **Windows Phone 8.1 Security Overview** document (which can be downloaded from `https://download.microsoft.com/download/B/9/A/B9A` `269-28D5-4ACA-9E8E-E2E722B35A7D/Windows-Phone-8-1-Security-Overview.pdf`), internal storage can only be encrypted via a corporate security policy by implementing the**Require Device Encryption** policy. When activated, the policy prevents users from disabling device encryption and forces encryption of internal storage. No escrow keys are created or uploaded to anywhere on the network to allow decrypting the encrypted partition. When enabled, Windows Phone 8.1 devices are encrypted with BitLocker technology using**Advanced Encryption Standard (AES)** 128-bit encryption.

 Important: There is no user-accessible option anywhere in Windows Phone 8.x settings to enable or disable encryption. Encryption can be only enabled via a pushed corporate policy. As a result, the majority of end-user devices remain unencrypted with no possibility for the user to encrypt data.

Windows 10 Mobile device encryption

This system has changed in Windows 10 Mobile. In this version of the OS, users can enable encryption manually via **Settings** | **System** | **Device encryption**:

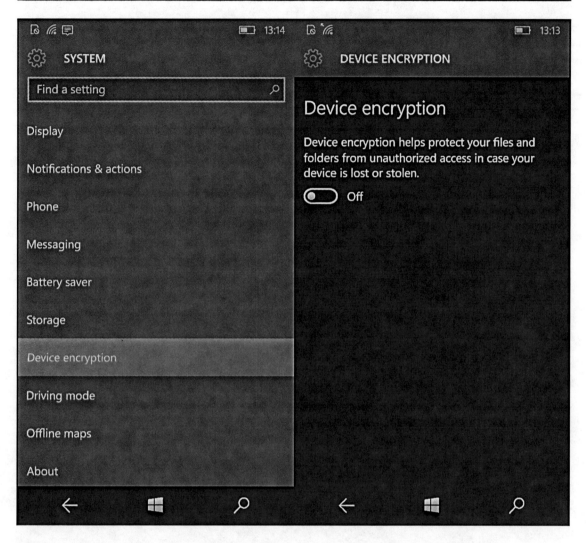

Interestingly, Windows 10 Mobile allows users to disable device encryption after it's been enabled. This is something that is not possible in Android. In order to disable device encryption, users simply turn the slider **Off** on the same configuration screen.

With regard to JTAG acquisition, encrypted devices present little interest and must be decrypted prior to acquisition. In order to decrypt the device, the correct PIN code must be entered to unlock the device; however, Windows 10 Mobile makes encryption possible even without a PIN code. In Windows 10 Mobile, there is no user-configurable provision to wipe device memory after n unsuccessful login attempts; therefore, hardware-based PIN recovery options are possible for such devices.

Windows Phone 8/8.1 and Windows 10 Mobile cloud forensics

Windows Phone 8 and 8.1 devices, as well as devices running Windows 10 Mobile, can use Microsoft OneDrive (formerly SkyDrive) via a Microsoft account (formerly My Windows Phone). Microsoft backups contain information in separate pieces in an obscure format. Manually analyzing this data is difficult even if you happen to know the user's Live ID and password or obtain the backup directly from Microsoft.

When acquiring data from Microsoft cloud, **Elcomsoft Phone Breaker** downloads information by chunks and creates an artificial backup. This backup mostly utilizes the SQLite format, thus enabling experts to use standard forensic tools to analyze its content. The tool also extracts a list of devices registered with a certain Microsoft account.

Elcomsoft Phone Breaker can extract the following data for Windows Phone and Windows 10 Mobile devices:

- Contacts
- Notes
- SMS messages

Downloaded data is saved as an archive that contains SQLite databases, as well as a `Manifest.xml` file containing information about every device from this user's Microsoft account and listing filenames for every database file.

Acquiring Windows Phone backups over the air

Elcomsoft Phone Breaker allows downloading Windows Phone data backed up in the cloud under the user's Microsoft account (provided that you know the user's Microsoft account login and password).

To download Windows Phone data from Microsoft OneDrive, perform the following steps:

1. In the **Tools** menu, select the **Microsoft** tab, and click on **Download Windows Phone data**:

2. Define the **User name** and **Password** for the Microsoft account that was used for backing the data up. Toggle the view button to display or hide the password:

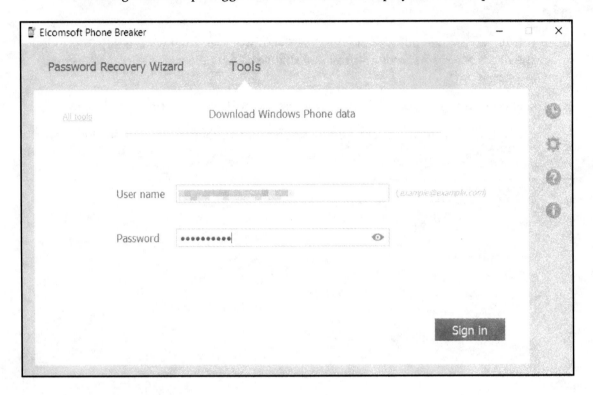

3. Select a location for saving data downloaded from the Microsoft account.

- Click on **Change user** to access data stored under a different Microsoft account
- Click on **Download** to start downloading data:

4. The download process begins. You can view the number of processed files and the number of errors received during decryption:

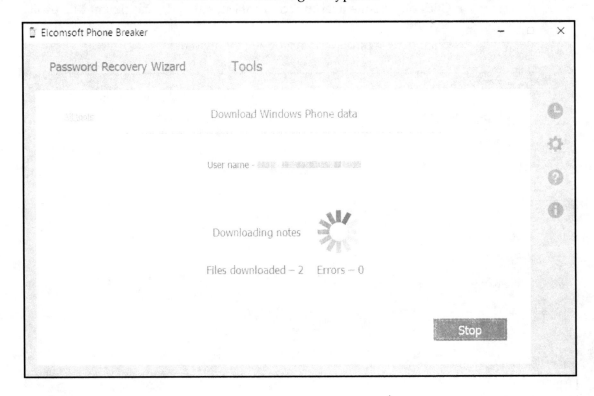

5. When the decryption is finished, you can view the backup in the location on the local computer to which it was saved by clicking on the **View** button. To view detailed information about decrypted files and errors that occurred during decryption, click on **Details**:

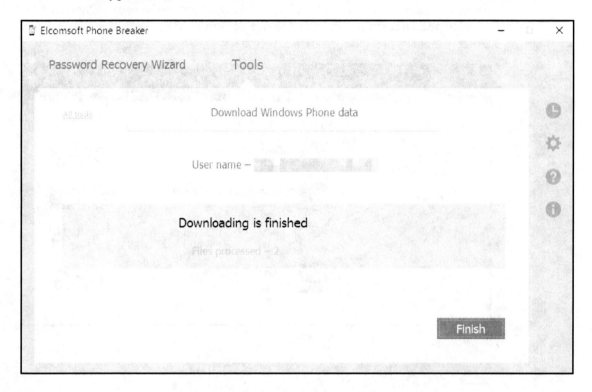

6. Click on **Finish** to close the wizard.

The artificially created backup file is now available on your computer for further analysis. You can use **Elcomsoft Phone Viewer** to browse and view the content of this backup. At this time, the tool extracts contacts, messages, and notes (in the MS OneNote format); Elcomsoft Phone Viewer can extract these notes into individual * . one files.

Note: You can use the same Microsoft account credentials to access other information stored in the user's Microsoft account. This includes e-mail (Hotmail), online cloud storage (OneDrive), Skype contacts and history (Skype), and other services managed under the **Microsoft Live** umbrella. A list of available backups can be viewed by signing into the user's OneDrive account and choosing **Settings | Device backups** (`https://onedrive.live.com/Options/DeviceBackups`):

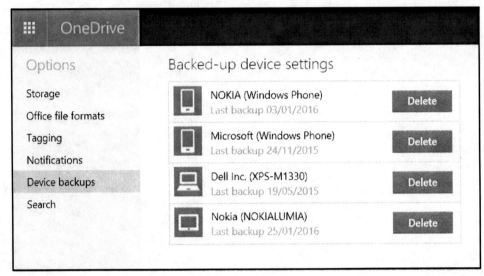

You can now open the backup in Elcomsoft Phone Viewer. You'll be able to access contacts, messages, and notes created on all devices synced with the same Microsoft Account:

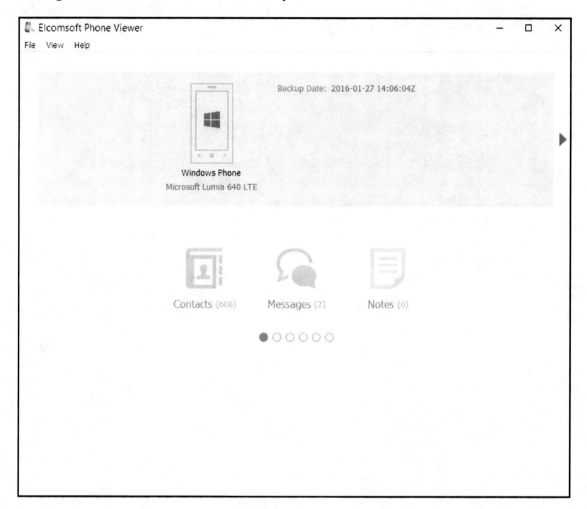

The account captured during this session contains backups made by six Windows devices, including Microsoft Lumia 640 and Nokia Lumia 930 phones, a ThinkPad 8 tablet, a Nokia Lumia 2520 tablet running Windows RT, a desktop PC, and a laptop. Once downloaded, the backup can be accessed via the following interface:

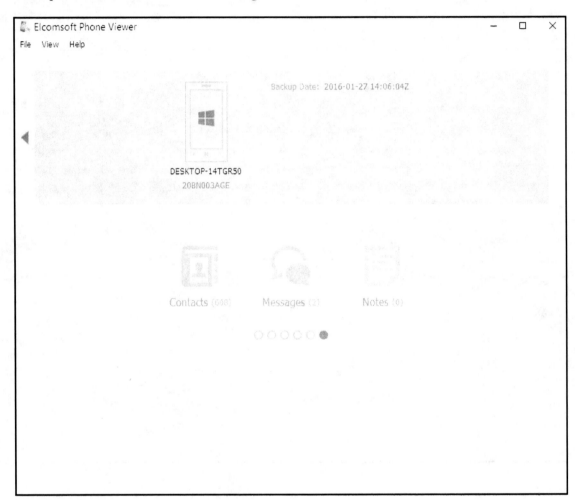

Messages are only available when downloading the information backed up by a Windows smartphone:

Contacts, on the other hand, are available on all devices and are synced with the user's Outlook / Hotmail / Windows Live account:

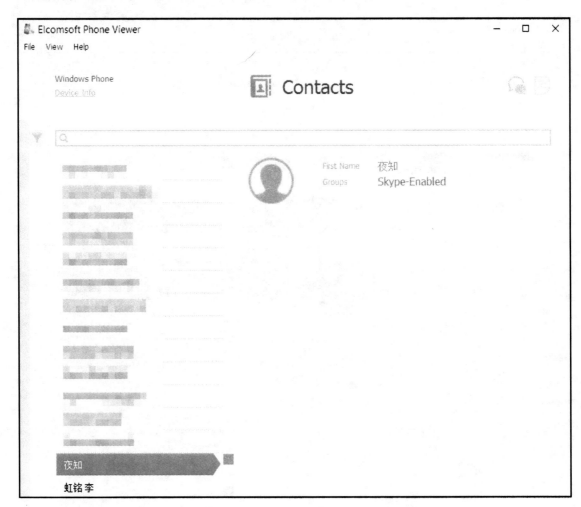

At this time, cloud acquisition options for Windows devices are limited to information seen earlier. The actual device backups (`https://onedrive.live.com/Options/DeviceBackup s`) are securely encrypted. Further research is required in order to be able to retrieve and decrypt these backups:

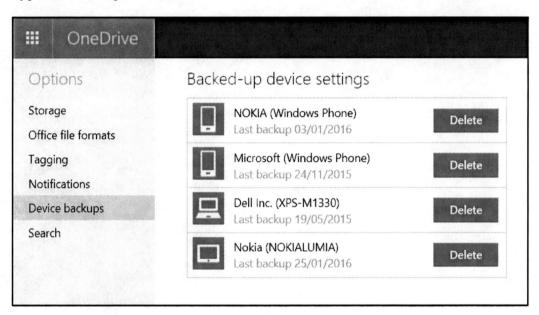

Summary

In this chapter, we talked about Windows forensics as applicable to mobile devices. We also covered the acquisition of Windows Phone 8.x and Windows 10 Mobile smartphones. We discussed cloud acquisition and its limitation on the Windows platform, and learned how to use Elcomsoft Phone Breaker to extract backup data from Microsoft OneDrive. In the next chapter, we'll continue discussing the Windows platform, although this time we'll look into the next class of devices—tablets running the Windows and Windows RT OS.

8
Acquisition – Approaching Windows 8, 8.1, 10, and RT Tablets

This is not a book on Windows forensics. Acquiring, imaging, and analyzing Windows data is one of the most developed areas in digital forensics. In this book, we'll be covering major points that make tablet forensics different from the traditional PC and laptop acquisition approach. In this chapter, we'll cover the new Connected Standby mode replacing traditional Sleep and Hibernate modes of Windows laptops, discuss **Secure Boot** on various Windows tablet platforms, review UEFI BIOS settings, and learn how to start the tablet from a bootable USB media. We'll also cover techniques on capturing the content of the device's RAM and imaging non-removable eMMC media. But first let's have a look at what Windows tablets are and what they aren't.

Things we will not be covering in this book include the general steps to create a bootable USB media (this is well covered elsewhere including official Microsoft sources) and the use of bootable USB media made with any particular forensic tool. We will, however, describe these steps for Windows RT devices as standard Windows recovery media cannot be used with RT devices.

Windows 8, 8.1, 10, and RT on portable touchscreen devices

Since the release of Windows 8 back in 2012, Microsoft has been targeting the market of portable electronics. The new tile-based user interface was optimized for touch use, and intended to be used mainly on tablets and portable computers with touchscreens.

Microsoft wanted to be part of the tablet market so bad that they even built a special version of Windows called Windows RT to run on hardware with ARM instruction sets (Snapdragon 800 and NVIDIA Tegra 4 chip sets in Nokia Lumia 2520, Microsoft Surface RT, and Surface 2 among others). Today, Microsoft has officially stated that this was a stopgap measure, while many customers and the IT press have long considered it to be a dead end.

Coincidentally, at about the same time, Intel decided to conquer the market of portable electronic devices and promote x86 architecture by subsidizing manufacturers who opted to use Intel CPUs in their phones and tablets instead of going for the then-prevailing ARM architecture. This lured manufacturers into building tablets and phones featuring Intel processors and running Android. Now, with many portable devices featuring x86 architecture, there was no longer need for Microsoft to go with RT and ARM architecture.

In order to compete with Android being installed on tablets with x86 processors, Microsoft decided to give Windows away to manufacturers of small and inexpensive devices. As a result, Microsoft released a special edition of Windows called Windows 8.1 with Bing, giving it away free of charge to manufacturers of small tablets with display sizes of up to 8 inches. Additional incentives Microsoft offers to manufacturers who install Windows on their tablets are zero licensing fees for its exFAT file system (exFAT is the default file system on 64 GB and larger SDXC cards) and no licensing fees (which manufacturers of Android devices would otherwise have to pay Microsoft).

These incentives actually worked. While there aren't that many Windows tablets around in absolute terms, there are more of those every year. HP Stream 7, Dell Venue 8 Pro, and many other 7″ and 8″ Windows tablets are available for extremely low prices.

Today, there are hundreds of thousands of these devices sold all over the world. While most of these tablets run full Windows (with few Windows RT devices still around), the approach to their acquisition is very different compared to acquiring desktop and laptop computers of yesterday.

Acquisition of Windows tablets

Windows desktop and laptop computers can be relatively easy to acquire. The procedure is well known, and experts have long experience dealing with these machines. For example, in order to obtain a memory dump one can simply plug a USB drive and run a small utility. If that's not possible, one can always exploit a FireWire port (if installed), or even install an add-on FireWire adapter if no IEEE.1394 port is available. This same operation would involve a different technique as far as a tablet PC is concerned.

The relatively new class of Windows devices consists of portable electronic devices, which includes tablets and convertibles (laptops with a detachable keyboard). From a forensic standpoint, these devices are similar to Windows desktops in some aspects, yet very different in other aspects. Let's see how one can approach a tablet computer.

Understanding Secure Boot

Most computers and laptops manufactured during recent years, and pretty much every Windows 8, 8.1, and Windows 10 tablet ever marketed has a feature in their UEFI BIOS called Secure Boot. Secure Boot was developed by members of the PC industry to help secure devices' bootloader against booting non-trusted (or, rather, unsigned) systems. If configured, Secure Boot allows tablets to boot using only software that is trusted by the manufacturer.

The concept of Secure Boot is similar to the concept of locked bootloaders that we've seen on Apple iOS and many Android devices, even if its operation and technical implementation is different. If Secure Boot is enabled in the computer's UEFI BIOS, the computer's firmware verifies digital signatures of each link of the boot chain, including firmware drivers and the operating system during the boot. The computer will only boot if the signatures pass the check.

It is important to understand that disabling Secure Boot is *not* required in order to boot into a Windows 8.x/Windows 10 recovery image, even if that image is stored on an external flash drive. The function of Secure Boot is preventing untrusted, unsigned code to run, so if enabled, it will prevent booting into Linux or another system.

 Secure Boot is still an optional feature that is supported, but not required by Microsoft Windows 8, 8.1, and Windows 10. All Windows RT devices ship locked with non-removable Secure Boot protection, making forensic analysis of these machines much more difficult.

Connected Standby (InstantGo)

Portable Windows devices such as tablets and convertibles are designed around the concept of **Connected Standby**, which means the device never really sleeps or shuts down by itself unless the user specifically invokes the *Power Off* command or the battery is nearly depleted.

In Connected Standby mode, the device consumes as little as five percent of battery per 16 hours of sleep (according to Microsoft specifications). In this mode, the device remains connected to the wireless network, and performs most of the usual background activities such as checking and receiving e-mail, syncing social networks, and updating news feeds.

For digital forensic purposes, this means that any Windows tablet being seized must be treated exactly like an active cell phone. In other words, one must take precautions and place the device immediately into a Faraday bag to block its wireless connectivity. However, it also means that the portable device being acquired is almost definitely in the *On* state, and can be used to acquire a memory dump.

Importantly, **InstantGo** (Connected Standby) is one of the requirements for automatic activation of BitLocker device encryption on Windows tablets.

BitLocker device encryption

BitLocker device encryption is an essential part of the Windows 8.x and Windows 10 security model. Device encryption is essentially a feature-limited version of BitLocker that encrypts the entire C drive partition. Unlike on desktop and laptop computers that are still mostly running on Windows 7, BitLocker device encryption is available to users of all versions of Windows 8.x and 10, including the core edition and Windows with Bing.

Essentially for digital forensics, BitLocker device encryption is activated automatically when the user logs in with their Microsoft Account with administrative privileges. After the first login, the system automatically begins the encryption process. The encryption process runs in the background. The process is transparent and invisible to the end user. The Recovery Key is automatically saved in the user's Microsoft Account, and can be retrieved from that account in order to decrypt the device. In corporate environments, BitLocker escrow keys are saved in the active directory.

Important: The Recovery Key (BitLocker escrow key) saved to the user's Microsoft Account can be deleted by the user at any time. Microsoft states that Recovery Keys deleted from the user's Microsoft Account are permanently destroyed and not retained by the company. As a result, consideration should be taken to prevent the suspect from accessing their Microsoft Account and deleting BitLocker Recovery Keys stored in that account.

BitLocker device encryption is offered on all versions of 8.1 and Windows 10. However, unlike full BitLocker, device encryption requires that the device meet all of the following specifications:

- InstantGo (formerly Connected Standby) support
- Solid-state drive or eMMC storage
- Soldered (non-removable) RAM to protect against cold boot attacks
- **Trusted Platform Module (TPM)** 2.0 chip

All of the above specifications must be met in order for BitLocker device encryption to be activated. Notably, all Windows RT devices and most Windows 8.1 and Windows 10 tablets will naturally meet all of the above specifications, with the exception of a TPM chip that may be missing on some of the cheaper tablets. As a result, BitLocker device encryption is not automatically activated on budget Windows 8.1/Windows 10 devices without a TPM chip.

BitLocker and Encrypting File System

While BitLocker protects the entire operating system drive against offline attacks, **Encrypting File System (EFS)** can provide additional file level security by encrypting individual files and folders on per-user basis. In other words, while BitLocker encryption protects the entire computer contents against outside attacks, EFS helps maintain security separation between multiple users of the same computer. EFS can be used in combination with BitLocker to additionally encrypt files on a BitLocker-protected drive.

BitLocker and hibernation

As we already know, BitLocker stores its binary encryption/decryption keys in the computer's main RAM, which makes it susceptible to memory dumping attacks. However, the BitLocker decryption key may be available in the computer's hibernation file.

Mike Halsey, in his publication *Will Bitlocker's Security Flaw Remain in Windows 8?* (`http://w ww.ghacks.net/212/3/15/will-bitlockers-security-flaw-remain-in-windows-8/`) claims that hibernation is perhaps BitLocker's biggest security flaw. All versions of Windows (up to and including Windows 8.1) will store the hibernation file unencrypted at a certain location on the hard disk. This, in turn, allows using forensic tools (for example, Elcomsoft Forensic Disk Decryptor) to extract the binary decryption keys from the hibernation file itself, and use those keys to instantly unlock the encrypted volume. This is confirmed by Microsoft (`https://technet.microsoft.com/en-us/library/ee449438(v= ws.1).aspx#BKMK_Sleep`) who recommend using additional authentication steps to secure BitLocker encrypted images if hibernate power management is enabled.

Notably, many Windows 8 systems ship with hibernation disabled by default. However, Windows 8.x tablets usually have an option that Microsoft calls *Fast Startup*, a new power management mode that is a method of a hybrid shutdown (or partial hibernate). Since Fast Startup is enabled by default, every time the user shuts down the tablet via the Power charm (as opposed to doing the same via the Windows + *X* menu, which will, counter-intuitively, engage the full shutdown) the system will save its kernel and drivers into a smaller version of the hibernation file (`hiberfil.sys`). By using that file, the system will be able to start up faster when it's next booted.

The partial hibernate file does not contain BitLocker decryption keys.

 Note: If the target computer was turned off or hibernated and the encrypted volume was dismounted during the hibernation, the hibernation file will not contain the encryption keys, and instant decryption of the BitLocker volume will not be possible.

BitLocker acquisition summary

To sum up the content of the previous chapter, if the C drive of hard disk is protected with BitLocker, one has the following acquisition alternatives:

If you have the BitLocker escrow key (Recovery Key), you can do either of the following:

1. Unlock BitLocker partition and image decrypted volume.
2. Image *as is*, decrypt captured image (for example, by saving the image onto a physical hard drive, using a Windows virtual machine or using a forensic product of your choice to decrypt the image).

If you don't have the BitLocker escrow key (Recovery Key):

1. Attempt to capture a memory dump (RAM dump) to acquire the binary decryption key:
    1. For this to work, the computer must be seized in the ON and unlocked state.
    2. If a FireWire (IEEE.1394) port is available, attempt capturing RAM via the FireWire attack.
2. If the tablet was locked, capturing a memory dump is not possible since memory chips are soldered to prevent cold-boot attacks and a FireWire port is usually unavailable on Windows tablets. However, hibernating (if available) or shutting down (if Windows fast startup is enabled) the tablet may produce a usable hibernation file from which the decryption key can be extracted.
3. If the device was seized in the hibernated state, attempt obtaining the hibernation file (`hiberfil.sys`).
4. Use Elcomsoft Forensic Disk Decryptor (`https://www.elcomsoft.com/efdd.html`) to analyze the memory dump or hibernation file, extract the BitLocker binary decryption key, and mount the encrypted volumes.
5. Image decrypted volume.

Capturing a memory dump

Attempting to capture a memory dump of a Windows device is essential for digital investigations. It is also a recommended practice by ACPO Guidelines.

Until recently, law enforcement officials would simply power down computers being seized, losing a large amount of potentially vital evidence stored in the computer's volatile memory. In the world of Windows, this information includes recent activities in social networks, data on running processes, open network connections, cached passwords, and private browsing sessions. Of particular interest are binary encryption keys that can be used to unlock access to encrypted volumes such as those maintained by BitLocker, TrueCrypt, and PGP WDE (Elcomsoft Forensic Disk Decryptor can be used to extract such keys and use them to mount encrypted volumes). These and many other types of evidence can be recovered if the investigator is able to capture and analyze the content of the computer's volatile memory.

This is exactly the reason for ACPO to recommend the capturing and analysis of a computer's RAM at the time of acquisition. Dumping the content of volatile memory has already become a standard operating procedure when acquiring digital evidence just before imaging the computer's persistent storage.

While dumping and analyzing the content of the computer's volatile memory is important, one must realize that due to its very nature RAM is highly volatile and highly fragmented. As a result, one may never find the complete conversation or the entire document being edited. Instead, there could be chunks, bits, and broken parts—which, in turn, can be reassembled into something usable with certain smart carving algorithms (such as Belkasoft Smart Carving). What can be realistically discovered in the computer's RAM?

Types of evidence available in volatile memory

Certain types of evidence are available exclusively in the computer's RAM. This evidence includes:

- Running processes and services
- Unpacked/decrypted versions of protected programs
- System information (for example, time lapsed since last reboot)
- Information about logged in users
- Registry information
- Open network connections and ARP cache
- Remnants of chats, communications in social networks, and MMORPG games
- Recent web browsing activities including IE InPrivate mode and similar privacy-oriented modes in other Web browsers
- Recent communications via Webmail systems
- Information from cloud services
- Decryption keys for encrypted volumes mounted at the time of the capture
- Recently viewed images
- Running malware/Trojans

Special case – Windows RT devices

While many say that Windows RT has never caught up, there were multiple devices sold featuring this little known platform. Microsoft Surface RT and Surface 2 and Nokia Lumia 2520 were among the most popular devices running on the RT platform. So what exactly is Windows RT, and what, if anything, can be done to acquire it?

In fact, Windows RT is simply a variation of Windows 8 or 8.1 running on the ARM processor architecture instead of the familiar x86 or x64. RT features the same modern UI and runs most of the same Metro-style apps as the full Windows, and has access to all of the same system updates as the 'big' Windows. Windows RT has a desktop, and can technically run applications (`.exe` files) compiled for the ARM instruction set. What it can't do is run desktop applications compiled for the Intel x86 architecture.

In addition, Microsoft decided to lock Windows RT desktop mode to only allow running .exe files signed by Microsoft, which means you cannot compile your own application with an ARM compiler and just run it in desktop mode. This effectively rules out live box analysis, and makes it next to impossible to capture live memory dumps with any known forensic tool.

How can one deal with a Windows RT device then? Since we cannot install anything other than Metro-style apps downloaded from Windows Store, we're pretty much limited to offline analysis of its built-in storage.

A live memory dump cannot be easily captured with built-in Windows tools (more information at *How to generate a kernel or a complete memory dump file in Windows Server 2008 and Windows Server 2008 R2*: `https://support.microsoft.com/en-us/kb/96928`; techniques described in this article equally apply to Windows RT). However, the system's default behavior is creating a full memory dump in the case of system failure. If one can make the system crash, there is a good chance that a memory dump will be created.

If making a memory dump is impossible, your best bet is making the system hibernate instead of using connected standby, and even that may not be an option as described in *Shut down, sleep, or hibernate your PC*: `http://windows.microsoft.com/en-us/windows-8/how-shut-down-turn-off-pc`.

However, if you manage to hibernate the device, you will be able to proceed to the next step: making a forensic disk image of the device's built-in storage.

SD cards and Windows File History

As a reminder, most Windows tablets including Windows RT devices come equipped with an SD card slot. A typical configuration allows using one micro SDHC (up to 32 GB) or one micro SDXC (64 GB and larger) memory card. By default, these memory cards are formatted with FAT32 (SDHC) or exFAT (SDXC) and are not encrypted with either BitLocker or built-in NTFS encryption. Therefore, these memory cards are usually an easy target for forensic analysis.

On recent Android devices, memory cards are not normally used to contain application data. Instead, their intended use is storing multimedia files such as large amounts of music and video for offline access. This is not the case with Windows, where the entire content of an SD card is accessible and can be used to keep pretty much everything from user documents, OneDrive contents and data backups, to desktop applications and page files.

The other factor contributing to the use of SD cards in Windows tablets is the fact that the majority of Windows tablets are sold with 32 GB of storage. Of those 32 GB, a measly 6 to 11 GB is available to the end user after the installation of all current Windows updates.

As a result, the users of Windows tablets are more likely to actively use an SD card as secondary (or even primary) storage for their documents, camera roll, and other files.

One Windows feature that's particularly interesting for experts investigating tablet devices is a little known feature called Windows **File History**. If enabled, this feature (available in Windows 8, 8.1, and RT) automatically backs up versions of user files in the Documents, Music, Pictures, Videos, and Desktop folders as well as the OneDrive files available offline to a storage device other than the system partition. If the originals are lost, damaged, or deleted, users can restore them by using copies stored in the File History.

File History contains different versions of user files such as working copies of documents, spreadsheets, old, deleted and unedited versions of pictures, and so on, arranged in a convenient timeline.

There are two important points here:

- Windows File History uses a drive other than the system partition. On Windows tablets, this is almost inevitably the unprotected, unencrypted, and easily removable SD card.
- File History contains current and historic versions of user files.

You may find these quite handy for your investigation.

Imaging Built-in eMMC Storage

In this chapter, we won't be talking about the use of forensic write-blocking hard drive imaging devices. We won't cover any disk imaging software, too, as such tools are readily available with all major forensic suites and you most probably have spent more time with one of those tools than either author of this book. Instead, we'll discuss how to approach a Windows tablet and make it available for imaging with the tool of your choice.

Note: As with smartphones and Android/iOS tablets, eMMC chips used in Windows devices can be unsoldered and placed into an eMMC reader. This destructive method is called chip-off acquisition. Such techniques are widely covered elsewhere. In this book, we'll talk about non-destructive, software-based acquisition.

Most Windows tablets (and all Windows RT devices) come with non-removable storage in the form of eMMC chips. **eMMC** stands for **embedded MMC**, or **embedded MultiMedia Card**, and is closer in operation to a standard SD (Secure Digital) card rather than an SSD drive. In other words, eMMC is a non-removable, BGA flash memory chip soldered onto a circuit board. If the tablet features 32 GB of storage, those 32 GB are located in the eMMC chip.

What does that mean for digital forensics?

As we already know, most Windows tablets (with very few exceptions) feature built-in, non-removable (unless one uses a BGA soldering station) eMMC storage. Let's think for a moment about the fact that the eMMC chip is soldered onto the circuit board. It cannot be removed and put into a write-blocking imaging device. It cannot be connected to another computer. In order to image the built-in storage, the investigator will have to boot into the system and run an imaging tool on the very same device being investigated. This can present challenges due to security settings of some models.

If we're talking about a full Windows tablet, best practice would be booting the system from an external bootable media. Most probably, you have one in your lab already. If not, there are plenty of tools and tutorials to help experts do exactly that, for example, *Create installation media for Windows*: http://windows.microsoft.com/en-us/windows-8/create-reset-refresh-media or http://windows.microsoft.com/en-us/windows-8/create-usb-recovery-drive.

Note: Due to the bug in early builds of 64-bit versions of Windows 8 and 8.1 preventing Connected Standby from functioning properly, many manufacturers of Windows tablets chose to install 32-bit editions onto their devices and provide 32-bit versions of UEFI BIOS. This, in turn, can mean that the system may not be able to boot from a 64-bit recovery media even if the CPU and other hardware is fully 64-bit compatible. On such systems, investigators must use 32-bit recovery media.

eMMC and deleted data recovery

While eMMC memory does not constitute a full replacement for SSD drives, the two types of storage have one thing in common: support for trimming deleted data.

If you think for a moment about how Windows (and most other modern operating systems) manage deleted files, you'll realize that information such as deleted files and folders is not permanently erased. Instead, the system will simply mark files and folders being deleted with a corresponding attribute in the filesystem. Disk space originally occupied by these files will be released to the pool of available disk space. To reiterate, Windows won't do anything to actually wipe or erase data blocks that were previously occupied with deleted data.

This behavior had to change with the introduction of solid-state storage media. NAND flash-based solid-state storage media is much slower to erase data compared to writing to an empty block. In addition, NAND flash cells can be only written to a limited number of times, which made some form of wear leveling necessary. In order to deal with the two issues, the industry adopted a certain protocol for dealing with released data blocks.

A compatible operating system (Windows 7, 8, 8.1 or newer) working with a compatible SSD or eMMC storage formatted with the only compatible file system (NTFS) will issue the TRIM command to instruct the storage controller that certain data blocks no longer contain data. After receiving the TRIM command, the controller will add data blocks passed in that command to the list of *dirty* blocks, while remapping them (assigning their logical addresses) to already erased blocks from the reserve pool. The *dirty* blocks will be slowly erased in the background. Effectively, the TRIM command serves as a garbage collection tool, helping SSDs prevent future slowdowns to write operations.

For the purpose of digital forensics, this means you can no longer count on deleted files being available for recovery after they've been deleted. Due to the use of the TRIM command by the operating system and the ongoing operation of wear leveling and garbage collection processes in the background, the empty blocks will, in most cases, be completely erased without any further interaction. In other words, if the user deletes certain files, they'll be truly gone—with a few exceptions.

More information regarding solid-state storage and data recovery can be obtained from Belkasoft whitepaper *SSD Forensics 2014. Recovering Evidence from SSD Drives: Understanding TRIM, Garbage Collection and Exclusions* at `http://belkasoft.com/en/ssd-214`.

Windows 8 and Windows 10 encryption – TRIM versus BitLocker

Considering the nature of full-disk encryption and taking into account performance and lifespan issues of solid-state media such as SSD and eMMC storage, one inevitably arrives to a logical question: what happens to deleted data if full-disk encryption is enabled on a solid-state volume? Particularly, will the system sacrifice performance by keeping deleted data encrypted, or will it sacrifice security by exposing empty (erased) parts of the encrypted volume?

The answer to this question depends on which combination of hardware and whole-disk encryption software is used in a particular system. However, in the case of BitLocker and eMMC storage, there is a simple—and official—answer. According to Microsoft (`https://b logs.msdn.microsoft.com/e7/29/5/5/support-and-qa-for-solid-state-drives/`), *Bitlocker's encryption process [is] optimized to work on SSDs [...] on NTFS. When Bitlocker is first configured on a partition, the entire partition is read, encrypted and written back out. As this is done, the NTFS file system will issue Trim commands to help the SSD optimize its behavior.* As we can see, in this particular case Microsoft has decided to go after performance while sacrificing a little bit of security. As a result, you will *not* be able to recover deleted files even if you image the entire BitLocker volume.

Historically, however, this has not always been the case. In the early days of SSD's, the then-current whole-disk encryption providers such as TrueCrypt went all the way after security, never letting TRIM commands reach the underlying physical storage. As a result, TrueCrypt used to have a hugely negative impact on performance if whole-disk encryption was used because the SSD controller could no longer tell the difference between free space and used up space because on an encrypted disk both free space and used space is treated as (encrypted) data. This approach defeated the very purpose of TRIM, and effectively disabled wear-leveling optimizations.

In order to mitigate this issue, developers of whole-disk encryption products introduced so-called *TRIM Pass-through*. With this feature enabled, the encryption product would pass information about free data blocks to the SSD controller, allowing it to trim released data blocks. This had a huge positive effect on performance and longevity of solid-state media, but exposed information about which data blocks were actually occupied by encrypted data to an outside attacker. This was seen as a security weakness, and for this reason alone, some WDE manufacturers chose not to enable the feature by default.

After some years, self-encrypting SSDs became available. These SSDs encrypt data blocks before writing them at the physical level. The TGS Opal full disk encryption standard allows the keys to be set by the OS (providing that both the operating system and hardware support the system), effectively fixing the issue mentioned above. Therefore, if the Windows device being investigated has a storage device (whether SSD or eMMC) that meets the right encryption standards, BitLocker makes use of the hardware encryption engine, effectively bypassing the software-based encryption in favor of a hardware-based one.

Booting Windows tablets from recovery media

In order to boot from recovery media, one needs several things. Firstly, the tablet must hold enough charge to be able to survive through the recovery process. As most tablets share a single USB port for charging and for connecting peripherals such as USB flash drives, fully charging the tablet before the recovery is recommended.

Secondly, only a few tablets offer full-size USB ports. One is more likely to encounter a micro USB port (USB2.0 or USB3.0 depending on the tablet). As a result, you'll need a matching USB **On-The-Go** (OTG) cable to connect the flash drive.

Finally, the tablet will not boot from an external device unless it's instructed to do so in its UEFI BIOS.

Special case – recovery media for Windows RT

Windows RT devices were supplied with UEFI Secure Boot permanently activated, which makes it impossible to boot these devices into anything other than Windows RT. Theoretically, with Secure Boot disabled, one could use an ARM version of Linux or a custom build of Android to boot and image the device. This, however, is not an option since Secure Boot cannot be disabled on any Windows RT device.

As a result, one can either boot from the tablet's recovery partition or use custom recovery. Since Windows RT is a rather crippled OS, obtaining or making a usable recovery image is significantly more difficult compared to x86 or x64 Windows builds.

If no recovery partition is available, one can usually obtain a Windows RT recovery image from the manufacturer. For example, Microsoft offers such images for its Surface RT and Surface 2 tablets at `http://www.microsoft.com/surface/en-us/support/warranty-serv ice-and-recovery/downloadablerecoveryimage`.

After following the download instructions, one can make a bootable flash media.

Steps to boot from recovery media

Microsoft published step-by-step instructions on how to boot a Windows tablet from USB recovery media at `http://www.microsoft.com/surface/en-ca/support/storage-files- and-folders/boot-surface-pro-from-usb-recovery-device?lc=415`. While these instructions apply to Microsoft Surface RT devices, they work just as well for most other Windows tablets. If not, refer to the manufacturer's manual for the particular device being acquired.

How to start from a bootable USB device when the tablet is off:

Microsoft published the following walkthroughs:

- *Boot Surface from a USB device* (`https://www.microsoft.com/surface/en-us/su pport/storage-files-and-folders/boot-surface-from-usb-recovery-devic e?os=windows-1`)
- *Using a Surface USB recovery drive* (`https://www.microsoft.com/surface/en-us /support/warranty-service-and-recovery/usbrecovery?os=windows-1`)

While the two guides are mainly aimed at Microsoft Surface users, they are also applicable to users of other Windows-based tablets:

1. Attach a bootable USB device containing a Windows Recovery image to the USB port.

   Use a USB OTG cable if no full-size USB port is available.

2. Press and hold the volume down button.

3. Press and release the power button.
4. When the logo appears, release the volume down button.

> The tablet will start the software on your USB device.

If the tablet is on and you are logged in, the startup procedure is different.

How to start from a bootable USB device when the tablet is on:

1. Attach a bootable USB device to the USB port.

> Use a USB OTG cable if no full-size USB port is available.

2. Swipe in from the right and then tap **Settings** (if you're using a mouse, point to the upper-right corner of the screen, move the mouse pointer down, and then click **Settings**).
3. Tap or click **Change PC Settings**.
4. Tap or click **Update and recovery**, and then tap or click **Recovery**.
5. Under **Advanced Startup**, tap or click **Restart now**.
6. On the **Choose an option** screen, tap or click **Use a device**.
7. On the **Troubleshoot** screen, tap or click **Advanced options**.
8. On the **Advanced options** screen, tap or click the name of the USB device. The tablet will restart and boot from the USB device.

Configuring UEFI BIOS to boot from recovery media

Depending on the manufacturer (and user-performed adjustments) of a particular Windows tablet, UEFI setup changes may be necessary if booting from an external device. If this is the case, you'll have to enter its UEFI BIOS and enable external boot mode.

Unlike Windows, which looks pretty much the same from one computer to another, there are endless variations of UEFI BIOS. Options and settings may be named differently across manufacturers.

Windows tablets do not have BIOS. Instead, they feature UEFI firmware that can be accessed by holding the **volume down** button while turning the tablet on with the **power** key. Once you are in the UEFI, look for Startup options to specify the order of devices your tablet will be allowed to boot from (a comprehensive tutorial on how to boot any Windows tablet into UEFI is available at `http://www.7tutorials.com/how-boot-uefi-bios-any-wi ndows-81-tablet-or-device`).

If your external boot device contains a secure boot key (like Windows 8.1 or Windows PE 5.1), you won't need to change Secure Boot settings in the UEFI BIOS setup. If, however, you are using an unsigned bootable recovery image, you will need to disable Secure Boot first.

Depending on the manufacturer, you may need to change the option called **Secure Boot** to **disabled** and the **UEFI Boot** to **CSM Boot** (or **Setup Mode** in some tablets) in order to allow the system to boot from external devices. After this, you should be able to boot from custom (unsigned) recovery media.

Note that disabling Secure Boot is not available on Windows RT devices.

Acquiring a BitLocker encryption key

BitLocker encryption is optional on Windows devices. Moreover, many budget-oriented tablets (such as those equipped with Intel Z3735 and 1 GB RAM) lack TPM (Trusted Platform Module) support, which makes the use of BitLocker complicated on such devices. By default, BitLocker encryption is not enabled in Windows 8.x, and is only activated when (and if) the user signs in to their Windows 8 machine with their Microsoft Account (as opposed to using a local Windows account). If you are using a Surface RT/2 with a Microsoft account and admin rights then Bitlocker (or Device Encryption) was automatically turned on for you the first time you logged in.

If enabled, BitLocker encryption will effectively prevent an investigator from accessing the content of the device – even if booting from a recovery drive.

Important: BitLocker is an essential part of the Windows security model, and a major obstacle to an investigation. All efforts shall be taken in order to preserve and recover BitLocker keys. It is essential to attempt capturing the dump of the computer's volatile memory, which will contain binary decryption keys to BitLocker volumes (if used). Finally, BitLocker encryption is still optional, and will not automatically activate if the computer only has local Windows accounts and does not use an administrative Microsoft Account.

When using a USB recovery drive, especially if that recovery drive was not created on the particular device being imaged, you may not be able to access the content of its storage because of BitLocker encryption. When using command prompt, you might be prompted to enter the encryption key. Without this key, the volume with all user data will remain securely encrypted.

BitLocker protection can be unlocked with the correct Recovery Key. This key is unique per computer, and is stored in the user's Microsoft Account. You will need to have the user's Microsoft Account login and password in order to retrieve the Recovery Key. The following steps describe how to extract the Recovery Key from the user's Microsoft Account:

1. If prompted for a Recovery Key, make a note of the **Key ID** mentioned on the screen of the device.
2. Use another computer to go to `http://windows.microsoft.com/recoverykey`.
3. Locate the device with the same Key ID noted above.
4. Use the Recovery Key corresponding to the given Key ID to unlock the encrypted drive.

Important: Microsoft holds Recovery Keys to users' BitLocker-encrypted storage devices. These keys are available in and can be obtained from the user's Microsoft Account unless explicitly deleted by the user. Consideration should be taken to prevent the suspect from destroying the Recovery Key after their encrypted device has been seized. If you know the user's Microsoft Account credentials, the Recovery Keys can be obtained in a matter of minutes. The Recovery Keys can be obtained directly from Microsoft by submitting a written request accompanied with a court order.

More information about BitLocker Recovery Key is available at `https://technet.microso ft.com/en-us/library/ee449438(v=ws.1).aspx`.

Microsoft has also published instructions on regaining access to computers locked by BitLocker Drive Encryption here: `https://technet.microsoft.com/en-us/library/cc73 2774(v=ws.11).aspx`.

Note that you'll still need a Recovery Key to unlock the disk when using Microsoft instructions. Alternatively, you can use third-party software to mount BitLocker-encrypted volumes if you manage to capture the content of the tablet's volatile memory while the encrypted partition was mounted. More on that in the next chapter.

Breaking into Microsoft Account to acquire the BitLocker Recovery Key

Acquiring BitLocker Recovery Key is easy once you have access to the user's Microsoft Account. A valid password is required in order to log in to Microsoft Account. If you don't know the password, brute-forcing your way into an online service is not going to work.

Starting with Windows 8, users can opt to sign in to their computers with their online account credentials instead of using a local Windows account and password. By using Microsoft Account, they get automatic cloud backups, the ability to sync settings and data (such as browser passwords) across multiple devices, and, most importantly, the ability to back up their BitLocker Recovery Keys to the cloud.

Signing in to Microsoft Account takes an e-mail and password (as opposed to a username and password). It is easy to see whether a local or Microsoft Account was used. Logins such as `username@live.com`, `username@hotmail.com`, or `username@outlook.com` are sure giveaways of Microsoft Account sign ins. Microsoft Account is used as a single sign-in solution for various Microsoft services such as Outlook.com, OneDrive, and Skype.

Since Microsoft Account is a cloud-based online authentication service, normally you would not be able to break in. Trying more than a handful of wrong passwords would lock out subsequent login attempts. However (and this is great news), Microsoft Account password hash is cached locally on all computers using these credentials.

This, in turn, allows for an interesting twist. You can acquire a local hash of that password and use it to brute-force your way into the online Microsoft Account by running an offline attack.

In order to do that, you can use two tools: Elcomsoft System Recovery (`https://www.elcom soft.com/esr.html`) to create bootable media (for example, a USB drive) to export the locally cached Microsoft Account password hash, and Elcomsoft Distributed Password Recovery (`https://www.elcomsoft.com/edpr.html`) to actually brute-force the password using a GPU-assisted attack distributed among multiple computers. A combination of dictionary and brute-force attacks may result in the recovery of the original plain-text password to the user's Microsoft Account, unlocking access to BitLocker Recovery Keys saved in that account and allowing us to decrypt the BitLocker volume.

Using Elcomsoft Forensic Disk Decryptor to unlock BitLocker partitions

Since many Windows tablets ship with BitLocker protection activated for the C drive partition, you will need a way to unlock protected volumes. BitLocker volumes can be unlocked automatically if you enter the correct user login and password. You can also unlock BitLocker volumes by supplying the correct Recovery Key which, in turn, can be often retrieved from the user's Microsoft Account.

But what if you don't know either password, and don't have access to the Recovery Key? If this is the case, you still have the option to extract the key from the computer's volatile memory dump. This is one of the reasons why you absolutely must try your best to make a dump of the computer's RAM before trying anything else.

If the Windows device you are about to acquire is active or sleeping (Connected Standby), do not allow it to power off. Try capturing a RAM image first. If the device uses BitLocker Device Protection, capturing a live memory dump can be the only chance to obtain the BitLocker decryption key. If you can extract that key, you will be able to use**Elcomsoft Forensic Disk Decryptor** (`https://www.elcomsoft.com/efdd.html`) to mount BitLocker-protected partitions even if you cannot sign in to the device.

BitLocker keys and Trusted Platform Module

While many budget tablets running Windows 8 and 8.1 (and some Windows 10 devices) lack **Trusted Platform Module (TPM)** support, one can encounter devices with and without the TPM module. It is important to realize that, because the keys needed to decrypt data remain locked by the TPM, one cannot read the data just by removing the storage device and installing it in another computer (source: `https://technet.microsoft.com/library/cc732774.aspx`). More importantly, the TPM has its own memory that is separate from the memory accessible by the operating system. This means that private portions of key pairs are kept separated from the memory controlled by the operating system, are not exposed to any part of the OS or software, and cannot be captured with memory dumping tools.

The actual drive encryption key, however, is released to the operating system, stored in the system's RAM, and can be retrieved by capturing a snapshot of the computer's volatile memory and examining the snapshot with Elcomsoft Forensic Disk Decryptor.

TPM facts summary:

- TPM is not available on many budget Windows tablets
- If TPM is not installed, BitLocker encryption is not immediately available (yet it can be manually activated by the user via `gpedit.msc` *Allow BitLocker without a compatible TPM* option)
- If TPM is available, the drive remains locked until the key is released
- Once the encrypted drive is unlocked, the decryption key remains in the computer's RAM, is accessible to the OS, and can be acquired by capturing a memory dump and analyzing with Elcomsoft Forensic Disk Decryptor

Imaging Windows RT tablets

While we said a lot about creating a bootable USB device for Windows RT tablets, how or even if it's possible to image one is still a big question. Windows RT is an inherently crippled platform with platform-level security measures that are extremely effective in disallowing anything but signed code to boot or execute on RT devices. Pre-activated Secure Boot that cannot be disabled, ARM architecture instead of x86, and system-level trusted signature checks for all desktop applications make traditional acquisition techniques ineffective.

As all known Windows RT devices are using eMMC, a soldered-on BGA chip, it is technically possible to perform chip-off or ISP acquisition.

This, however, is a time-consuming, labor-intensive, and destructive process which is not always available as an option during routine investigations. BitLocker disk encryption, if enabled, can make the acquisition process difficult or impossible. Even in Windows RT, other imaging options are available.

BitLocker encryption

Windows RT is a crippled and secure platform. By default, the C drive partition where all the user files reside is protected with BitLocker. Booting from the recovery media, accessing the **Windows Recovery Environment (WinRE)** Command Prompt or otherwise attempting to log in without supplying the correct account password or PIN code will result in being locked out and unable to access information stored on the partition of interest. As a result, Windows RT forensics requires you to know either a password to an administrative account (or, in a worst-case scenario, to any local account at all) or to have access to the BitLocker Recovery Key. More information about this in the *Acquiring BitLocker Encryption Key* section.

BitLocker To Go is partially supported in Windows RT. According to Microsoft (`https://t echnet.microsoft.com/en-us/library/dn73641.aspx#BKMK_bitlockertogo`), *"Although Windows RT 8.1 cannot create encrypted BitLocker To Go USB drives or SD cards, it is able to use these drives or cards after they have been encrypted from Windows 8 Pro or Windows 8 Enterprise (or even Windows 7) computers. When inserting the BitLocker To Go USB drive or SD card, the user will be prompted to provide the required password before they can access or update the data on the USB drive or SD card."*

Important: By default, Windows RT will create BitLocker escrow keys and upload them to the user's Microsoft Account. Microsoft holds Recovery Keys to users' BitLocker-encrypted storage devices. These keys are available in and can be obtained from the user's Microsoft Account unless explicitly deleted by the user. If you know the user's Microsoft Account credentials, the Recovery Keys can be obtained in a matter of minutes via h ttps://onedrive.live.com/recoverykey. The Recovery Keys can also be obtained directly from Microsoft by submitting a written request accompanied with a court order.

DISM – a built-in tool to image Windows RT

As we know, Windows RT disallows booting into anything other than Windows RT. The system does not allow running any unsigned desktop apps either.

So let's say you have a Microsoft Surface RT, Surface 2, Nokia Lumia 2520, or any other RT tablet. You managed to boot the device from a USB recovery media containing Windows RT, and have full access to the command line. As with Android or iOS tablets, there's not a lot you can do to image it since the tablet is running on an ARM CPU and is locked to only allow built-in desktop tools to run. Since Windows RT tablets can't execute x86 code (and can't run unsigned ARM code), support from manufacturers of forensic tools is non-existent. This all means that, in your forensic needs, you are limited to using command-line tools that are built into Windows.

Fortunately, there is a tool that does exactly what we need. Microsoft's Deployment Image Servicing and Management (DISM.exe) is fully capable of creating images of Windows partitions and saving them in the WIM format.

In order to image the tablet, do the following.

Note: The preceding described techniques are not limited to Windows RT. They can be applied to any tablet running Windows 8, 8.1, Windows Server 2012, or Windows RT. However, better acquisition methods are available for non-RE systems. DISM imaging should only be used as a last-resort measure.

Must be logged in with an administrative account

If you are logged in already and have administrative privileges, you may skip directly to the *Using DISM.exe to image the drive* section. If not, you'll need to boot your system into recovery mode to gain access to the administrative-level command prompt.

Must be logged in

Since Windows PE does not exist for RT architecture, you are limited to using Windows Recovery (Repair) Environment (WinRE) in order to gain administrative access to the computer. In particular, you'll need to access the command prompt. After booting to the command prompt, you'll have access to Windows built-in command-line tools. In particular, we'll be using the DISM tool to image partitions on the device.

If you are logged in, you can configure your system to boot into Windows Recovery Environment with command prompt.

Booting to the WinRE command prompt

In order to boot into WinRE Command Prompt, do the following:

1. Start the tablet.
2. At the login prompt, tap the Ease of Access icon.
3. Select **On-Screen Keyboard**.
4. Tap the *Shift* key, the *Shift* key should remain lit.
5. In the lower right corner, tap the power key and select **Restart**.
6. When the unit reboots, select the **Troubleshoot** option.
7. From here, select **Advanced** options.
8. Select **Command Prompt**.

Entering BitLocker Recovery Key

You may be prompted for a Recovery Key for the primary partition. In case you see the message **Enter the recovery key to get going again**, enter the Recovery Key and press Enter. If you don't have the Recovery Key, you will still have access to the command prompt by using the **Skip this drive** option, but you won't be able to read the encrypted volume. More information in *BitLocker recovery keys: Frequently asked questions*: `http://wind ows.microsoft.com/en-us/windows-8/bitlocker-recovery-keys-faq`.

If you have your own bootable USB drive, you can similarly configure the system to boot from that drive.

Using DISM.exe to image the drive

Microsoft TechNet has a comprehensive guide on how to capture Windows partitions using the DISM.exe tool (see the preceding link to *Capture Images of Hard Disk Partitions Using DISM*):

1. **Determine which partitions to capture**: Most commonly, Windows RT tablets are equipped with a single System partition, a single Primary partition, and one or more Reserved partitions (containing the recovery image). What you need is the Primary partition (and all Logical partitions, if any).

2. **Assign drive letters to partitions**: If one or more partitions you want to capture don't already have a drive letter assigned, assign a letter using the DiskPart tool. The partition will be mounted in R/W mode.

3. **Capture images with the DISM command-line tool:** You'll be using the DISM command together with the /capture-Image option. Example:

```
Dism /Capture-Image /ImageFile:c:\partition0.wim /CaptureDir:C:\
/Name:"partition0"
```

 Note: if your attached storage does not have the required amount of space to receive the entire partition, you may save images to the network disk by running the net use n: \\Server\Share command and substituting the path of the /ImageFile parameter with the newly mapped network drive.

You can read more about DISM command-line tools and its options and parameters on Microsoft TechNet:

- *DISM Image Management Command-Line Options*: https://technet.microsoft.com/en-in/library/hh825258.aspx
- *Capture Images of Hard Disk Partitions Using DISM*: https://technet.microsoft.com/en-us/library/hh82572.aspx
- *Capture and Apply Windows, System, and Recovery Partitions*: https://technet.microsoft.com/en-us/library/hh82541.aspx

Cloud Acquisition

Windows RT is a Windows 8/8.1-based OS. As such, the system has the ability to maintain cloud backups in Microsoft OneDrive. Information backed up into the cloud includes contacts, messages, synced Internet Explorer passwords, list of installed applications, and some application settings such as stored passwords (for example, reinstalling a previously installed Pocket client after a full factory reset does not require logging in; the app will work immediately. However, any downloaded content will be re-downloaded).

The data is only automatically backed up if the user is logged in with a Microsoft Account (as opposed to using a local Windows account) and has the Backup option enabled in the settings. This, however, is a typical usage scenario for Windows RT tablets.

In order to download Windows RT data, use the **Download Windows Phone data** acquisition option in Elcomsoft Phone Breaker:

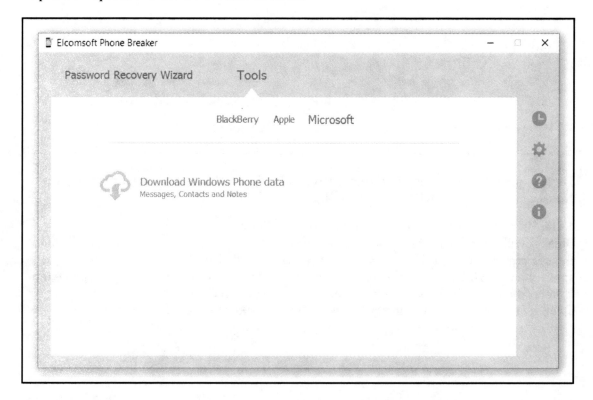

You will need to specify the user's Microsoft Account login and password.

The tool downloads information from Microsoft Live! servers (at this time, only Contacts, Notes, and Messages can be downloaded).

Note: Since the user may own more than a single Microsoft device, Elcomsoft Phone Breaker will download information synced by all devices where the user signed in with their Microsoft Account. This includes Windows Phone 8.1 and Windows 10 Mobile smartphones, Windows RT tablets, Windows 8, 8.1, and Windows 10 desktops, laptops, and tablet computers. The list of available backups can be viewed by signing into the user's OneDrive account and choosing **Settings** | **Device Backups** (`https://onedrive.live.com /Options/DeviceBackups`).

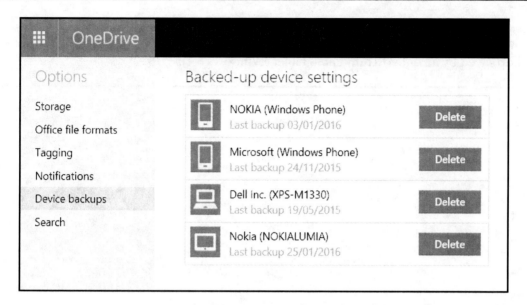

Elcomsoft Phone Breaker downloads information:

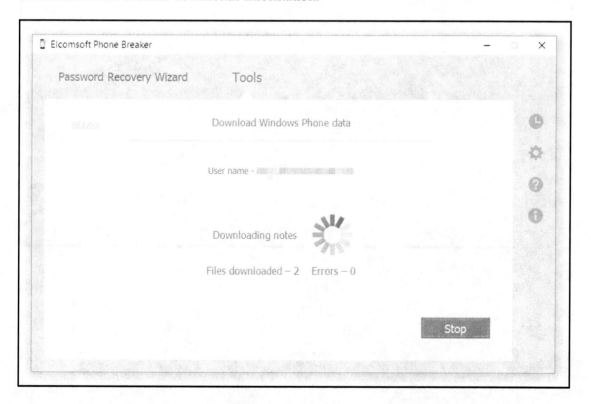

After the extraction is finished, you'll be able to view the downloaded backup in Elcomsoft Phone Viewer. The following screenshot demonstrates information extracted from a cloud backup saved by a Lenovo ThinkPad 8 tablet (Windows 8.1):

Summary

In this chapter, we talked about acquiring Windows tablets. We covered the acquisition of Windows 8.x and Windows 10 tablets, and addressed the issues of ARM-based Windows tablets running the dedicated ARM-based version of Windows, Windows RT. We learned about automatic BitLocker encryption and reviewed methods of circumventing BitLocker protection by extracting BitLocker Recovery Keys from the user's Microsoft Account. Finally, we learned how to break in to Microsoft Account by executing an offline password recovery attack on the user's cached password. In the next chapter, we'll move back to smartphones and look into acquisition options available for BlackBerry smartphones.

9
Acquisition – Approaching BlackBerry

While BlackBerry's global market share fell to less than one per cent according to Bloomberg (`http://www.bloomberg.com/news/214-5-28/blackberry-market-share-to-fall-to--3-in-218-idc-says.html`), many BlackBerry devices are still used in corporate environments.

Security was always one of the BlackBerry's key points. Information stored in encrypted BlackBerry devices was impossible to extract or decrypt without knowing the correct passcode. However, attacking BlackBerry backups offers a way to recover user data.

Recovering information from BlackBerry devices depends on which version of the BlackBerry OS the device is running. If the device uses any version of BlackBerry OS prior to BlackBerry 10, the users can configure it to produce offline backups protected with a user-selectable password. If, however, the device is running BlackBerry 10, the backups are stored in an online cloud, and require the original BlackBerry ID and password to access.

 A comprehensive whitepaper on BlackBerry forensics by Shafik Punja (Teel Technologies) and Cindy Murphy (Gillware Digital Forensics) is available at `http://www.nist.gov/forensics/upload/5-Punja-nist-214-bb-forensics-FULL.pdf` (Blackberry Forensics, NIST Mobile Forensics Workshop June 2014).

The history of the BlackBerry OS – BlackBerry 1.0-7.1

Prior to the release of BlackBerry 10, the now current version of BlackBerry OS, BlackBerry devices could be configured to produce password-protected offline backups (`*.ipd` or `*.bbb` backup files) when connected to an authorized computer running BlackBerry Desktop Software. It is important to note that these backups were only protected with a user-selectable password. Unlike Apple, BlackBerry has not specified the use of any additional hardware-based encryption keys. As a result, successfully recovering a password is all that is needed to decrypt a BlackBerry backup.

BlackBerry backups (OS 1.0 to 7.0) are not password protected/encrypted by default. This option must be enabled by the user within the BlackBerry Desktop Software interface. Unencrypted BlackBerry devices can be also acquired via JTAG (compatible models) or chip-off.

BlackBerry 7 JTAG, ISP, and chip-off acquisition

Depending on whether or not **Content Protection** (data encryption, **Options | Security | Encryption** in BB7) was enabled in a given device, it may or may not be susceptible to advanced acquisition techniques such as JTAG, **In-system programming (ISP)**, or chip-off. Moreover, these older BlackBerry devices can be unlocked via BES they are attached to. Note that JTAG only works for older devices.

Depending on whether or not a BlackBerry 7 device was on a BES, decrypting the chip-off dump may or may not be possible. In certain cases, non-BES devices using the built-in encryption (Content Protection) can be dumped via chip-off and successfully decoded by recovering the original password from the SHA1 hash file.

 More information: PGP Encrypted BlackBerrys and Chip-off Forensics `htt p://securemobile.me/yes-the-blackberry-can-be-cracked-but-how-easily/`.

Acquiring BlackBerry desktop backups

We'll use Elcomsoft Phone Breaker to recover the password protecting a BlackBerry backup by performing an attack on the backup files. It is important to note that this attack is only applicable to the *classic* BlackBerry OS up to and including version 7. You can specify one or more different attacks, for example, wordlist (known as password attack), dictionary, brute force,and so on. A combination of attacks makes up a recovery pipeline.

To recover the password in Elcomsoft Phone Breaker, do the following:

1. Open the **Password Recovery Wizard** page.

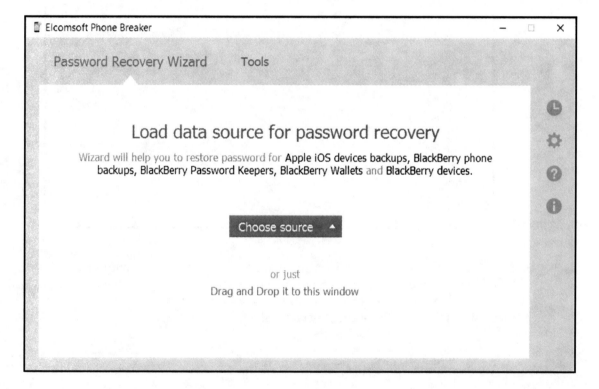

2. Specify the backup file (`.ipd` or `.bbb`) by either selecting the file with the **Choose source** command or by dragging and dropping the backup file onto the **Password Recovery Wizard** window.

> **Note**: Alternatively, you may use the **Tools** | **BlackBerry** | **Decrypt backup** route, as seen in the following screenshot:

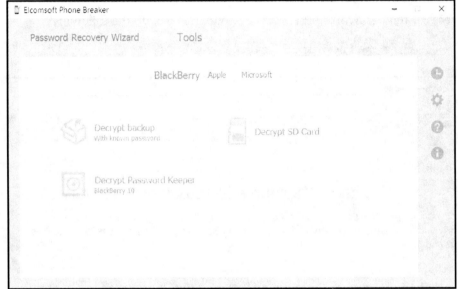

3. By default, the tool will list all locally available backups created with BlackBerry Desktop Software. If you are recovering a backup located on the suspect's hard drive, external device, or mounted forensic disk image, you will need to manually specify the location of backup files.

4. After specifying the backup file, you will need to define the attacks that will be used to break the password. Click on the plus + sign to add various attacks for breaking the password. By default, Dictionary and Brute-Force attacks are added automatically. For more information about attacks and their settings, see the *Password recovery attacks* topic in the online manual.

5. You can optionally configure both the Dictionary Attack and Brute-Force by clicking on the gear icon to the right of each method.

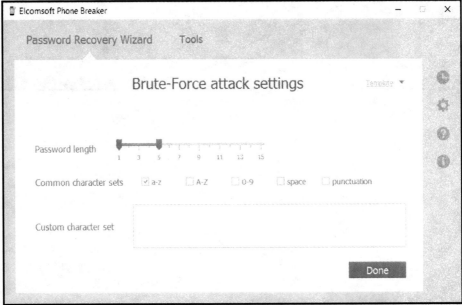

6. Click **Start recovery**. Elcomsoft Phone Breaker will begin attacking the password. Estimated time left as well as the currently processed word will be displayed. You can click **More Info** next to the name of the attack to see additional information, such as the number of attempted passwords and the average attack speed.

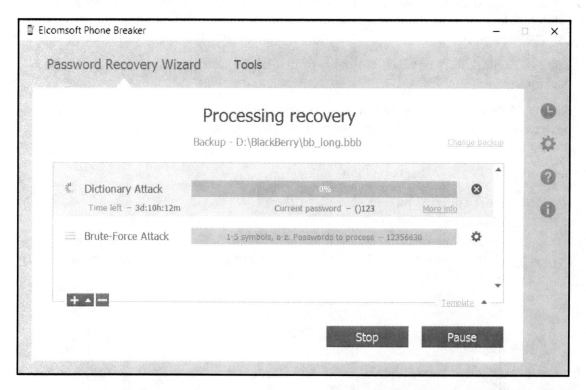

7. If the attack is successful, the discovered password will be displayed in the **Recovery results** window. At this time, you can either decrypt the backup to open it in **Elcomsoft BlackBerry Backup Explorer** (https://www.elcomsoft.com /ebbe.html), or use a third-party forensic tool to decrypt the backup with the discovered password.

That's it, we have successfully recovered a password. This password can now be used to decrypt the backup. In addition, you can break passwords protecting BlackBerry Wallet and Keeper data.

Decrypting the backup

The following section is applicable to BlackBerry OS backups (BB OS 7 and older).BlackBerry 10 backups are acquired using a different process.

If you already know (or have previously recovered) the password to BlackBerry backup, EPPB can decrypt it, so you will be able to open decrypted backup files in other software (we recommend usingElcomsoft Blackberry Backup Explorer).

You need a BlackBerry database`*.ipd` file or BlackBerry backup `*.bbb` file to decrypt the backup.

Only BlackBerry smartphone backups can be decrypted; backups made from PlayBook devices have different formats and are not supported yet, so EPPB can only recover the passwords for such files, but cannot decrypt them.

To decrypt a BlackBerry backup, do the following:

1. In the **Tools** menu, select the **BlackBerry** tab.
2. Select Decrypt backup.
3. Select either a BlackBerry database file (`*.ipd`) or BlackBerry backup file (`*.bbb`) by drag-and-dropping it to the **Decrypt backup** window, or click **Choose backup** to navigate to the necessary file manually.

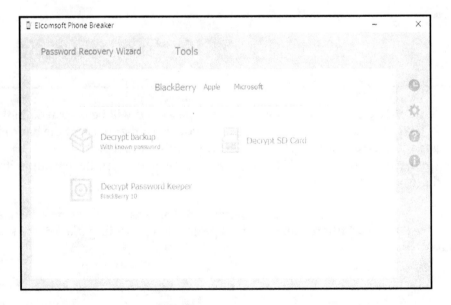

4. When the backup is loaded, you can view the following information about backup:
   - Backup date
   - Product type
5. You can select a different backup by clicking **Change backup** next to the backup name.

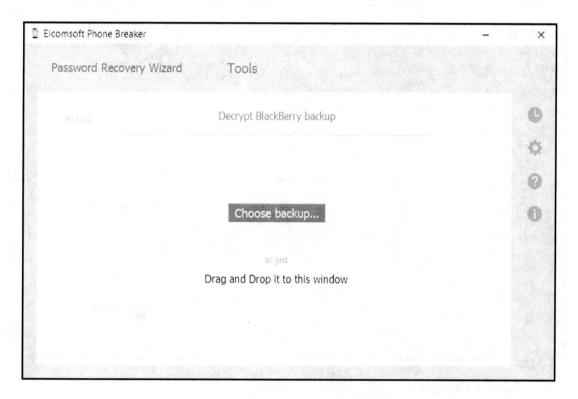

6. Define options for backup decryption:
    - **Save decrypted to**: Select location for saving the decrypted backup.
    - **Backup password**: Enter the password for the backup. Toggle the **View** button to display the password as characters or in asterisks (*). Click **Restore password** if you have not restored it yet.

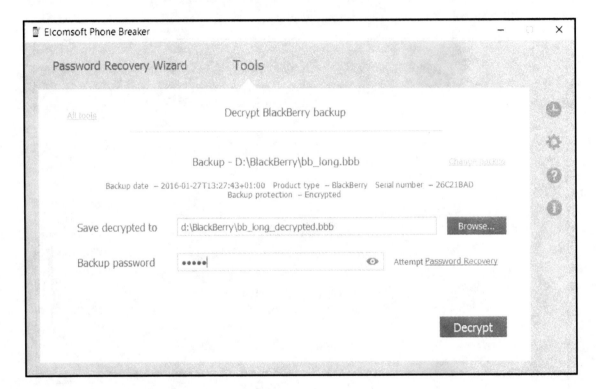

7. Click **Decrypt**.
8. The decryption process starts. You can view the number of processed files and the number of errors received during decryption.

9. When the decryption is finished, you can view the backup in the location on the local computer to which it was saved by clicking the **View** button.

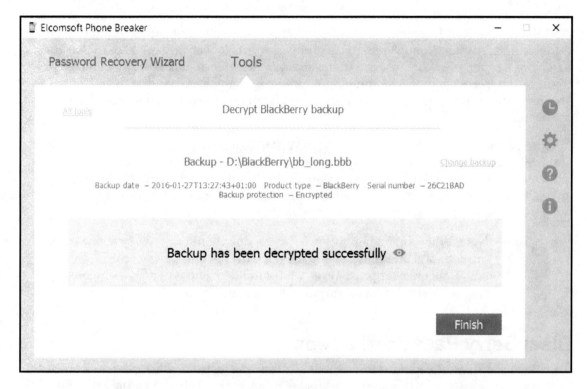

10. Click **Finish** to close the Decrypt backup page.

You have now successfully decrypted the backup, and may proceed to recovering BlackBerry Keeper and Wallet data.

Note: If you are viewing a backup file produced by an older version of Blackberry (before BlackBerry 10), you may use Elcomsoft Blackberry Backup Explorer: http://www.elcomsoft.com/ebbe.html.

BlackBerry Password Keeper and BlackBerry Wallet

BlackBerry Password Keeper and BlackBerry Wallet are two built-in apps containing lots of valuable data. Authentication credentials and passwords to websites are kept in BlackBerry Password Keeper, providing users with faster login experience. BlackBerry Wallet keeps credit card numbers, billing and shipping addresses, loyalty and frequent flyer programs,and so on. In general, this information is encrypted with an additional master password.

BlackBerry Password Keeper and BlackBerry Wallet do not share master passwords (yet nothing prevents users from setting them up with the same password). If a wrong password is entered 10 times in a row, information stored in BlackBerry Password Keeper or Wallet can be permanently erased if a corresponding setting is selected by the user (which is default behavior).

 Note: When analyzing offline backups, one should not worry about the 10 unsuccessful attempts erasing the data. In fact, when recovering Keeper and Wallet master passwords, we try millions of passwords—obviously without losing any data stored in the backup.

BlackBerry Password Keeper

BlackBerry Password Keeper protects access to users' passwords with a master password. With only one password to remember, users are much more likely to maintain unique passwords to different resources such as Web sites, applications, and services. BlackBerry encourages the use of Password Keeper for generating extremely secure random passwords that contain long sequences of letters, numbers, and symbols. The Keeper encrypts users' passwords, and can only decryptthem with the correct Password Keeper master password.

Passwords stored in BlackBerry Password Keeper are included into full offline backups by default (unless explicitly excluded at the time of backup). The backups themselves are encrypted; however, even when the backup is decrypted, Keeper passwords are still protected with the additional master password.

BlackBerry Wallet

BlackBerry Wallet keeps certain financial information such as credit card numbers, billing and shipping addresses, frequent flyer numbers, loyalty rewards, and membership card numbers. Wallet is designed to speed up mobile checkout andmake the online purchasing process easier by automatically filling out the required fields.

Data stored in BlackBerry Wallet is highly sensitive, and is securely encrypted with the Wallet master password. This password is normally different from the BlackBerry backup password, which adds an extra layer of protection.

BlackBerry security model – breaking a device password

Information stored in classic BlackBerry OS devices is secured with a device password. A device password is requested every time the device is turned on, as well as every time on expiration of Security Timeout (if this option is selected). 10incorrect attempts cause full data wipe, leaving no chance of subsequent recovery. This security feature is one of the hallmarks of the BlackBerry security model. However, the individual security password is **not enforced** and is optional. In other words, a BlackBerry device user does NOT have to enable a device password for BlackBerry devices (this includes BlackBerry 10) unless such protection is enforced via corporate policy (BES, Exchange services,and so on).

ElcomSoft has discovered a way around the device password. In certain cases, it is possible to attack and recover the device password offline if a user-selectable option to encrypt the contents of a removable media card is selected. If this is the case, investigators can useElcomsoft Phone Breaker to analyze information stored on the media card (microSD) and attack the original device password without the need to use the BlackBerry device itself.

What is media encryption, and why can it be used to attack a device password? BlackBerry smartphones can optionally encrypt the contents of the SD card. Theoretically, this would not allow attackers to gain access to information stored on the SD card without knowing the correct device password. In reality, the encryption scheme is dependent on the device password and allows attacking said password without using the device itself. It is important to note that SD card encryption is disabled by default, but some users opt for enabling the extra security layer.

Note that this method only works if the removable media card is encrypted with the **Security Password** option (as opposed to using a hardware-dependent encryption key). An estimated 30 percent of BlackBerry users opt to protect their media cards with this option, making their devices open to this attack.

There are three possible combinations of this option as defined by BlackBerry, namely the following:

- **Device Key**: Encrypts files using an encryption key for a media card generated by the BlackBerry smartphone

- **Security Password** or **Device Password** (depending on OS version): Encrypts files using the BlackBerry smartphone password

- **Security Password and Device Key** or **Device Password and Device Key** (depending on OS version):Encrypts files using an encryption key for a media card and the BlackBerry smartphone password

Elcomsoft Phone Breaker can successfully recover the password if either **Security Password** (Device Password) or **Security Password and Device Key** (Device Password and Device Key) option is specified. However, if the **Security Password and Device Key** was activated, decrypting the content of the media card without the BlackBerry device it was used in is not possible even after recovering the original password.

BlackBerry 10 always uses media card encryption based on theDevice Key, which has two consequences. Firstly, we can no longer attack device passwords by using the encrypted media card. Secondly, if the user removes the card from the BlackBerry 10 device it was originally used in, no other BlackBerry 10 device will be able to access information stored on that card. As a result, backing up information stored on a media card before moving it to another BlackBerry device is essential.

More information can be found at:

- `http://blackberry.com/btsc/kb12999`
- `http://blackberry.com/btsc/kb25484`

When using this option, the actual BlackBerry device is not required to perform the attack. All you need is a single file from the SD card. Offline recovery speeds when using a modern computer are extremely high (considering how slow the hardware used in classic BlackBerry OS devices was), delivering tens of millions passwords per second. This means that a reasonably secure seven-character password can be unlocked in less than an hour.

Knowing the original device password, investigators gain access to information stored in the original BlackBerry device, or can produce a backup file for offline analysis.

Acquiring BlackBerry 10

For many years, the QNX-based BlackBerry 10 remained BlackBerry's bread-and-butter operating system. It's used on all new devices; older devices did not receive an upgrade to BB 10 (`http://www.theinquirer.net/inquirer/news/2145581/rim-current-devices-w on-t-upgraded-blackberry`).

In January 2013, BlackBerry released a new, revamped version of the OS dubbed BlackBerry 10. Initially only available on a single touchscreen device, BlackBerry Z10, the new OS made it to subsequent devices including BlackBerry Q5, Q10, Q20 (Classic) and Q30 (Passport and Passport SE), touch-screen Z30 and Leap, as well as a counted number of Porsche design models.

BlackBerry 10 comes with the ability to run Android apps (installable via Amazon app store or Amazon Underground in latest releases); however, the OS lacks support for **Google Mobile Services (GMS)** and does not, in general, collect as much information about the user as Google-powered Android.

Getting started

Much like iOS, BlackBerry 10 is a closed-source OS. Similar to Apple, BlackBerry manufactures all BB10 handsets in-house using just two chip sets of a single manufacturer. All BlackBerry 10 devices with the exception of BlackBerry passport feature variations of the Qualcomm Snapdragon S4 chip set (found in BlackBerry Q5, Q10, Q20 Classic, Z10, Z30, Z3, Leap, and limited production run Porsche Design units). The Passport is equipped with Snapdragon 801. Just like iOS, all BlackBerry 10 devices are updated at the same time to the latest version of BlackBerry OS. Therefore, there is no platform fragmentation as such, and no platform or manufacturer specific considerations. As such, only a few simple iterations allow determining the best acquisition method.

Do you know if the device is encrypted? If you do know, and the device *is not encrypted*, then ISP or chip-off will deliver the maximum amount of information including deleted data. If you know that the device *is encrypted*, then low-level acquisition techniques will likely not work.

Note: In existing versions of BlackBerry 10, encryption is not enforced unless the device is on a BES, and the BES enforces device encryption policy. In addition, on consumer devices that are not on a BES, encryption is off by default. Encryption status of any BlackBerry 10 handset has to be proven on a case by case basis. Please note that this does NOT apply to BlackBerry Android devices (BlackBerry Priv and DTEK50), which have full-disk encryption enforced out of the box.

Is the device on a BES? Depending on the version of BB10 OS, the device may only be able to employ PGP encryption if it's on a BES; user-selectable **Data protection** may use a different encryption scheme.While decrypting a device that is on a BES can be possible remotely via the BES, breaking through user-selectable encryption is not possible without knowing the correct device password.

Do you know the password? If you know the device password, you may be able to log into the device and make it produce a full backup through BlackBerry Link or a third-party tool. The backup will be encrypted with a key stored online; you will only be able to decrypt the backup if you know the correct BlackBerry ID password.

Do you have access to a backup? If you have access to an existing backup file, you may be able to decrypt it if the original BlackBerry ID password is known. Without this password, decrypting the backup is impossible, as the decryption key is stored on the server.

BlackBerry 10 backups

Despite the similar naming convention, BlackBerry 10 is a completely new system that differs from BlackBerry OS in every imaginable way. How much different? It's on the same level as the differences between Symbian and Android.

The newOS is based on a **micro kernel architecture (QNX)**, which is substantially different from mono-kernel architectures such as those used in Android and iOS. No wonder that BlackBerry 10 introduced major changes to the OS security model. SD card encryption no longer compromises the device password. Local backups are now handled by BlackBerry Link, and are always encrypted with a highly secure encryption key based on the user's BlackBerry ID as opposed to a user-selectable password. The encryption key is stored deep in the device and cannot be extracted with a chip-off. However, this key can be used to restore (and decrypt) backups on new BlackBerry devices, and thus it can be obtained from BlackBerry servers.

What exactly happens when the user creates a backup with BlackBerry Link?

Using BlackBerry Link to back up a BlackBerry Passport

When setting up a new BlackBerry device with an existing BlackBerry ID, the device connects to a BlackBerry server and receives a binary encryption key tied to that BlackBerry ID. This key is then stored in a secure area in the device. This area is not accessible from the outside and cannot be obtained from eMMC dumps or via chip-off; only BlackBerry OS has access to this key.

The encryption key is quite secure. Unlike Apple's `securityd`, BlackBerry's encryption scheme does not depend on hardware. Instead, the key is tied to the user's BlackBerry ID and is stored on the server. All this allows users to restore a new device with exactly the same data complete with sensitive information. The encryption key is not changed when the user changes or resets their BlackBerry password. The same key is used after hardware upgrades, which proves that the key is not hardware-dependent.

When the user makes a backup with BlackBerry Link or a third-party tool such as Sachesi or Darcy's BlackBerry Tools, the tool does not receive unencrypted data. Instead, the tool passes a command to the BlackBerry device, and the device itself encrypts information on the fly. The encrypted data is streamed to BlackBerry Link (or an alternative application). Similar to Apple iTunes, BlackBerry Link is not responsible for making backups; it simply receives an encrypted data stream and saves it to a file.

When restoring the same or new BlackBerry device, the device is initialized with a BlackBerry ID via the BlackBerry server. The encryption key is transmitted from the serverto the device. Only after receiving the encryption key can the device decrypt backups restored via BlackBerry Link. The decryption occurs in the device itself. In BlackBerry 10,the decrypted data never leaves the device.

The initialization request can be intercepted by emulating a BlackBerry device being activated with a given BlackBerry ID. The BlackBerry ID is stored in the backup file in plain text. If you know the correct password protecting the user's BlackBerry ID account, you can then use Elcomsoft Phone Breaker to acquire the encryption key from the BlackBerry server and instantly decrypt local backups.

After supplying the user's BlackBerry ID and password, you can decrypt the offline backup with Elcomsoft Phone Breaker. The following categories are available and will be produced:

- Application data
- Media files (pictures and videos)
- Settings

 Note: BlackBerry 10 can also backup application files (.bar files). The .bar files will not be extracted due to copyright reasons.

Most information in BlackBerry 10 backups is available in plain text or SQLite format. This can be analyzed with general mobile forensic software.

BlackBerry 10 – considering ISP and chip-off forensics

A JTAG port is not available in BlackBerry 10 handsets. However, advanced acquisition techniques such as ISP and chip-off may still be available depending on the device's encryption status.

With BlackBerry losing its market share, the main reason to buy a BlackBerry is security. As a result, encryption is likely to be enabled on a BlackBerry 10 device being acquired. With encryption enabled, chip-off acquisition of a BlackBerry 10 phone is pointless without a valid decryption key, which cannot be dumped during chip-off.

 Important: In current versions of BlackBerry 10, encryption is not enabled by default, and needs to be activated by the end user or on the **BlackBerry Enterprise Server** (**BES**) administrator. Encryption status of any BlackBerry 10 handset has to be proven on a case by case basis.

If a passcode is known for a particular device, checking whether encryption is enabled is easy:

1. Turn on and unlock the device.
2. On the home screen of the device, swipe down from the top of the screen.

3. Tap **Settings** | **Security and** Privacy | **Encryption**:

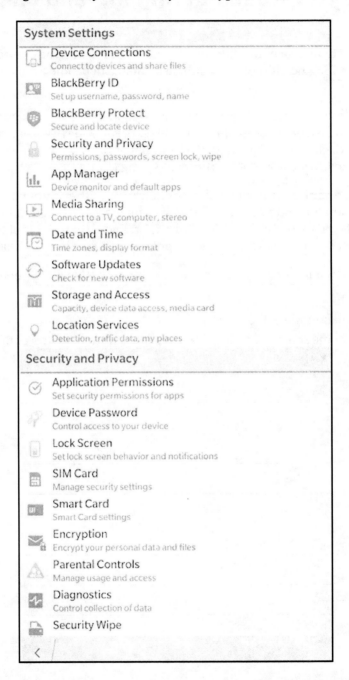

4. Check if any of the following switches are set to **On**:

- Device Encryption
- Media Card Encryption

If a BlackBerry 10 device is locked with an unknown passcode, there is no easy way to verify if its encryption features are activated. One can then attempt performing a chip-off on the phone, in the hope to obtain an unencrypted image.

We encounter unencrypted BlackBerry 10 devices every once in a while. Statistically, it is extremely rare to see a non-encrypted BlackBerry. However, we've seen multiple reports of successful chip-off acquisitions on new BlackBerry's including BlackBerry Classic, Z10, and Z30 with no issues.

Acquiring BlackBerry 10 backups

BlackBerry 10 devices use BlackBerry Link to make offline backups. In addition, BlackBerry 10 no longer has the Wallet. However, the Keeper app is still available, and is part of the BlackBerry operating system starting with version 10.3.

Using Elcomsoft Phone Breaker

You will need a BlackBerry backup *.bbb file to decrypt the BlackBerry Link backup. You will also need a password for the BlackBerry ID of the user who created the backup.

To decrypt a BlackBerry Link backup, do as follows:

1. When the backup is loaded, you can view the following information about the backup:
2. Select the BlackBerry backup file (*.bbb) by drag-and-dropping it to the **Decrypt backup** window, or click **Choose backup** to navigate to the necessary file manually.
3. Select **Decrypt backup**.
4. In the **Tools** menu, select the **BlackBerry** tab.
    *   **Backup date**: The local time on the PC/Mac, where backup has been created (we simply do not modify that field as it is extracted from the backup file, that is, show it as is)
    *   **Product type**: The type of BlackBerry device that was backed up
    *   **PIN**: The ID of the BlackBerry device

5. You can select a different backup by clicking**Change backup** next to the backup name.

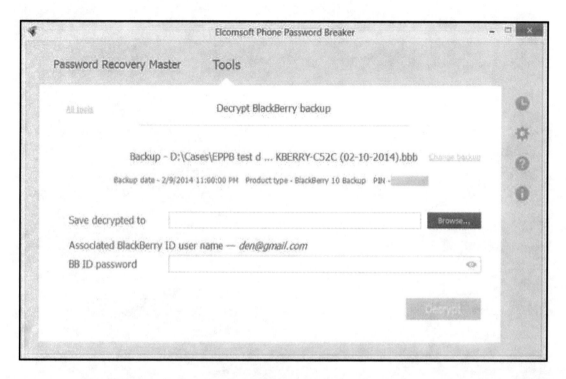

6. Define options for backup decryption:
   - **Save decrypted to**: Select the location for saving the decrypted backup.
   - **Associated BlackBerry ID user name**: The BlackBerry ID (email) of the user who created a backup.
   - **BB ID password**: Enter the password to the BlackBerry ID displayed in italics in **Associated BlackBerry ID user name**. Toggle the **View** button to display the password as characters or in asterisks (*).
7. Click **Decrypt**.
8. The decryption process starts.

9. When the decryption is finished, you can view the backup in the location on the local computer to which it was saved by clicking the **View** button.

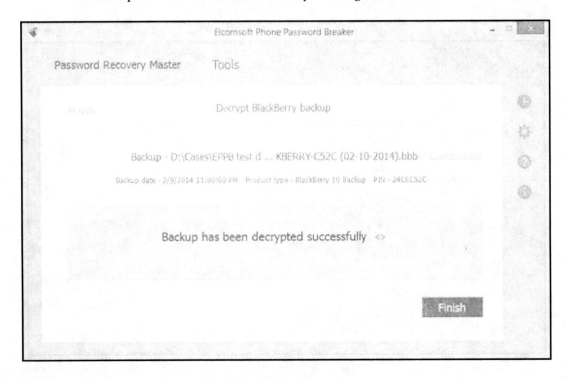

10. Click **Finish** to close the **Decrypt backup** window.

The backup is now available on your computer for further analysis. You can use Elcomsoft Phone Viewer to browse and view the content of the backup.

Using Oxygen Forensic Suite

If you own a license to Oxygen Forensic Suite, you can use the tool's built-in acquisition wizard to import encrypted BlackBerry 10 backups. Oxygen Forensic Suite uses technology from Elcomsoft Phone Breaker to obtain the decryption key from BlackBerry servers using the correct BlackBerry ID and password.

1. Use **Import File** | **Import Blackberry backup** | **Import BB10 backup....**

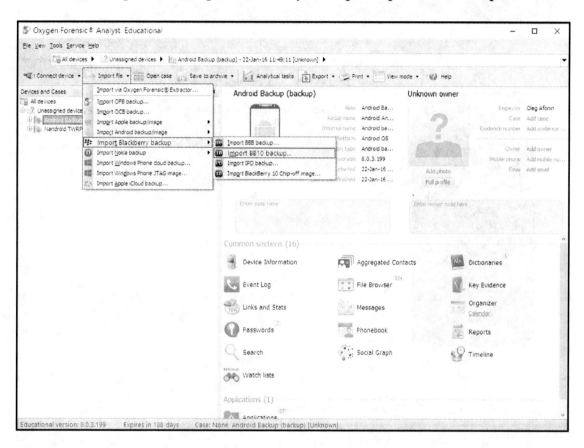

2. You will be prompted to enter the BlackBerry ID password (*not* the device password):

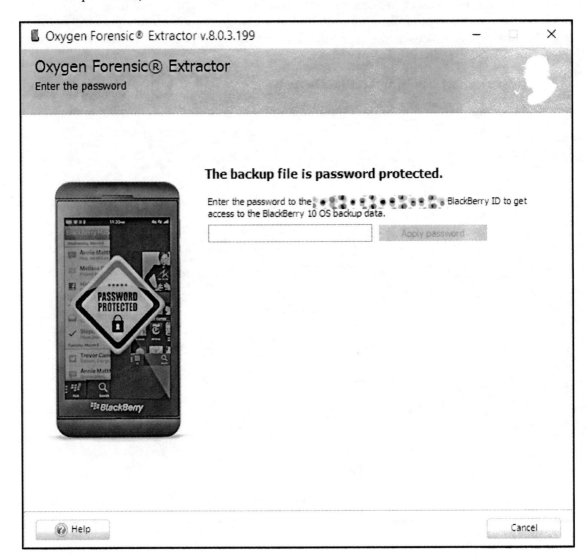

3. If the correct password is entered (the tool checks it immediately after you click the **Apply password** button), you will be able to fill in case details, after which the following summary screen will appear:

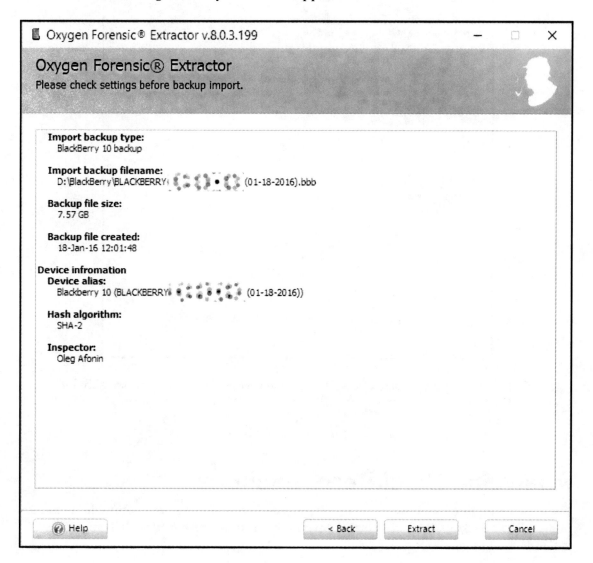

4. Click **Extract**, and the tool will begin decrypting the backup:

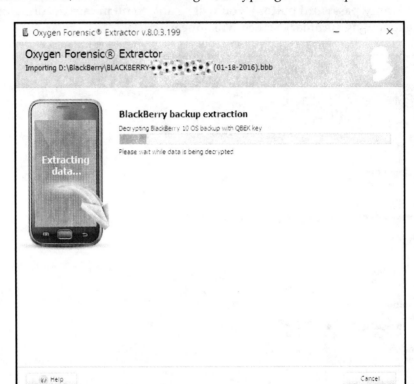

5. Depending on the size of the backup, the process may take a reasonably long time. For example, the decryption of a 7.57 GB backup took approximately 25 minutes.

Analyzing BlackBerry backups

There are many forensic tools on the market that can parse and analyze information stored in BlackBerry backups (provided that the password is known or recovered). ElcomSoft makes the following tools:

- **Elcomsoft BlackBerry Backup Explorer** (BlackBerry 1.0-7.1 only) at http://www.elcomsoft.com/ebbe.html

- **Elcomsoft Phone Viewer** (BlackBerry 10, iOS, and Windows Phone) at http://www.elcomsoft.com/epv.html

Elcomsoft BlackBerry Backup Explorer (for backups produced with BlackBerry 1.0 through 7.1) can access encrypted information stored in password-protection backups if the original password is known or recovered with Elcomsoft Phone Breaker. With the tool, you can extract essential information available in BlackBerry backups, analyze, print, and export information. Elcomsoft BlackBerry Backup Explorer is one of the few tools that can take an encrypted backup and decrypt it on-the-fly with the supplied password.

Elcomsoft Phone Viewer can access decrypted BlackBerry 10 backups. In order to view a BlackBerry 10 backup, first decrypt it with Elcomsoft Phone Breaker. Then open Elcomsoft Phone Viewer and click **Choose backup**:

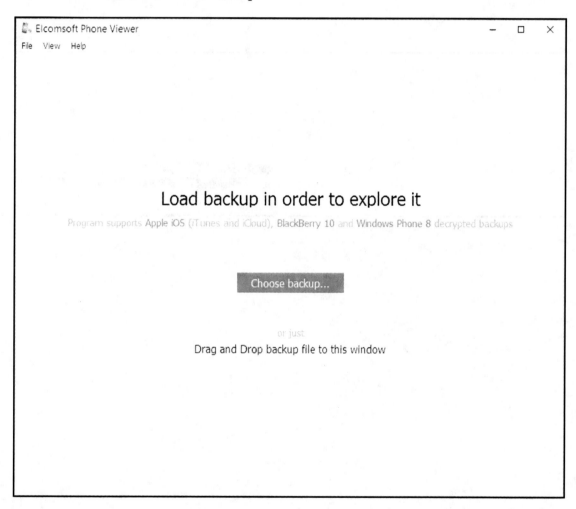

The tool defaults to displaying the list of iTunes backups (if available). To load a BlackBerry 10 backup, click **Choose another**:

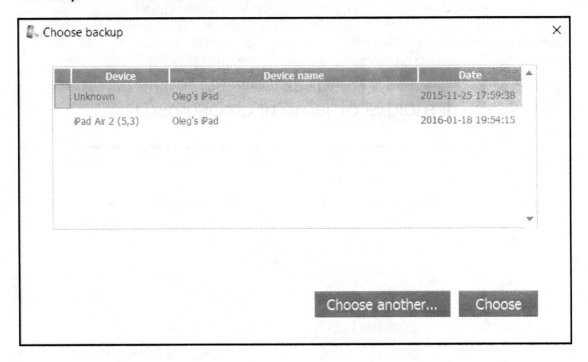

From the file dialog that appears, select the BlackBerry 10 backup you are about to view.
The tool will import the backup.

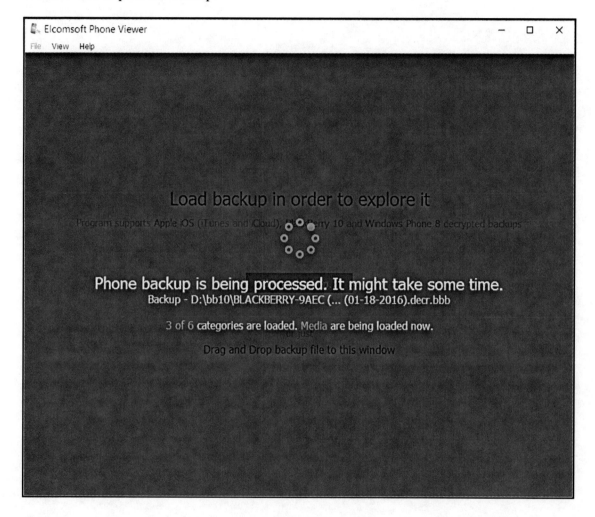

Once the backup is imported, you will see an overview of information available in the device.

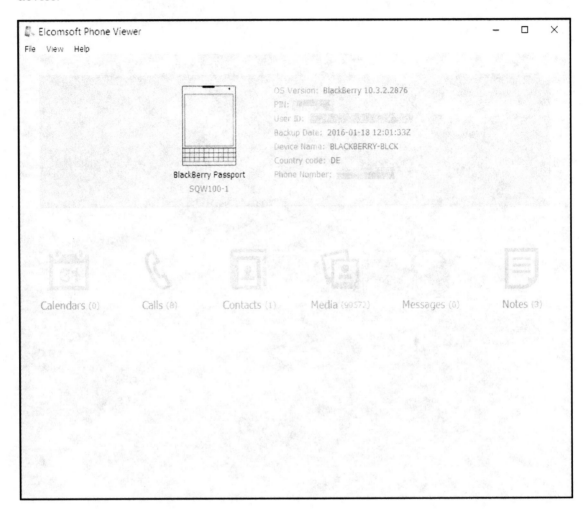

Elcomsoft Phone Viewer allows viewing **Calendars**, **Calls**, **Contacts**, **Media** (pictures and video, including cached images and map tiles), **Messages**, and **Notes**. You'll be able to use filters specifying date range, incoming/outgoing,and so on.

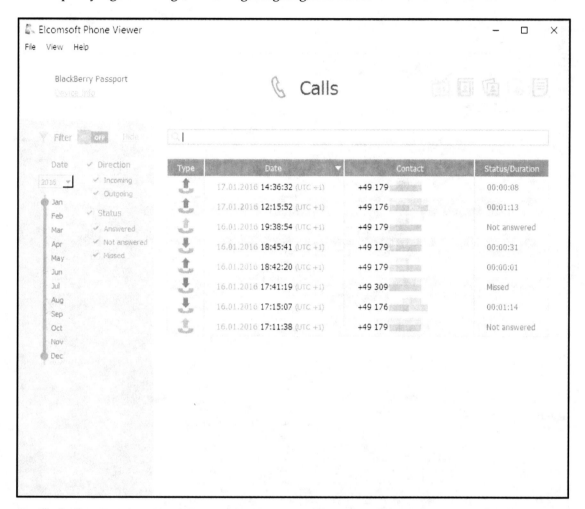

If you need more analytic features, you can use one of the fully featured mobile forensic tools such as Oxygen Forensic Suite. In particular, Oxygen Forensic Suite enables full-text search through the entire filesystem of the backup.

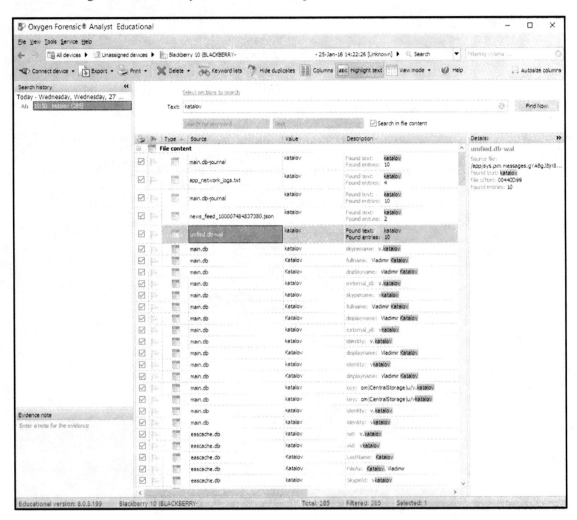

Summary

In this chapter, we reviewed acquisition methods for two distinct generations of BlackBerry devices: BlackBerry OS 1 through 7 and BlackBerry 10. We learned how to acquire BlackBerry backups depending on the OS, and reviewed a vulnerability allowing us to recover a device passcode if its media card was encrypted in legacy BlackBerry OS devices. We did not look at BlackBerry Android devices, as their acquisition approach would be similar to acquiring any other Android device.

The next chapter discusses obstacles, special cases, and considerations when acquiring mobile devices.

10
Dealing with Issues, Obstacles, and Special Cases

Each acquisition case is unlike others. Different manufacturers, hardware, and ecosystems; different versions of the mobile OS; different on-device security settings; and many other things make every case unique. In this chapter, we'll have a look at some common obstacles that may become roadblocks on the way to successful acquisition. We'll learn how to deal with some issues and understand restrictions and limitations imposed by some things specific to various platforms.

Cloud acquisition and two-factor authentication

Two-factor authentication is probably the best security feature since passwords were invented. Two-factor authentication goes a long way towards protecting one's accounts against being hacked. A password alone, no matter how long or secure, is no longer enough to provide sufficient protection. Social engineering, linked security breaches (`http://blog.elcomsoft.com/213/2/yahoo-dropbox-and-battle-net-hacked-stopping-the-chain-reaction/`), leaked passwords, and hacked mailboxes all contribute to the insecurity of password-based protection. Once the intruder gets a hold of someone's password, they can access the account without a fuss. Even worse, they can gain access to other accounts by, for example, using a hacked e-mail address to request password resets on other connected services. Two-factor authentication aims to address this problem.

LinkedIn. Yahoo! Mail. Dropbox. Battle.net. IEEE. Adobe Connect. PayPal. eBay. Twitter. These are just a few recent examples of big name service providers being hacked, with literally millions of passwords leaked.

The infamous celebrity photo leak (`http://www.mirror.co.uk/3am/celebrity-news/cele brity-4chan-shock-naked-picture-4395155`) was huge. It demonstrated how susceptible iCloud users are to remote hacks. Thousands of explicit images that celebrities captured with their iPhones were stolen straight from their iCloud accounts. Apparently, hackers were able to get passwords from celebrities' Apple ID, and gained access to the linked iCloud accounts using a copy of Elcomsoft Phone Breaker. Should Apple enforce two-factor authentication on iCloud account holders, the problem would probably occur on a much lesser scale. Even though two-factor authentication is not infallible and is susceptible to social engineering, it does require significantly greater effort to obtain a quickly expiring security code from the victim, and poses a much higher risk to an attacker.

As an expert in mobile forensics, you may face similar obstacles when attempting to acquire information from the suspect's cloud account over the air.

Two-factor authentication – Apple, Google, and Microsoft

All three major mobile service providers (Apple, Google, and Microsoft) use similar approaches to two-factor authentication. The two most common approaches are online and offline.

Online authentication works by approving authentication requests on a trusted device or entering a code that is pushed to the user or delivered via a text message. Offline authentication apps must be initialized with a cryptographic seed once; they will generate time-sensitive authentication codes afterwards without the need for an Internet connection.

Google mostly uses offline authentication via its Google Authenticator app (or via Microsoft Authenticator on Windows Phone devices). However, push authentication was added by Google in June 2016.

Apple is mostly relying on online authentication, pushing codes to trusted iOS devices, or delivering server-generated single-use codes via text messages. The ability to use time-dependent offline codes was added in iOS 9 with two-factor authentication support.

Finally, Microsoft users have access to both authentication methods at the same time. Windows users verifying their Microsoft Account can choose online or offline authentication at any given time. In addition, users can set up two-step verification with an e-mail address or phone number. Microsoft will send a security code to enter on the sign-in page when the user attempts to sign in on a new device or from a new location.

	Microsoft	Apple	Google
Push authentication	Yes: Windows 10 Mobile and Android apps only	Yes: iOS 9 and newer	Yes: unspecified versions of Android running the latest Google Play Services
Offline authentication	Yes	Yes: iOS 9, via Settings	Yes
Text/SMS authentication	Yes, as a backup	Yes, as a backup	Yes, as a backup

Online versus offline authentication

When using online authentication, users must approve a notification on one of their trusted devices. With this type of authentication, users don't have to enter security codes. Instead, they will be pushed a verification request to all of their trusted devices. By approving the request, they will successfully confirm their identity.

Offline authentication apps are based on a different principle. They don't require an active Internet connection or mobile service. A new time-sensitive single-use code is generated every few seconds by the authenticator app. The codes are automatically generated even when the trusted device is offline.

While it is generally possible to de-authorize individual trusted devices with online authentication apps, de-authorizing offline authentication is only possible for all offline authentication apps at the same time. Once a new cryptographic seed is generated, codes generated by offline authentication apps using the old seed will fail to verify.

App passwords and two-factor authentication

Two-factor authentication is still relatively new. As a result, some devices and some third-party applications are unable to properly authenticate accounts if two-factor authentication is enabled. If this is the case, the user will see an incorrect password error when trying to set up an account. This happens because these older apps do not support additional security codes.

This issue was immediately recognized by developers of two-factor authentication schemes. A neat workaround was implemented. If a certain app or device does not support two-factor authentication, the user can create a unique app password allowing these apps to sign in and effectively bypass the second authentication step. Users can generate as many app passwords as needed. Microsoft, Apple, and Google all support app-specific passwords. Users are recommended to create new app passwords for each app or device not supporting the two-factor authentication scheme.

App passwords can be revoked by the user at any time. Apps using revoked passwords will not be able to sign in or authenticate (for example, via a stored token). Interestingly, app-specific passwords will not work for web sign-ins or with each company's respective apps.

A typical app password generated by Google 2FA looks like this: `asdg skgf dsks ezck` (it should be entered without spaces).

Forensically, these app passwords, once extracted, can be used for effectively bypassing two-factor authentication. However, their forensic use is limited. For example, Apple does not allow downloading iCloud backups using an app password, but does allow accessing certain types of data (such as notes and messages). Microsoft does not allow accessing its backups with app passwords either. Google, on the other hand, allows limited access to certain types of data even when using an app password. Notably, app passwords can be used as a last resort when the expert has no access to the second authentication factor.

Google's two-factor authentication

Google implements consistent two-factor authentication, protecting access to all interactions with any of its services that involve the use of the user's Google Account. If two-factor authentication is enabled, users have to verify their identity as they attempt to access any of the services provided under the Google Account umbrella if they initiate access from a new device, app, or web browser. Authenticating Gmail in Internet Explorer does not automatically grant access to the same Gmail account if the user tries to open it in Chrome, and vice versa.

Protected services include (but are not limited to) logging in to the Google Account, using Gmail, accessing files or documents in Google Drive, or setting up a new device (for example, an Android phone) to access Google Play services. All in all, Google's implementation of two-factor authentication is the most consistent and straightforward compared to Apple and Microsoft.

Google relies mostly on offline, non-interactive two-factor authentication. An authenticator app is readily available on Android and iOS. The app can be initialized by scanning a color code displayed while the user sets up two-factor authentication. Once initialized, the app will continuously generate and display six-digit codes. The codes are valid for a short period of time (30 seconds).

Technically speaking, the app implements TOTP or HOTP security tokens as defined in the RFC 6238 standard. As a result, similar two-factor authentication apps based on the same standard may be compatible with Google, generating exactly the same codes that will be valid for authenticating the account. As an example, Microsoft Authenticator, available in Windows Store for the Windows Phone platform, is fully compatible with both Microsoft's and Google's two-factor authentication schemes, and can be used to authenticate both types of accounts.

Offline authentication in general is convenient because it does not require an active Internet connection. However, since it serves for authenticating account access (which is inherently an online operation), this point is moot. The drawback of this type of authentication is that the user cannot de-authorize an individual device or app that was previously authorized to generate authentication codes. Instead, if the user needs to de-authorize an app on any one of their devices, a new initialization image must be generated and used to re-initialize all authenticator apps running on all devices.

Since an initialized authentication app may not always be available, Google offers two backup options for receiving authentication codes. The user can authorize one or several phone numbers to receive single-time codes as text messages (SMS). In addition, the user can print 10 pre-generated eight-digit backup codes. These codes do not expire. These codes are disposable; each code can be used only once. If all codes are used, or if the user loses them, a different bunch of backup codes can be generated (which automatically invalidates all unused codes from the previous batch) at `https://www.google.com/landing/2step/`.

Google offers a plethora of authentication options ranging from printable verification codes to app-specific passwords, push authentication on trusted devices, and security keys (electronic tokens).

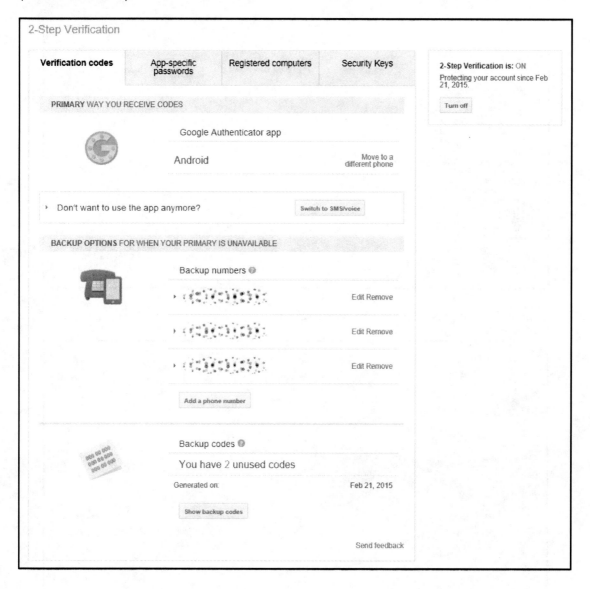

Elcomsoft Cloud Explorer (`https://www.elcomsoft.com/ecx.html`) supports Google's two-factor authentication. If the Google authentication server requests a verification code, the tool automatically requests that code from the user:

The code will be requested after you click **Sign in**:

You can request the code from a trusted device (a list of trusted devices will appear if you choose **Secure Code** as the authentication type) or use a **Recovery Key**, if available. Enter the code and click **Verify** to proceed:

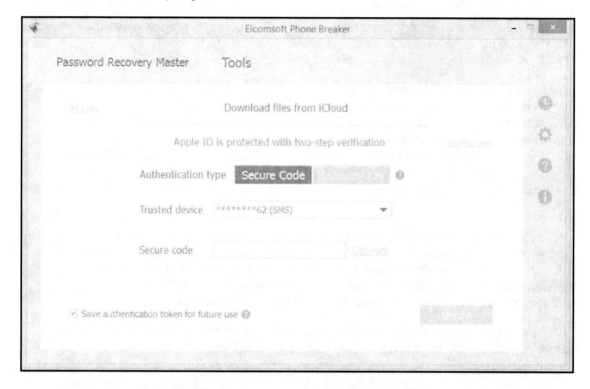

 More information about Google Authenticator can be found at `https://g arbagecollected.org/214/9/14/how-google-authenticator-works/`.

Microsoft's implementation

In the world of Microsoft Windows, the company protects Microsoft Account login with several security measures. Microsoft uses the same 2FA configuration for restoring Windows 8, 8.1, Windows 10, Windows Phone 8.1, and Windows 10 Mobile. The number of systems running one of those operating systems is huge, so it's important to understand the implications of Microsoft two-factor authentication.

Why should forensic experts be concerned about two-factor authentication in Microsoft systems? At the very least, two-factor authentication protects access to online backups made by all compatible systems listed previously. These backups contain comprehensive information about the user including bits such as stored Internet Explorer and Edge browser passwords, application data, contacts, calls, and text messages. While the amount of data available in Microsoft backups is somewhat less than that captured by Apple iOS, it is still much more than available in Android backups (even in the latest Android 6.0.1).

When setting up a new Windows 8, 8.1, or Windows 10 PC and attempting to sign in with a Microsoft Account (as opposed to using a local login), the system may prompt you to complete identity verification. The user's identity can be verified by either approving the verification request on a trusted device or by entering a code generated by the Authenticator app. The verification request can be pushed to an authorized Microsoft Account app running on a trusted PC or mobile device (an Android version of the app is available). Once the request is approved with an app, the new device is added to the list of trusted devices.

The Windows Phone 8 and 8.1 platforms use an offline Microsoft Authenticator app that works similarly to Google Authenticator (generating time-sensitive single-use codes). The difference between the two types of authentication is that the former requires an active Internet connection to receive authentication requests, while the latter works completely offline. Both authentication methods can be active at the same time.

The different authentication types may not be available on all platforms. Microsoft has compiled a comprehensive FAQ on how to configure authentication apps on the different mobile platforms.

Identity verification apps: FAQs at `http://windows.microsoft.com/en-US/Windows/identity-verification-apps-faq`.

Did you know? Microsoft and Google offline authentication apps are compatible. One can use Microsoft Authenticator running on a Windows Phone device to authenticate Google accounts, or Google Authenticator running on iOS or Android to authenticate Microsoft accounts.

The following are types of identity verification apps available on the different platforms:

- **Apple iOS**: It is an offline authenticator. Microsoft recommends using Google Authenticator, which is compatible.
- **Android**: It authenticates apps offline and online. Microsoft Account handles online authentication requests, while Google Authenticator can be used to generate authentication codes offline.
- **Windows Phone**: It is an offline authenticator. Microsoft Authenticator can be used to verify both Microsoft and Google accounts.

Verification methods can be configured at `https://account.live.com/proofs/Manage`.

Two-step verification

Two-step verification is an advanced security feature that makes it harder for someone to break in to your account with just a stolen password. Learn more about whether this is right for you.

Set up two-step verification

Identity verification apps

You've set up the Microsoft account app and an authenticator app. Learn more about identity verification apps.

Set up identity verification app

Turn off existing apps

Recovery code

You can use your recovery code if you lose access to your security info. You need to print out your recovery code and keep it in a safe place.

Replace recovery code

Trusted devices

On your trusted devices, you don't have to enter a security code to access sensitive info (such as your credit card details). Learn more about trusted devices.

Remove all the trusted devices associated with my account

More about Microsoft two-step verification: http://windows.microsoft .com/en-us/windows/two-step-verification-faq.

Microsoft allows using two-factor authentication to protect all interactions with Microsoft Account. However, the user can choose to only enable this type of authentication for accessing sensitive information such as establishing Microsoft Account on a Windows 10 device (which automatically enables full access to all files synced via Microsoft OneDrive, access to stored passwords, and the ability to restore backups including configuration settings and application data).

Apple's two-step verification

Up until recently, Apple used its very own approach to multi-factor authentication. Dubbed as two-step verification (https://support.apple.com/en-us/HT24152), the extra security layer was only meant to cover certain activities that could be performed with the user's Apple ID. Namely, two-step verification covered (and still covers, if you're dealing with iOS older than 9.0) all of the following activities:

1. Sign in to Apple ID account page.
2. Sign in to iCloud on a new device or at https://www.icloud.com/.
3. Sign in to iMessage, Game Center, or FaceTime.
4. Make an iTunes, iBooks, or App Store purchase from a new device.
5. Get Apple ID-related support from Apple.

According to Apple, this is how two-step verification works:

1. You enter your Apple ID and password as usual.
2. Apple sends a verification code to one of your devices.
3. You enter the code to verify your identity and finish signing in.

Source: https://support.apple.com/kb/PH14668?locale=en_US

Two-step verification only supports a single secondary authentication factor: a trusted iOS device. A verification code will be pushed by Apple to a trusted device, allowing users to validate requests protected with two-step verification.

Backup verification methods include SMS verification and an offline**Recovery Key** that can be created, printed out, and stored in a safe place.

With iOS 9, Apple moved from this proprietary scheme to a different method: the more open two-factor authentication.

Apple's two-factor authentication

Since iOS 9, Apple switched from two-step verification to a different, improved security mechanism. Apple's two-factor authentication is built directly into iOS 9, designed to protect access to all the photos, documents, and other important data stored with Apple.

Two-factor authentication is being gradually rolled out by Apple to eligible users since fall 2015 (`https://support.apple.com/en-us/HT2575`). Unlike the older two-step verification, the new two-factor authentication mechanism protects iOS devices from the ground up. If two-factor authentication is enabled, users will be required to enter a unique, single-use six-digit authentication code every time they access their Apple ID from a new device. The code is displayed automatically on the user's other devices, or sent to a trusted (and verified) phone number (`https://support.apple.com/en-us/HT24915`).

The code is only requested once per device. It remains valid until the user signs out completely, erases the device, or changes the password. Web sign-ins can be remembered by offering the user an option to trust the browser.

Bypassing Apple's two-factor authentication

When it comes to digital forensics, the secondary authentication factor may or may not be available. If the secondary authentication factor is a trusted iOS device, being able to unlock the device (by entering the correct passcode) is required in order to access the pushed authentication code. Such access may or may not be available to the investigator.

When performing cloud acquisition of Apple accounts protected with either two-step verification or two-factor authentication, investigators have the ability to bypass authentication requirements by using a cached authentication token. The authentication token is a piece of cached data that helps authenticate requests to Apple servers without requiring the user to enter their credentials every time.

At this time, only authentication tokens produced by Apple iTunes can be used to bypass authentication.

Comprehensive information on how to acquire and use binary authentication tokens to access the user's iCloud and iCloud Drive data is available in our blog:

Breaking Into iCloud: No Password Required at `http://blog.elcomsoft` `.com/214/6/breaking-into-icloud-no-password-required/`.

If no binary authentication token is available, it may still be possible to extract the correct Apple ID and password from the computer:

Acquiring and Utilizing Apple ID Passwords, Mitigating the Risks and Protecting Personal Information at `http://blog.elcomsoft.com/215/3/` `acquiring-and-utilizing-apple-id-passwords-mitigating-the-risk` `s-and-protecting-personal-information/`.

Further reading: Apple Two-Factor Authentication and the iCloud at `http` `://blog.elcomsoft.com/213/5/apple-two-factor-authentication-an` `d-the-icloud/` (published back in 2013, so some things have changed since then).

Two-factor authentication – a real roadblock

Two-factor authentication goes a long way towards securing user accounts. Even if a weak password is used, third parties may not be able to access information protected with two-factor authentication if they don't have physical access to the secondary authentication factor.

Two-factor authentication is a roadblock to performing over-the-air acquisition. Since acquisition is normally performed on what's considered to be a new device, the authentication system will require verifying a user's identity with the second factor. As such, tools such as Elcomsoft Cloud Explorer will require entering the correct authentication code.

There are exceptions. For example, Apple's authentication tokens can be extracted from a previously authorized computer and used with a tool such as Elcomsoft Phone Breaker. This allows accessing information stored in the user's iCloud, including iOS backups and uploaded files, even without having a trusted device.

Unallocated space

While we cover the issue of unallocated space separately for each individual mobile platform, this chapter gathers all information we have about the issue in a single place. In order to allow our readers to use this chapter as a reference, we included some information about internal (eMMC) and external (SD card) storage, as well as some basic information about encryption and its effect on unallocated space. We separately reviewed encryption options available for internal and external storage, as their effect on unallocated space can be quite different. If you just want an idea on whether or not unallocated space can be recovered from a particular device, carry on reading!

The issue of unallocated space

What happens to information that was deleted from a smartphone? Is there life after a full factory reset? Is there anything left on the device after a remote wipe? What is the best method to recover information stored in unallocated space; what tools and equipment are required? With six major mobile platforms and countless variations, there is no single answer to any of those questions. Let's look at the issue from the very beginning.

Accessing destroyed evidence in different mobile platforms

At this time, we have several distinctly different mobile platforms: Apple iOS, Android, Windows Phone 8, Windows RT, Windows 8/8.1/10, and BlackBerry 10. To say that these platforms handle deleted data differently is not saying much at all. Android and iOS are poles apart when it comes to handling deleted data and recovering information. Windows Phone 8 is somewhere in between, while Windows RT and the full versions of Windows 8/8.1/10 have their own share of issues.

Apple iOS – impossible

This chapter is easy to write. Recovering data stored in unallocated space in iOS 5 and newer is impossible, even on jailbroken devices. Not even if you send it to Apple, and not if you give them the passcode. Once the data is gone, it's gone. A factory reset erases everything completely and irrecoverably.

A theoretical concept exists allowing you to restore the state of the filesystem to a certain moment in the past. A proof-of-concept tool was developed, but it never made it to a truly usable state.

The reason for this is how Apple implements encryption. Since iOS 5, Apple used full disk encryption in iOS devices. The decryption keys are only maintained for the file system (allocated data blocks). iOS immediately discards decryption keys for unallocated (released) data blocks. This means that once a file is deleted, decryption keys to those encrypted data blocks are destroyed.

You may be able to extract the complete disk image. You may be able to extract decryption keys. But you still won't be able to decrypt unallocated areas because there will be no decryption keys for those data blocks. While the actual (encrypted) data may still be there, there is absolutely no possibility to decrypt it.

Since no Apple device uses external storage (SD cards), there is no way to recover information from SD cards either.

What about *data recovery* tools from the Cydia repository available to users of jailbroken devices? Those are fakes. On recent iOS devices, deleted files cannot be recovered, and any tool or service offering such recovery is an imposter.

Note that you may still be able to access some recently deleted files by retrieving the device's iCloud backups. Since iCloud keeps the three most recent backups, downloading the earliest backup with Elcomsoft Phone Breaker (`https://www.elcomsoft.com/eppb.html`) may result in finding those files before they've been deleted.

BlackBerry – Iffy

Security is the hallmark of BlackBerry smartphones. While previous versions of BlackBerry OS used to offer user-selectable security and data encryption levels, this is not the case with the newest BlackBerry 10.

By design, BlackBerry 10 employs optional full-disk encryption activated by either the end user or provisioned by the corporate **BES (BlackBerry Enterprise Server)**. There is no jailbreak for BlackBerry 10. Physical acquisition methods for BlackBerry 10 devices are limited (Cellerbrite UFED via a bootloader exploits certain devices if no device password is set). There is no way to extract a decrypted raw image of an encrypted BlackBerry 10 smartphone. Chip-off acquisition will only produce an encrypted disk image; all data will remain securely encrypted. The BlackBerry security model is exemplary, and there is no way of accessing (encrypted) unallocated space data in BlackBerry 10 smartphones.

In reality, BlackBerry 10 phones sold to end users don't come with encryption activated out-of-the-box. Since many users won't bother activating encryption (or are concerned with the slower performance of the storage subsystem after encryption), we've encountered quite a few BlackBerry 10 smartphones that were not encrypted.

As there is no physical acquisition and no JTAG extraction available on newer BlackBerry devices, chip-off is the only extraction method available for BlackBerry 10 devices. There is no known way to determine if a particular BlackBerry is encrypted or not. As a result, the encryption status of a particular BlackBerry 10 phone has to be decided on a case by case basis.

SD cards

Some BlackBerry 10 devices can use SD cards for additional storage. Those SD cards can be encrypted, or they can be left unencrypted. Unencrypted SD cards can be acquired in the usual way. There is nothing available to decrypt the content of encrypted SD cards though (unless you instruct the original BlackBerry 10 device to do so, which will require you to unlock it first with a passcode).

Samsung devices are known to encrypt SD cards with encryption keys stored in the device's internal memory. As a result, encrypted SD cards can only be used in the same device. Windows 10 Mobile applies similar technique to encrypt SD cards.

Android – possible with limitations

Android is a highly fragmented platform that implements many things in the opposite way to iOS. Let's have a look at what happens in Android devices when a file is deleted.

Android – built-in storage

Many Android devices can have two distinctly separate types of memory: built-in storage (typically an eMMC chip) and optional external storage (typically a micro SD card).

Before Android 2.3 Gingerbread, Android smartphones commonly used plain flash chips as their main storage. A flash-friendly file system called f2fs was used for wear leveling. Since Android 2.3 and in all later versions, the overwhelming majority of Android smartphones use eMMC storage. Typically, the data partition is formatted with one of the Linux file systems such as ext3 or ext4, but f2fs is also frequently encountered. In the past, the YAFFS2 file system was also a common choice. Several Samsung models used RFS, a FAT-based file system.

Note that a large number of ultra-budget Chinese smartphones are still manufactured equipped with raw NAND chips instead of eMMC flash. While chip-off acquisition would allow capturing the complete raw dump of those chips, less advanced acquisition such as physical and JTAG is often available on those devices. Such devices are relatively rare outside China.

Unencrypted storage

If the data partition is not encrypted, capturing a full disk image via physical acquisition, JTAG, **ISP (In-system programming)**, or chip-off will enable the investigator to perform unallocated space analysis by using a tool supporting Linux file systems. Limitations common to all eMMC storage apply (as described in the *eMMC and Deleted Data* section). Note that full-disk physical acquisition may require rooting the device or using an acquisition tool that can temporarily root the device. None of these methods are able to extract overprovisioned areas from eMMC chips.

Encrypted storage

Android is the exact opposite of iOS in many ways, including its approach to encryption. As opposed to Apple iOS, which employs full-disk encryption and destroys decryption keys for unused blocks, Android encryption is sector-based. As a result, if decrypting the user partition was successful, unallocated areas are automatically decrypted as well.

Since Android is a highly fragmented platform, OEMs can implement various parts of the system in many different ways. Some manufacturers (for example, Samsung) are known to vary their implementations widely between devices, even changing encryption types on the same device with OTA updates. As a result, it is impossible to predict whether or not a particular encrypted partition could be extracted via physical acquisition (with or without knowing the right passcode). One thing is for certain: encryption can make low-level attacks, such as JTAG and chip-off, complicated.

Encryption in different versions of Android

Speaking of stock Android, Google implemented encryption as early as Android 3.0 Honeycomb. However, most OEMs started implementing encryption with effect from Android 4.0. Based on the Linux `dm-crypt`, first-generation encryption was easy to brute force. The second version was much tougher to break, but brute-forcing passcodes was still possible (by swapping the function to scrypt). Initial implementations of Android encryption were inherently insecure, as encryption metadata was stored alongside encrypted data.

Samsung used to use stock Android encryption in its early devices. However, the company was never happy about its security, so Samsung started experimenting with its own implementations. Early implementations of Samsung proprietary encryption still kept encryption metadata openly accessible. However, with time the company learned to encrypt metadata and moved the master key into a protected area (inaccessible during chip-off).

Android 5.0 implements encryption in a way that's very similar to what Samsung does. Encryption metadata is now protected with a master key which, in turn, is now stored in a protected area inaccessible to chip-off. Google had plans to enforce encryption on all devices released with Android 5.x; however, this never materialized, and device encryption remains optional on most Android 5.x devices except for the Nexus line.

If you manage to pull an unprotected image of the encrypted partition (for example, via physical acquisition) or succeed in decrypting a protected image, you may be able to gain access to unallocated areas. Note that most encryption implementations also implement Trim pass-through, allowing the eMMC controller to clear (erase) data blocks that are no longer used. Such data blocks will be apparently visible as empty (zeroed) areas. However, since the Trim operation is not instant on eMMC controllers (as opposed to most SSD drives), you may still have time to analyze and recover data from those unallocated areas.

Android – SD cards

Since many Android devices have SD card slots, and those SD cards are rarely encrypted (see the next chapter for details), retrieving and analyzing the external SD card is an easy way of recovering information. Naturally, recovering information from an SD card is best done by removing the card and inserting it into a micro SD reader, in a write-protected manner, connected directly to the investigator's computer.

Since Android is a highly fragmented platform, the many different versions of the system (as well as many vendor customizations) implement varying approaches as to what types of data can or cannot be stored on an SD card. Android has the following policies, which cannot be changed by the user without rooting the device but can be overridden by individual OEMs:

- **Android 2.3, 4.0-4.2**: Apps are allowed to write to the external SD card. Many OEM implementations leave external SD cards unprotected. Applications can be moved to an SD card. Applications can be installed onto an SD card. Applications moved to or installed on the SD card can keep their data on that SD card.
- **Android 4.4**: Due to changes in security policies, only system apps have full access to the external SD card. Regular applications cannot keep data on an SD card unless they used the new **SAF** (**Storage Access Framework**) API. SD cards can still be used for storing multimedia files (music and videos) or keeping information such as map data (for example, HERE Maps).
- **Android 5.0-5.1**: New APIs (SAF extensions) now allow full access to SD card directories and files.
- **Android 6.0**: Access to external storage (SD cards and OTG sticks) integrated with internal storage.

The different APIs were introduced in order to secure information stored on SD cards. Unlike internal partitions that are usually formatted with ext3 or ext4 (a file system with built-in permission management and access control), external SD cards are normally formatted with FAT32 (SDHC, up to and including 32 GB) or exFAT (SDXC, 64GB, and larger cards). Neither of these implement any type of permissions or access control, requiring the operating system to take full control of who can access what areas on the SD card.

Note: 64GB (and larger) SDXC cards are formatted with exFAT out of the box. You will need an exFAT-compliant tool to recover deleted information and analyze unallocated areas on these SD cards. While you can still carve those cards with tools not supporting exFAT, such tools will not be able to tell unallocated and allocated areas apart, and provide messy results. Do check your tool's capabilities as exFAT support is not a given.

Android – SD card encryption

Encrypted SD cards are relatively uncommon in Android phones. Stock Android didn't implement the encryption of external SD cards in any version before Android M (although SD card encryption will be part of Android M).

Many Samsung phones as well as certain OEM ROMs offer optional SD card encryption. The corresponding setting is typically located under **Settings | More | Security | Encrypt external SD card** or **Settings | Control | Security**, and can only be activated if the phone is protected with a passcode. Similar to internal storage, there is no `full disk` encryption on SD cards. Instead, only the file system is encrypted. Unallocated (empty) areas are commonly left unencrypted, which, for one, enables investigators to recover deleted information stored on SD cards prior to encryption. Samsung devices are known to encrypt SD cards with encryption keys stored in the device's internal memory. As a result, encrypted SD cards can only be used in the same device that was used to encrypt the card.

 Android M implements the new concept of adoptable storage, allowing us to use an external SD card or USB drive in the same manner as internal storage. This, in particular, means that the same encryption is applicable to adopted external storage as it is used to protect the internal storage. More information can be found at `http://nelenkov.blogspot.fi/215/6/decr ypting-android-m-adopted-storage.html`.

A factory reset renders data stored on an encrypted SD card unusable (even if the SD card is stored separately from the device) as the encryption master key is destroyed during the reset.

Windows Phone 8 and 8.1 – possible for end-user devices with limitations

Windows Phone is a unique system. All three other systems are Unix-based. Apple iOS is based on BSD UNIX, Google Android is based on Linux, and BlackBerry 10 is based on QNX. Windows Phone 8/8.1, on the other hand, is based on Microsoft Windows, and shares its system architecture and the file system (NTFS).

Windows Phone 8/8.1 is a well-balanced operating system that learned a lot from Android and iOS. Somewhat similar to iOS, it offers the ability to create cloud backups (although these backups contain less information compared to iOS, with almost no application data being restored, save for login data). The OS features separate data space (sandbox) for each application and leaves no residual garbage after removing an app. However, it allows access to shared files (for example, music and videos can be played by any supported application and not just that one app the user imported the data to), which is similar to Android. Just like iOS, Windows Phone does not normally allow installing applications from sources other than Windows Store.

Windows Phone devices can be officially developer-unlocked to allow installing a limited number of unsigned applications from third-party sources. However, unlike in Android, there is no way for a user-installable app to obtain administrative access. Since Windows Phone devices cannot be rooted or jailbroken, there is no way to install an executable file with administrative-level access either.

As a result, it is impossible to develop a user-level application to launch on the phone in order to gain access to unallocated space. The issue is the result of both insufficient privileges and missing low-level disk access APIs.

Windows Phone 8/8.1 devices sold to end users don't come with pre-activated encryption. Unlike in Android, users cannot manually activate encryption on their devices, and there is no encryption option available anywhere in the settings. This allows using JTAG and chip-off acquisition methods to extract the device's full disk image. In addition, acquisition methods exist that allow reading the eMMC chip directly without removing it from the circuit board. Limitations common to all eMMC storage will apply (as described in the *eMMC and Deleted Data* section). Windows 10 Mobile changed this behavior and allows full user control over encryption (and decryption) of the device.

Some Windows Phone 8 devices of fairly recent generations (for example, Nokia Lumia 520) can be acquired via physical acquisition by exploiting a bootloader hack. Cellerbrite offers a tool (**UFED**) that can perform physical acquisitions of selected Windows Phones. Images acquired via this method (if the device is not encrypted) will contain full, raw dumps of the phone's storage including unallocated areas.

Windows Phone BitLocker encryption

In general, the Windows Phone OS (versions 8 and 8.1, as well as Windows 10 Mobile) supports using BitLocker technology to encrypt user data. The technology effectively protects information (including unallocated areas) against hardware attacks such as JTAG and chip-off extraction.

In Windows Phone 8 and 8.1, end users have no control over device encryption. There is no option to activate or deactivate encryption anywhere in the phone settings.

In Windows 10 Mobile, Microsoft added a user-accessible Device Encryption setting. Interestingly, Microsoft allows both enabling and disabling encryption, allowing investigators to actually decrypt encrypted devices with a simple change of a setting. Needless to say, any data stored in unallocated space is **permanently lost** during the decryption process.

Windows 10 Device Encryption

Windows Phone devices used in corporate environments will normally have BitLocker encryption activated out of the box, according to Microsoft (`https://dev.windowsphone.com/en-US/OEM/docs/Phone_Bring-Up/Secure_boot_and_device_encryption_overview`). Device encryption is not enabled by default. Device encryption is automatically enabled in the following scenarios:

- The user adds an Outlook account to the phone, and the Microsoft Exchange server that it connects to is configured to require device encryption
- The user connects the phone to a company apps account, and the enterprise device management server for the account pushes down a policy to the phone that requires device encryption

In either of these scenarios, the phone automatically begins encrypting the main OS and internal user data store partitions after the device encryption policy change is configured on the phone. The device encryption work is throttled to minimize the impact to end users.

This encryption effectively prevents capturing the full disk image via physical acquisition, and makes unallocated space analysis impossible. JTAG/chip-off acquisitions can still be done, but becomes useless.

According to Microsoft, *Unlike BitLocker for desktop Windows, there is no recovery key backup and no UI option for end users to enable or disable device encryption on Windows Phones. Microsoft Exchange servers and enterprise device management servers cannot disable device encryption after it has been enabled.*

`https://dev.windowsphone.com/en-US/OEM/docs/Phone_Bring-Up/Secure_boot_and_device_encryption_overview`

Windows Phone SD cards

Many Windows Phone smartphones (with a few exceptions) have support for external storage via an SD card slot. The Windows Phone OS implements advanced support for external storage, allowing users to not only store music and videos on an SD card, but use the external storage to install applications. Unlike in Android, this functionality is standard on all Windows Phone devices equipped with an SD card slot regardless of OEM. In particular, entry-level Windows Phone devices with a limited amount of internal storage (for example, 8 GB models) are very likely to have an SD card installed, which makes acquisition easier.

Windows Phone offers no separate options to encrypt the content of SD cards. Instead, SD card encryption is triggered by the same corporate policy provisioned to the phone, meaning that most end user devices will remain completely unencrypted while most corporate devices will have encrypted internal partitions and activated encryption for SD cards.

Even if the security policy provisioned to the device demands SD card encryption, user files such as photos and videos will remain unencrypted as per Microsoft policy.

More information on SD card encryption in Windows Phone 8.1 is available in `Chapter 8,` *Acquisition – Approaching Windows 8, 8.1, 10, and RT Tablets.*

Windows RT, Windows 8/8.1, and Windows 10

Since Windows RT is a closed platform that does not allow running unsigned desktop applications, acquisition options other than sending the device to the manufacturer (accompanied with a government request) are limited.

Since most Windows RT devices (as well as many tablets running Windows 8/8.1/10) are properly equipped for BitLocker drive encryption, the chance of encountering a device with an encrypted system partition is higher. (To recoup, BitLocker full disk protection is activated automatically by default, without user intervention, if the device is equipped with a TPM module, has non-removable (soldered) RAM, and the user logs in with their Microsoft Account as opposed to using a local Windows account.) More on BitLocker protection in **BITLOCKER DEVICE ENCRYPTION**. Note that BitLocker Recovery Keys can be obtained from Microsoft with a government request.

BitLocker encryption is volume-based. On eMMC and SSD drives, BitLocker provides trim pass-through, and does not encrypt unallocated space. Released data blocks will remain encrypted until they are trimmed by the SSD or eMMC controller.

If BitLocker encryption is not activated, the usual acquisition techniques, and all considerations applicable to eMMC in general, will apply. However, Windows RT acquisition may be tricky, with chip-off extraction possibly being the best possible course of action.

Most Windows RT devices (and practically all Windows 8/8.1 tablets) support SD cards. While Windows RT can access (and decrypt) SD cards with BitLocker To Go, the system does not come with tools to encrypt the SD card. (Users can still encrypt their SD card with a password on a different PC running the full version of Windows 8/8.1/10, and use that card, encrypted, with Windows RT.) As a result, you will most likely see an unencrypted SD card. Since many Windows and Windows RT devices are equipped with barely enough storage to keep Windows installation as well as Metro apps (32 GB is barely enough for that purpose), it is very likely that the user will have a micro SD card installed.

Note that in *full* (non-RT) versions of Windows, BitLocker To Go is only supported in the Pro and Enterprise editions of Windows 8 and 8.1.

Also note that Windows RT and Windows 8/8.1/10 maintain a OneDrive backup of the user's documents (if the user is logged in with their Microsoft Account), and a full application backup (with app data) is maintained in the user's Microsoft Account. Providing that the user's Microsoft Account login and password are known, examiners can extract information from the cloud. Alternatively, a government request can be sent to Microsoft to obtain information they have including all BitLocker Recovery Keys stored in the cloud.

eMMC and deleted data

One of the few things that all mobile devices have in common is the choice of the type of internal storage. All Apple smartphones and tablets, most Android devices since Android 2.3 Gingerbread, all BlackBerry 10 smartphones, Windows Phone 8, Windows RT, and a lot of Windows 8/8.1 tablets use eMMC chips as their storage.

eMMC stands for **embedded MMC**, or **embedded MultiMedia Card**. To put it simply, eMMC is a non-removable memory card that is soldered onto a circuit board. Unlike *plain* flash memory chips, the eMMC standard uses a combination of NAND modules and an integrated storage controller built into a single chip. It is the storage controller that makes things so different to traditional storage media when it comes to recovering deleted information.

In broad general terms, the embedded storage controller takes care of all the reading and writing operations. In addition (and this is the important part), the eMMC specification defines a number of maintenance routines designed to maintain performance and keep flash memory in good health in a way that's very similar to how SSD drives perform.

eMMC and SSD – similarities

Technically speaking, eMMC memory is similar to SSD drives in that it relies on solid-state NAND flash chips to store data, and uses an integrated controller to perform read, writes, and all maintenance operations.

NAND flash chips used in both eMMC and SSD drives have two inherent properties:

- Solid-state storage based on NAND flash chips can only write data to an empty block. If the block contains information, it must be erased before it can accept new data. Erasing a non-empty block is much slower compared to writing into an empty one. These properties are shared between eMMC and SSD drives because they use underlying physical media of the same type.
- NAND flash chips have a limited lifespan. Each cell can only sustain a finite number of writes. Every time new data is written to a cell, the cell starts leaking slightly more current than before. After a certain number of write cycles, the leak will become significant enough to severely affect the ability of the cell to retain data. Most manufacturers rate their flash cells to a certain number of write operations, assuming three-month data retention while powered off.

Because of the underlying technology, the eMMC standard defines performance optimization and wear leveling measures similar to those used in SSD drives. Overprovisioning, instant remapping, wear leveling, trim, and background garbage collection are properties of both eMMC and SSD drives. This, in turn, means that we'll observe issues with eMMC media self-destructing evidence as a result of those background processes.

However, despite similarities, eMMC and SSD drives implement those technologies differently, still retaining remnants of information even after it's been deleted.

eMMC and SSD – differences

The main technical difference between eMMC memory and SSD drive is not the type, but the number of NAND flash chips used. SSD drives are so much faster compared to eMMC, not because they employ special types of ultra-fast flash memory (yet, in general, manufacturers tend to pick higher-quality chips for SSD drives compared to eMMC modules). Instead, SSD drives are equipped with multiple flash chips working in parallel. As a result, their controllers have the ability to read and write data from (or to) several flash cells at the same time. This ability dramatically increases SSD performance compared to single-chip solutions.

As we can see, SSD drives are equipped with faster, smarter, and much more complex controllers. These controllers are also much larger, taking more space and consuming more energy. eMMC chips are built for different requirements. Used in portable, battery-powered devices, they must be small and power-efficient. As a result, not only are they not equipped with parallel operations, but they employ simplified versions of some of the maintenance algorithms used in SSD drives. This includes:

- Unlike SSD drives, eMMC controllers may not start erasing trimmed data immediately. In many cases, deleted data may remain intact even after the trim command has been issued. For example, many Android phones will only trim data upon shutdown. For the purpose of forensic extraction, this means that eMMC chips may maintain deleted data for longer than SSD drives.
- Unlike SSD drives, the eMMC standard does not define a deterministic trim. Used in SSD drives, **DRAT (Deterministic Read After Trim)** defines that the controller will return the same data for all trimmed blocks. Its extended version**DZAT (Deterministic Zero After Trim)** means that the SSD controller will return all zeroes on any attempt to read trimmed blocks—even of the physical blocks that have not yet been erased. Now, eMMC controllers are NOT equipped with a deterministic trim. For that reason, the controller will return the actual content of the cell—even if it's marked as trimmed. For the purpose of mobile forensics, this means that deleted data can be stored in a recoverable state for a much longer time compared to SSD drives.

Overprovisioning and remapping

Of particular interest are overprovisioning (the fact that a memory chip has more physical storage than advertised to the outside world) and remapping (the ability of the embedded controller to instantly reassign logical addresses to different physical blocks).

Overprovisioning is used by manufacturers as a means to increase write performance and the effective lifespan of the flash storage. The controller can instantly push a logical data block out of service and into the overprovisioned area, where that block will be erased and prepared for future service. Importantly, overprovisioned data blocks are non-addressable and not accessible by any means except by the controller. There is no way to extract data blocks from the overprovisioned area by any logical or physical means. JTAG and chip-off acquisition methods will *only* return addressable space because they work through the eMMC controller (instead of accessing the NAND flash chips directly). The possibility of reading data directly off NAND chips is more of a theoretical one. It can be done, but at great expense and requiring extremely complex hardware.

Overprovisioned data blocks in eMMC chips are not accessible to any data recovery program or app. They will not become part of a raw image or dump. Overprovisioned areas remain invisible during JTAG and chip-off acquisition because JTAG and chip-off requests are served by the controller integrated into the eMMC chip (as opposed to directly accessing NAND flash chips). If the device is equipped with plain flash chips, JTAG, using the Boundary Scan technique or chip-off acquisition, will return the entire content of those chips complete with overprovisioned areas.

Overprovisioned blocks can be pulled to service by the controller integrated into the eMMC chip. The controller can instantly assign a logical address to any healthy physical block, including overprovisioned blocks. This, in turn, can mean that data block(s) belonging to a deleted file can be instantly pushed into the overprovisioned area by means of data remapping, while an already erased physical block will correspond to the logical address that used to belong to a deleted file.

User data in overprovisioned areas

We've been asked this question: *Have you determined if any user data is also found in this space? Is this like the bad sectors on the older NAND flash that may have contained older-dated user data that could only be obtained through chip-off? Or does the eMMC Controller allow user data to be stored there and one requires a process to gain access to these areas using chip-off, ISP, or JTAG?*

It is important to understand what overprovisioned space is, and what it isn't.

In the context of eMMC chips, an overprovisioned area represents a number of extra storage blocks that are not advertised as available storage capacity. These blocks don't have physical addresses that could be used by the OS to access. There is no standard way or process to gain access to them from the outside world. Only the eMMC controller embedded into the chip has access to these blocks. However, no standard mechanisms, commands, or processes are defined by the eMMC standard that could be used to make the controller dump the contents of the overprovisioned area.

Overprovisioned blocks can be one of the following:

- **Bad blocks**: Each and every eMMC chip, with no exceptions, contains a number of bad memory blocks out-of-the-factory. These are permanently mapped out. If any particular NAND block expires (reaches the maximum number of allowable write cycles) or gets bad, it can be permanently overprovisioned. Its physical address will be assigned to one of the healthy blocks from the overprovisioned area.

- **Trimmed (erased) blocks**: These are commonly used by the controller as quick substitutes for dirty blocks marked for trimming. If this happens, the controller maps the dirty block out of the addressable space, and assigns its address to a fresh block from the overprovisioned area.
- **Dirty blocks**: These blocks still contain information, waiting for their turn to be cleaned (trimmed, erased). Eventually, these blocks will be erased; however, there is no defined timeframe, so there is no way to know if a certain block will be erased at any particular time. If (or when) these blocks will be actually trimmed depends on the make and model of a particular eMMC chip, the controller used, and the current I/O load.

As can be seen, overprovisioned blocks may still contain user data. Due to the nature of eMMC chips, accessing the actual NAND flash modules is extremely difficult, and not possible without precise equipment.

Due to the constraints of eMMC, we've never been able to access a real, raw dump of the NAND chip (as opposed to dumps obtained via chip-off). However, our experience with SSD drives (which do contain individual NAND chips that can be dumped) suggests that there can be remnants of user data scattered around in both addressable trimmed blocks as well as in the overprovisioned area.

In the case of portable electronic devices, this will be actual user data as opposed to system files. In smartphones and tablets, system files are predominantly read-only and are not normally shuffled around or deleted, unless a recent OTA/firmware update was applied.

To conclude this chapter, it must be said that acquiring the content of overprovisioned areas (by capturing raw physical dumps of the NAND chips) is so complicated, yet the amount of potential user data is so negligible that the process is hardly worth it, except under extreme circumstances.

Delete operations on non-encrypted eMMC drives

Once a file is deleted from an unencrypted eMMC volume, the operating system will make changes to the file system to indicate that certain sectors (defined on a file system level) are no longer in use. The operating system will also send the Trim command to the eMMC controller, telling the device that certain physical data blocks are no longer used. The eMMC controller then assigns the special *do not care* status to those data blocks. So far, it's been pretty straightforward.

What happens next depends on the particular eMMC controller and its internal programs. As we mentioned earlier, NAND flash cells can be written much faster if previously erased (they must be erased before they can be written to). As a result, the eMMC controller will do two things:

- The controller will schedule trimmed blocks to be emptied (erased) to prepare them for accepting new data.
- The controller may remap those data blocks, assigning their logical addresses to already-emptied physical blocks. Those already-emptied data blocks can be taken from available (addressable) blocks, or pulled from the overprovisioned area. Such remapping has two goals: it allows the system to write new data to that logical address immediately without waiting for it to be erased (increasing effective write speeds), and allows the controller to write data to flash cells with the least number of write cycles on them (regardless of those cells' physical addresses).

As a result, the operating system (or any application attempting to read that particular sector) may discover that sectors belonging to a recently deleted file have become empty in an instant—much faster in fact that it takes for the flash chip to actually erase data.

As a forensic expert, you may wonder what happens to those data blocks that still contain information from that deleted file. Those data blocks can be remapped to another logical address (meaning that you should be able to carve the file after taking a full dump of the eMMC chip). Alternatively, those data blocks could be pushed out of the addressable space and placed into an overprovisioned area, where the integrated controller will erase their content in the background. If those data blocks end up in the overprovisioned area, there is no feasible way of extracting their content—even if you use JTAG or chip-off extraction.

eMMC conclusion

Before we start discussing the particular implementations of the different mobile platforms, we can already conclude that recovering unallocated space is going to be difficult and not always possible due to the underlying technology. The chances to retrieve information from an eMMC chip are substantially higher compared to the situation with SSD drives, but significantly lower compared to traditional hard drives or flash-based storage media without integrated controllers.

In other words, there still is a chance to recover deleted data from unallocated space… if the mobile operating system does not prevent it in one way or another.

SD cards

Many Android phones, most Windows Phone 8, Windows RT, Windows 8/8.1 devices, and BlackBerry 10 phones are equipped with micro SD card slots to allow users to increase available storage capacity. Depending on the platform, certain limitations apply as to what types of data the users are allowed to keep on an SD card. For example, the Windows Phone 8 platform enables full, unrestricted use of an SD card including an option to install applications, while the different versions of Android implement strikingly different policies to external storage.

SD cards are frequently used to store multimedia files (music and videos), Camera Roll, offline maps (for example, HERE Maps or other navigation applications), and additional data (for example, extra files belonging to larger games). In Android, not all applications are able to use external storage to keep their data.

Just like eMMC chips, SD cards are a combination of NAND flash chips and an integrated microcontroller. However, the built-in storage controller is much simpler than that of an eMMC drive. SD card controllers do have address remapping (as per manufacturing limitations, each NAND chip in every SD card contains a large number of unusable, faulty blocks that are simply mapped out); however, trimming erased data in the background is not part of the Secure Digital standard. As a result, data that belongs to files deleted from an unencrypted SD card will normally remain accessible until overwritten with new information.

Note: SDHC/SDXC specifications include support for **flash erase**, the command that permanently erases the content of data blocks. While some standard-sized SD cards support **flash erase**, mobile devices use the "micro" variety of SD cards. microSD cards are built to different specifications compared to standard-size SD cards. In particular, microSD cards do not support **flash erase**, meaning that background garbage collection is not possible. microSD cards do not support automatic wiping of released data blocks.

Another thing to note is the use of the file system. micro SD cards that conform to the SDHC standard (up to and including 32 GB cards) come formatted with FAT32, while the SDXC standard requires the use of exFAT, a new file system from Microsoft that lifts the 4 GB limitation for maximum file size. Microsoft collects licensing fees for supporting exFAT. This is the reason for many Android devices only supporting SD cards up to 32 GB (more often than not, these same devices will support a 64 GB memory card if reformatted to FAT32). At the same time, even the cheapest Windows Phones support SDXC memory cards with exFAT.

SD card encryption

Many mobile platforms have the ability to encrypt the content of external storage including micro-SD cards. While encryption policies and implementations vary widely among the different ecosystems, two things are in common between all of them:

- SD cards are almost never encrypted out of the box. The user (or system administrator, if the device is managed by a corporate policy) must explicitly encrypt the content of an SD card.
- SD card encryption is practically never full-disk encryption. This means that, when the user encrypts the SD card, only the file system is encrypted. Any free space (which may or may not contain remnants of deleted data) is left over.

Other than that, the following policies are observed.

Apple iOS

SD card support is not available in any Apple iOS device.

Android

Users can manually encrypt SD cards. Factory reset typically wipes the content of internal memory; the content of an external SD card is rarely wiped, although data becomes inaccessible after the wipe due to encryption metadata being destroyed. This behavior may be different due to platform fragmentation and various OEM implementations.

Most implementations make encryption of multimedia files (pictures, videos, and music) on SD cards optional. This opens the possibility for carving deleted pictures and videos from the SD card.

If an Android device has an SD card mounted, the system and some applications may automatically use the SD card to store information. For example, Foursquare keeps parts of its data on an SD card by default, while WhatsApp uses the SD card to create backups. HERE Maps and some other navigation tools can be configured to store maps, voices, and parts of their data on an SD card. There are many more applications that use SD cards to keep data, which enables experts to carve the content of an SD card for evidence.

Since Android does not come with the ability to format SD cards with a Linux file system such as ext3 or ext4, the majority of SD cards used in Android devices are formatted with either FAT32 (SDHC, cards up to and including 32 GB) or exFAT (SDXC, 64 GB and larger SD cards). Neither file system comes with access control or permission management. This, as well as the fact that the SD card can be easily removed, made some developers employ proprietary encryption to protect files stored on an SD card by their applications. This can become an extra obstacle when analyzing unallocated space from an SD card.

Windows Phone 8/8.1

Windows Phone 8.1 supports the ability to install apps on an SD card. According to Microsoft documentation (`http://download.microsoft.com/download/B/9/A/B9A269-28 D5-4ACA-9E8E-E2E722B35A7D/Windows-Phone-8-1-Security-Overview.pdf`), apps and their data are stored on a hidden partition on the SD card. If encryption is enabled on the device by the corresponding policy, this partition will be encrypted just like the internal storage. Notably, personal content such as photos and videos is stored on the SD card in an unencrypted partition so that the user can access the SD card on other devices. As a result, unallocated space can be carved at least for the unencrypted partition even if encryption is activated.

In reality, we were unable to prove the existence of a special hidden partition on Windows Phone 8.1 devices. Installing applications onto an SD card inserted into a Windows phone provisioned to support encryption has always resulted in clearly visible files and folders being created on the main partition on that card. The entire content of these folders, complete with application binaries, their data, and temporary files, was accessible in plain view. After a system update pushed by Microsoft in late 2014, the system fixed that behavior by enabling per-file encryption. The entire file system can still be browsed through, and filenames and sizes are visible, yet the content of those files is now encrypted. This behavior is significantly different from the mechanism described in the Microsoft whitepaper. Other researchers (for example, `http://www.insinuator.net/215/1/in-secu re-sd-cards-on-wp8-1/`) received similar results, so it's unlikely that our experience was an isolated incident.

It is essential that Windows Phone 8.x does not allow users to encrypt their devices (or SD cards) with a setting within the phone's menu. There is no such option available. Encryption can only be activated as provisioned by the corporate security policy (if the phone is used in a corporate environment and connected to an MDM system).

A factory reset may not render the SD card inaccessible since encryption escrow keys may be available in the MDM system.

Windows 10 Mobile

Windows 10 Mobile introduced the ability for end users to control device and SD card encryption. Users now have an option to encrypt and decrypt (!) the internal memory. A separate encryption option is available for SD cards.

Windows RT

Windows RT supports a somewhat restricted version of BitLocker that does not allow encrypting the SD card in a Windows RT device, but does allow using an already encrypted card (for example, if one was encrypted in a computer running the full version of Windows). Considering the number of Windows RT devices sold, the chances of encountering an encrypted SD card in one of those are slim to none.

Notably, a full factory reset of a Windows RT system will neither wipe the content of an SD card nor render the data inaccessible since information is encrypted with a password and can be accessed again if the correct password has been entered.

Windows 8 through 10

While most tablets running Windows 8, 8.1, and Windows 10 support BitLocker full disk protection (for encrypting partitions in the main eMMC storage), BitLocker To Go (for encrypting external storage such as USB flash drives and SD cards with a password) is only available in the Pro and Enterprise editions of Windows 8 and 8.1 and Windows 10 Pro. Since many budget Windows tablets use the most basic edition of Windows with Bing, SD card encryption is not available to their users (yet, similar to Windows RT, they can still access BitLocker-protected SD cards that were encrypted on a higher Windows edition that supports BitLocker). Even if the SD card is encrypted, BitLocker To Go only encrypts the file system, leaving unallocated space unencrypted. (This has changed in Windows 10, with the option to encrypt the entire content of the SD card now available.)

Notably, a full factory reset of a Windows system will neither wipe the content of an SD card nor render the data inaccessible since information is encrypted with a password and can be accessed again if the correct password has been entered.

BlackBerry OS 1 through 7

Early versions of BlackBerry OS offered three distinct options to encrypt SD cards:

- Using the device key
- Using the password
- Using the device key and the password

With the exception of the first encryption method, passwords can be attacked and recovered, and backups can be decrypted.

When it comes to SD encryption, the decryption key can be extracted from a physical image or chip-off dump of the device. Early versions of BlackBerry OS (prior to BlackBerry 10) used to have a security flaw related to encrypted SD cards. Encryption metadata could be derived by analyzing the content of the encrypted SD card and brute-forcing the security key. This weakness (used, for example, in Elcomsoft Phone Breaker) allowed investigators to decrypt encrypted partitions dumped from the device itself in addition to the content of the SD card itself. Effectively, the option to encrypt the content of an SD card became the system's Achilles heel. This, however, is no longer the case in BlackBerry 10.

BlackBerry 10

SD card encryption is optional in BlackBerry 10, even if the device is configured to encrypt its main memory. A factory reset destroys encryption metadata, rendering the content of such an SD card completely inaccessible.

Below is a comparison table of SD card encryption in various systems:

	Enabled by default	User configurable	Algorithm	Known vulnerabilities
Android	No	Yes	Version specific, AES	None
BlackBerry OS 1-7	No	Yes	Depends on user selectable settings	In some scenarios, attacking encrypted SD can recover device passcode
BlackBerry 10	No	Yes	AES	None

Windows Phone 8.x	No	No	BitLocker	Some versions don't enable encryption, but claim encryption is enabled
Windows 10 Mobile	No	Yes	BitLocker	None
Windows RT	No	No; must use different PC to encrypt (depends on Windows edition); can use already encrypted SD cards	BitLocker	None
Windows 8 through 10	No	Yes, depends on Windows edition	BitLocker	None

SD cards conclusion

While SD cards are equipped with an integrated storage controller, the built-in controllers are of a simple variety. While supporting data remapping, SD card controllers do not implement trim, which means that deleted data will remain available in unallocated areas, just like on most USB drives. The same acquisition methods that work for USB flash drives will work for SD cards. SDHC cards (up to and including 32 GB) are typically formatted with FAT32. Do note that larger SDXC cards (64 GB and up) come pre-formatted with exFAT, and will require a carving tool supporting that file system.

It is essential to note that mobile devices (smartphones and tablets) accept microSD cards as opposed to standard-size SD cards. microSD are built to different specifications compared to standard-size SD cards. In particular, microSD cards do not support the **flash erase** command, meaning no background collection and no automatic wiping of released data blocks.

SQLite databases (access to call logs, browsing history, and many more)

A special case (accessing deleted data on mobile platforms) applies to information stored inside SQLite databases. SQLite is a universally accepted database format employed by countless system and third-party apps running on all popular mobile platforms. Android and iOS keep call logs, message history, Web browsing logs, and many system settings in SQLite databases. Applications such as Chrome, Firefox, Skype, WhatsApp, and countless others also use SQLite.

Unlike files deleted from encrypted partitions, records deleted from SQLite databases may not immediately disappear. In a naive attempt to counter forensic efforts, users may clear call history, delete message logs, and clear the browsing history. These measures may not be as effective as users think.

The reason for these measures being unreliable is the way in which SQLite deletes records. Due to performance considerations, SQLite does not wipe deleted records (which can be quite big) unless flushed. Instead, the actual data is not moved anywhere. SQLite modifies pointers to deleted records to manifest that those records are now stored in a so-called **freelist**. By using a forensic SQLite analysis tool (for example, Belkasoft Evidence Center or Elcomsoft Phone Viewer), one can access and parse the database container, successfully extracting deleted records from the freelist and viewing them along with existing data.

Regularly cleaning call logs and removing text messages helps users maintain the illusion of privacy, while in fact deleted records may not immediately disappear. Instead, these records might be placed into a freelist. Records can be kept in the freelist for a long time—much longer in fact than most users realize because new calls and text messages that could potentially trigger a cleanup are relatively infrequent.

Summary

In this chapter, we had a look at the obstacles, special cases, and considerations when acquiring mobile devices. We reviewed SD card encryption and learned about the issues of unallocated space in flash-based storage media. We also reviewed the differences between two-factor authentication methods implemented in all major mobile ecosystems. The next chapter will present case studies and list forensic tools that can be used to acquire and analyze mobile devices.

11
Mobile Forensic Tools and Case Studies

In this book, we have covered a number of forensic tools by ElcomSoft and Oxygen Forensics. We covered these tools as we are involved in their development and we also have lengthy experience using them. However, the market for mobile forensic tools is not limited to the small bunch of products reviewed in this book. There are more well-known and truly excellent tools available.

Cellebrite

Cellebrite (http://www.cellebrite.com/) offers an extensive range of tools for mobile forensics under their **Universal Forensic Extraction Device (UFED)** umbrella. UFED Physical Analyzer, UFED Cloud Analyzer, UFED Logical Analyzer, UFED Phone Detective, and more are available from Cellebrite.

Cellebrite developed a number of unique technologies that are unmatched by competitors. This includes the ability to acquire a number of devices (such as those equipped with Qualcomm chipsets, a number of Lumia smartphones, and so on) via a company-developed bootloader exploit (http://blog.cellebrite.com/blog/tag/android-forensics/). This acquisition method is clean, robust, and forensically sound. In certain cases, UFED can be the only acquisition tool that can do the job.

Micro Systemation AB

Micro Systemation AB (https://www.msab.com/) offers a range of high-quality mobile forensic tools under the XRY umbrella. This includes XRY Physical, XRY Logical, XRY PinPoint, and XRY Viewer. XRY allows performing physical and logical extraction from a wide range of mobile devices, extracting all available raw data (physical only). XRY Logical allows recovering most of the live and filesystem data from the device and is the automated equivalent of manually examining each available screen on the device.

AccessData

AccessData (http://accessdata.com/) offers **Mobile Phone Examiner Plus (MPE+)**, an all-in-one acquisition and analysis toolkit supporting a wide range of mobile devices. The company claims support for over 7,000 device models. MPE+ is one of the better acquisition and analysis tools on the market.

Oxygen Forensic toolkit

Oxygen Forensics (http://www.oxygen-forensic.com/en/) offers one of the most advanced all-in-one acquisition and analysis toolkits on the market. Supporting more than 12,000 unique device models via physical, logical, and cloud acquisition techniques, Oxygen Forensic toolkit comes with the ability to exploit unique properties of certain chipsets and OEMs that allow investigators to dump the entire contents of the device while bypassing bootloader lock and screen lock altogether. Oxygen Forensic Suite has been thoroughly reviewed in this book.

Magnet ACQUIRE

Magnet ACQUIRE (https://www.magnetforensics.com/) can extract logical, filesystem, or physical Android and iOS data. The extraction is done in a manner that is agnostic, so any analysis tool can import the extracted data for analysis. This product is available at no cost to the forensic community.

BlackBag Mobilyze

BlackBag Mobilyze (`https://www.blackbagtech.com/`) can acquire Android and iOS. iOS is restricted to logical/filesystem, but for Android it can do all three levels of extraction based on the device type and other variables such as OS, operator customizations, and so on. Mac and Windows versions are available.

ElcomSoft tools

ElcomSoft Co. Ltd. (`https://www.elcomsoft.com/`) offers a number of mobile forensic tools, some of which have been reviewed in this book. The tools include the following:

- **Elcomsoft Phone Breaker**: This is helps in the logical acquisition and backup analysis of iOS, Windows Phone, and BlackBerry backups. It is used for the cloud acquisition of iOS and Windows Phone devices.
- **Elcomsoft iOS Forensic Toolkit**: This helps in the physical acquisition of iOS devices (32-bit and 64-bit, jailbreak required). At this time, the company's physical acquisition technology is unrivaled by competition.
- **Elcomsoft Blackberry Backup Explorer** and **Elcomsoft Phone Viewer**: This is a fast lightweight tool for viewing the content of mobile backups.
- **Elcomsoft Cloud Explorer**: This is used for the cloud acquisition of Google account data. Extensive acquisition and analysis features are available.

Case studies

In this chapter, we'll review some typical scenarios that call for different approaches and tools when handling mobile acquisition.

Mobile forensics

I have a ton of iPhones in my lab. Only get to spend about 40 minutes on each. What can you get me in 40 minutes?

This is a typical question coming from a police officer working in a busy environment. What can be done on these iPhones in such a restricted timeframe?

It depends on what's available. If all you have is a working but locked iPhone, and the passcode is not known, the only chance of extracting anything off the phone is to attempt physical acquisition. If the phone falls within the compatibility matrix, you can follow these steps to extract information out of the device. With its characteristic-guaranteed timeframe, physical acquisition is the only way to obtain information out of a locked device.

If you know the user's Apple ID and password, you can use Elcomsoft Phone Breaker to perform a selective download of essential information, such as call logs, geolocation information, address book, messages, and so on from iCloud. Selective downloading can help jump-start your investigation, while you can continue downloading the rest of the data in the background.

If you have the user's computer, hard drive, or forensic disk image of that hard drive, you may also have other options available. For example, the hard drive may contain a binary authentication token, allowing you to connect to iCloud and download information right away, without knowing the user's passcode, Apple ID, and account password.

The computer may also contain a local backup copy of information stored in the iOS device. If the backup is not password-protected, you can access data instantly with Elcomsoft Phone Viewer. If, however, the backup is protected with an unknown password, you can attempt to break this password, although there can be no timeframe guarantee.

Data recovery

Accessing information stored in employees' corporate smartphones is often required during internal investigations. Having real-time access to such data helps investigate or prevent leaks of sensitive information carried on or transmitted with a smartphone.

In corporate environments, breaking into employee devices is rarely a problem. With recovery key deposit and obligatory recovery procedures for corporate online phone accounts in place, combined with the complete ban on jailbroken devices demanded by most corporate security policies make physical acquisition impossible/unnecessary. Instead, corporations commonly use online access to phone data.

In the case of Apple iOS devices, companies can access data stored in their employee's corporate smartphones by downloading information from iCloud. iCloud downloads are performed transparently and without requiring the original Apple device.

Until very recently, one could use Elcomsoft Phone Breaker to download iCloud data without the end user's knowledge. However, Apple has modified its security policies. Apple automatically sends an e-mail notification to the user's registered Apple ID when someone attempts to download their iCloud backup. A notification is delivered to a registered e-mail address when accessing iCloud backups from a new IP address. However, the notification is not sent when accessing application data such as **Keynotes, Pages**, or **Numbers** documents. These notifications are designed to prevent spying on unsuspecting users, notifying the user that their data is being downloaded.

BlackBerry scenarios

The scenarios discussed in the following are based on real-life situations, encountered by *Shafik Punja* (TeelTech), either through a consulting engagement or during the course of examination of classic BlackBerry devices running BlackBerry OS 1 through 7.

Locked BlackBerry devices

In most situations, any BlackBerry device being acquired is locked. There are still methods available to deal with locked Blackberries.

Locked BlackBerry, not attached to BlackBerry Enterprise Server (BES)

Situation:

- Shows only one padlock in lower right
- Contains no memory card

Examiner considerations:

- Password *not* stored on computer or laptop that device is synced with
- Password is *not* found within the IPD or BBB backup file
- There is no **lockdown** type file
- In the absence of a password, the only recourse is chipoff (de-chipping) of the flash memory

Locked BlackBerry attached to BES

Situation:

- Internal investigation, device is managed by a BES
- Showing two padlocks: upper left and lower right
- BES is accessible to the examiner either directly or indirectly

Examiner considerations:

- Initiate a password reset to device through BES
- Password reset will not destroy the user data
- The physical image obtained with the UFED tool may not decrypt the encrypted content if BES encryption policies are in place, which may also be influenced by the BlackBerry OS version
- UFED **Physical Analyzer** (**PA**) decryption capability depends on the BB OS that was used; newer encryption methods are not supported
- Turning off/disabling encryption to the device will only affect new data and not existing data
- In any BES-related scenarios, don't forget to check the BES logs for call history and messaging and the e-mail server for e-mails

Locked BlackBerry attached to BES with Pretty Good Privacy (PGP) encryption

Situation:

- External BES, managed by hostile entity (read as criminal group)
- Showing two padlocks: upper left and lower right
- Investigators were lucky and found a sticky note with the password, *secret*
- A physical image (because of known password) was obtained through UFED tools. However, e-mail was discovered to be PGP-encrypted, and this data still shows as encrypted within UFED PA

Examiner considerations:

- UFED PA decryption capability depends on the BB OS that was used and newer encryption methods are not supported.
- When the passcode is entered on the BlackBerry, the e-mail is unlocked/decrypted. However, you have to unlock each e-mail individually (once you enter the passcode for that sender, it appears that the majority of the e-mails sent by that sender are unlocked then when you come across another sender, you have to enter the passcode again).
- You will have to take pictures of each e-mail item! There is no tool that presenters are aware of that will automatically decrypt all the PGP encrypted email content, with the supplied password.
- There has been success, by a Federal LE group, in setting up a new bogus account and new IT policy, then having the BB talk with an active directory server; only after the BB synchronization was completed was the e-mail downloaded in an unencrypted state.

Locked BlackBerry, not attached to BES

Situation:

- Showing two padlocks: upper left and lower right
- Contains a memory card

Examiner considerations:

- Password *not* stored on computer or laptop that device is synced with
- Password is *not* found within the IPD or BBB backup file
- There is no lockdown type file
- Image the memory card and locate the `info.mkf` file, use **Elcomsoft Phone Password Breaker (EPPB)** to analyze this card, and see if it can obtain the device password
- In the absence of the password, the only recourse is chipoff (dechipping) of the flash memory

Locked BlackBerry – completed successful chipoff

Situation:

- Showing two padlocks: upper left and lower right
- No success with memory card and attack of the `info.mkf` file
- Successful dechipping and reading of the chip
- During parsing by UFED PA, message is provided to examiner: ....*Please provide the password that matches the following SHA1 hash:....*

Examiner considerations:

- Copy the SHA1 value and use one of the several freely available online sources to decrypt the SHA1 value. Enter the decoded SHA1 value into the UFED PA screen.

Locked BlackBerry – password does not work

Situation:

- You have a BlackBerry device attached to a BES
- You are using the password provided to you as *exd0*
- You attach the BlackBerry device to your extraction tools, which requests for the password prior to data extraction, but any data extraction tool you try is not accepting the password

Examiner considerations:

- Keep it simple. Don't forget about the *Alt* key sequence, which changes the key character when *Alt* key is pressed.
- Verify the password based on the key sequences being used.
- In this case, *exd0* was actually meant to be interpreted as *2580*. The four-character key sequence requires the *Alt* key to be pressed for the first three characters in order for key press to be *258*, followed by releasing the *Alt* key and pressing the key for 0 to obtain *2580*.

Unlocked BlackBerry devices

On some occasions, you may have a BlackBerry device that is not locked with a passcode. Such devices are generally easier to acquire.

Unlocked BlackBerry device with no password

Situation:

- Contains memory card and SIM

Examiner considerations:

- Which type of data extraction should be performed and in what order?
- Physical, then logical? There are a variety of tools available to the examiner.
- However, performing a physical acquisition with UFED may, in rare cases, cause the device to reset itself back to the factory default. This is referred by Cellebrite as a cache memory reset.
- A data structure at the logical level, in the form of a logical backup/acquisition, is different from the same record at the physical level.

Unlocked BlackBerry device with password

Situation:

- Password not known and cannot be removed
- Fortunately, the desktop is accessible and can be navigated
- To prevent a timeout due to inactivity, the device must be *used* (that is, keep the mouse moving)

Examiner considerations:

- Password not known and cannot be removed
- Device data can be viewed, and your only recourse is to take pictures

Summary

In this chapter, we listed some of the many tools available to forensic experts. We reviewed some common scenarios affecting the choice of tools when handling mobile acquisition.

Index

B

X

CPSIA information can be obtained
at www.ICGtesting.com
Printed in the USA
LVOW09s1723100618
580221LV00003B/124/P